A TRANSLATOR'S GUIDE TO THE LETTERS FROM JAMES, PETER, AND JUDE

Helps for Translators Series

Technical Helps:

Old Testament Quotations in the New Testament
Section Headings for the New Testament
Short Bible Reference System
New Testament Index
Orthography Studies
Bible Translations for Popular Use
The Theory and Practice of Translation
Bible Index
Fauna and Flora of the Bible
Short Index to the Bible
Manuscript Preparation
Marginal Notes for the Old Testament
Marginal Notes for the New Testament
The Practice of Translating

Handbooks:

A Translator's Handbook on the Book of Joshua
A Translator's Handbook on the Book of Ruth
A Translator's Handbook on the Book of Amos
A Translator's Handbook on the Books of Obadiah and Micah
A Translator's Handbook on the Book of Jonah
A Translator's Handbook on the Gospel of Mark
A Translator's Handbook on the Gospel of Luke
A Translator's Handbook on the Gospel of John
A Translator's Handbook on the Acts of the Apostles
A Translator's Handbook on Paul's Letter to the Romans
A Translator's Handbook on Paul's Letter to the Galatians
A Translator's Handbook on Paul's Letter to the Ephesians
A Translator's Handbook on Paul's Letter to the Philippians
A Translator's Handbook on Paul's Letters to the Colossians and to Philemon
A Translator's Handbook on Paul's Letters to the Thessalonians
A Translator's Handbook on the Letter to the Hebrews
A Translator's Handbook on the First Letter from Peter
A Translator's Handbook on the Letters of John

Guides:

A Translator's Guide to Selections from the First Five Books of the Old Testament
A Translator's Guide to Selected Psalms
A Translator's Guide to the Gospel of Matthew
A Translator's Guide to the Gospel of Mark
A Translator's Guide to the Gospel of Luke
A Translator's Guide to Paul's First Letter to the Corinthians
A Translator's Guide to Paul's Second Letter to the Corinthians
A Translator's Guide to Paul's Letters to Timothy and to Titus
A Translator's Guide to the Letters from James, Peter, and Jude

HELPS FOR TRANSLATORS

A TRANSLATOR'S GUIDE TO THE LETTERS FROM JAMES, PETER, AND JUDE

by

ROBERT G. BRATCHER

UNITED BIBLE SOCIETIES

London, New York,

Stuttgart

Books in the series of Helps for Translators may be ordered from a national Bible Society or from either of the following centers:

United Bible Societies
European Production Fund
D-7000 Stuttgart 80
Postfach 81 03 40
West Germany

United Bible Societies
1865 Broadway
New York, New York
U.S.A.

L.C. Cataloging in Publication Data

Bratcher, Robert G.
A translator's guide to the letters from James, Peter, and Jude.

(Helps for translators)
Bibliography: p.
Includes index.
1. Bible. N.T. Catholic Epistles—Translating. 2. Bible. N.T. Catholic Epistles—Criticism, interpretation, etc. I. Bible. N.T. James. 1984. II. Bible. N.T. Peter. 1984. III. Bible. N.T. Jude. IV. Title. V. Series.
BS2777.B73 1984 227'.9077 83-18159
ISBN 0-8267-0192-2

ABS-1984-1,500-1-L-08572

Contents

Preface

A Translator's Guide to the Letters from James, Peter, and Jude is a commentary belonging to the series of Guides prepared as part of the general series, *Helps for Translators*. Two kinds of commentaries on biblical books are being prepared by the United Bible Societies for the use of translators: the Handbooks and the Guides.

The Handbooks have proven to be valuable for a good number of translators. They are full-range commentaries that deal with problems of the original text, interpretation, vocabulary analysis, and discourse structure. They also include analysis of translation problems that may occur, and they provide suggestions for dealing with such problems. Some translators, however, prefer material in a more condensed form and from which they can easily retrieve information. Therefore the Translator's Guides do not, for example, attempt in every case to explain the reasons for the exegesis of a passage nor for a suggested solution to a translation problem. A Guide does not take away from translators the responsibility to make their own decisions, but it does attempt to give them practical information and to alert them to pitfalls they may otherwise overlook. It is hoped that such information will enable a translator to prepare a translation that is faithful to the meaning of the original and that is presented in a style which is appropriate and effective in communicating the message to the reader.

Other Guides are in preparation, covering material from both the Old Testament and the New Testament. Meanwhile, preparation of the Handbooks continues, so that the needs of all translators may be met. The United Bible Societies Subcommittee on Translations will welcome any suggestions for making both the Handbooks and the Guides more effective and useful for translators.

Abbreviations Used in This Volume

Books of the Bible

Col	Colossians
1,2 Cor	1,2 Corinthians
Deut	Deuteronomy
Eph	Ephesians
Exo	Exodus
Gal	Galatians
Gen	Genesis
Hab	Habakkuk
Heb	Hebrews
Hos	Hosea
Isa	Isaiah
Jer	Jeremiah
1,2 Kgs	1,2 Kings
Lev	Leviticus
Matt	Matthew
Num	Numbers
Phil	Philippians
Prov	Proverbs
Psa	Psalms
Rev	Revelation
Rom	Romans
1,2 Tim	1,2 Timothy

Other Abbreviations:

A.D.	anno Domini (in the year of our Lord)
B.C.	Before Christ
KJV	King James Version
NEB	New English Bible
RSV	Revised Standard Version
SpCL	Spanish common language version
TEV	Today's English Version
UBS	United Bible Societies

Translating the Letters from James, Peter, and Jude

The purpose of this Guide is to help the translator recognize and solve some of the problems that will be encountered in translating these Letters. The Guide is not intended to replace standard commentaries or the Handbooks for Translators, published by the United Bible Societies. Rather it seeks to provide, in a simple and consistent way, guidance for the translators so that their finished work will be faithful to the meaning of the original and clear and simple for the readers. Every translator is urged to seek additional help from available commentaries and Bible dictionaries, and to consult other translations.

Each Letter is divided into sections, with a heading that indicates the content of the section, or its main idea. The translator should read the whole section before starting to translate it.

The texts of the Revised Standard Version (RSV) and the Today's English Version (TEV) are used. The TEV section headings are included, and other headings are proposed. The translator will notice that in many places RSV and TEV differ considerably in form, although in the vast majority of cases the meaning is the same. The differences are due mainly to the fact that RSV is a translation that tries to reflect the form of the original Greek in terms of vocabulary, word classes, word order, and grammatical constructions. TEV attempts to express the meaning of the original as simply and naturally as possible, using a vocabulary and grammatical constructions that will be easily understood by most people who read English.

The translator is encouraged to express the meaning of the text in a form that will be natural, clear, and easy for the readers to understand.

Each verse is printed in full in the RSV (left hand column) and the TEV (right hand column) texts. Key passages in each verse are selected for consideration: they are underlined, and suggestions are made about other ways of translating. Sometimes it is necessary to expand somewhat on the explanations given, so that the translator may understand why certain ways of translating are proposed. Quotations of the RSV text are underlined, and quotations from TEV and other translations are placed within quotation marks.

The Guide takes notice of places where there are important differences among the Greek manuscripts of the Letters. In some places RSV and TEV differ in their decision about the Greek text (see 1 Peter 5.2,10; 2 Peter 2.4; Jude 5,22); the Guide briefly evaluates the evidence and recommends what a translator should do.

It is important that the translator be thoroughly acquainted with the content of each Letter before starting to translate it, so as to reflect the author's style and his exposition and development of the subject.

ON THE RELATION BETWEEN FIRST PETER AND SECOND PETER AND BETWEEN SECOND PETER AND JUDE

A translator should be aware of the fact that there are different opinions about the relation between 1 Peter and 2 Peter, and the relation between 2 Peter and Jude. The purpose of this brief statement is simply to indicate the various explanations given to these two questions, without any discussion of the arguments for or against any particular explanation. Nor is it possible, in the compass of such a short treatment, to advance reasons for preferring a particular explanation for each of the two questions.

1. 1 Peter and 2 Peter. (1) Some scholars believe that the apostle Peter wrote both Letters, and that the different styles of the two are explained by the role that Silas had in writing 1 Peter (see 5.12), while the apostle himself wrote 2 Peter. Some believe that 2 Peter was written before 1 Peter. (2) Others believe the apostle wrote 1 Peter but not 2 Peter. 2 Peter was written in the apostle's name by a follower of his, after Peter's death. Dates proposed for this Letter range from 95 to 150 A.D. (3) Still others believe both Letters were written by a follower of the apostle sometime in the first half of the second century A.D.

2. 2 Peter and Jude. A given explanation of the relation between the two will be influenced in part by the conclusion as to the authorship and the date of each of the two Letters. The obvious similarity between the two—nearly all of Jude is to be found in 2 Peter—has received several explanations: (1) Both Letters are dependent upon a common source, either oral or written. (2) Jude is dependent upon 2 Peter; very few hold to this view. (3) 2 Peter is dependent on Jude; this is the view of the majority.

A translator is encouraged to consult a Bible dictionary or encyclopedia, or some commentaries, in order to become acquainted with the reasons given in the defense of the explanation adopted for each of these two questions.

List of Topics in the Letter from James

Practically all commentaries and articles on *James* find it impossible to give an outline of *James*, and simply list the various topics the author discusses, as is done below. One notable exception, however, is Euan Fry "The Testing of Faith. A Study of the Structure of the Book of James" in *The Bible Translator*, vol. 29, no. 4 (October 1978), pp. 427-435. Translators should study Fry's article before beginning to translate this Letter.

1. Introduction 1.1
2. Faith and Wisdom 1.2-8
3. Poverty and Wealth 1.9-11
4. Testing and Temptation 1.12-15
5. God's Gifts 1.16-18
6. Human Anger 1.19-21
7. Hearing and Doing 1.22-25
8. True Religion 1.26-27
9. Warning against Discrimination 2.1-13
10. Faith and Actions 2.14-26
11. Controlling the Tongue 3.1-12
12. True Wisdom 3.13-18
13. Friendship with the World 4.1-10
14. Judging a Fellow Christian 4.11-12
15. Presuming on God's Goodness 4.13-17
16. Warning to the Rich 5.1-6
17. Patience 5.7-11
18. Making Promises 5.12
19. Prayer 5.13-18
20. Church Discipline 5.19-20

Title

THE LETTER FROM JAMES

It may be necessary to expand the title of the book somewhat: "The Letter that James Wrote to His Fellow Christians." It is not recommended that "Saint James" be used. Since this Letter is not addressed to any particular group of Christians (see 1.1), it is called a "General Epistle" or "Catholic Epistle" in some Bibles. The word "Catholic" in this sense means "general," "for all Christians."

Chapter 1

1.1

Revised Standard Version	Today's English Version
James, a servant of God and of the Lord Jesus Christ, To the twelve tribes in the Dispersion: Greeting.	From James, a servant of God and of the Lord Jesus Christ: Greetings to all God's people scattered over the whole world.

The Letter begins in the usual way, with the writer's name, the recipients, and a greeting.

Like the other Letters in the New Testament, a decision must be made here whether to retain the third person form, James...to the twelve tribes (or "From James..."), or to use the first person, "I, James... write this letter to." The third person can be retained, "This letter is from James...to...," but this may give the impression that someone other than James is writing these words.

James: the same as the Hebrew "Jacob." The traditional interpretation is that this James is the brother of Jesus (see Mark 6.3; Acts 15.13; Gal 1.19), but this is not certain.

a servant: "one who serves," or "I serve." The "service" is that of Christian ministry, and the word identifies the writer as a Christian leader. Since he does not identify himself further, it is assumed that he was quite well known. If the verb form is used it may be necessary to repeat it: "I serve God and I also serve the Lord Jesus Christ."

the twelve tribes in the Dispersion: the literal meaning would be "the Jewish people of the Dispersion (or, Diaspora)," that is, the Jewish people living outside Palestine. After the Babylonian captivity in the sixth century B.C., many Jews continued to live in countries outside Palestine, and they were known as the Diaspora (literally "scattered") Jews. But this Letter, in its present form, is addressed not to Jews but to Christians, so the language is figurative. (Some scholars, however, take the expression to refer specifically to Jewish Christians.) That is why TEV translates "all God's people scattered over the whole world." If the passive "scattered" is a problem, something like "who are living away from their true home," "who are living in exile" can be used. This world is not the true homeland of Christians; while here, they are in "exile" from their heavenly homeland (see Gal 4.26; Phil 3.20; 1 Peter 2.11). 1 Peter 1.1 has a similar phrase.

Greeting: this is not a distinctively Christian greeting, but the normal one used in Greek at that time (see Acts 15.23).

The verse may be translated as follows: "I am James, a servant of God and of the Lord Jesus Christ. I write this letter to all my fellow believers, in all the world. Greeting." Or, "I, James, a servant of God and of the Lord Jesus Christ, write this letter to...." In some languages it will be more natural to begin with the greeting.

SECTION HEADING

Faith and Wisdom: "Patience, Faith, and Wisdom," "True Wisdom Comes from God." The division of the Letter into sections is somewhat arbitrary, and a given heading may not adequately identify the material in the section. At best, the main subject should be given in the heading. It seems better to keep the sections fairly short, as TEV has done.

In this section, verses 2-8, James begins by referring to possible difficulties the readers may face on account of their faith (verses 2-4). Then he turns at once to the matter of true wisdom, for which a believer should pray, fully confident that God will give it (verses 5-8).

1.2-3 RSV	TEV
Count it all joy, my brethren, when you meet various trials, 3 for you know that the testing of your faith produces steadfastness.	**My brothers, consider yourselves fortunate when all kinds of trials come your way, 3 for you know that when your faith succeeds in facing such trials, the result is the ability to endure.**

Count it all joy: "Regard all times of testing as something to be happy about," or, more simply, "Be happy when you go through times of testing." TEV "consider yourselves fortunate when..." conveys the sense well enough in modern English; it would be better to say "Consider yourselves very fortunate."

my brethren: "my Christian brothers and sisters," "my fellow believers." The letter was not addressed only to male Christians.

when you meet various trials: "when various trials come your way." The Greek verb is "to fall among" and is used especially of dangers and difficulties; see Luke 10.30 (among thieves); Acts 27.41 (a ship running into a reef).

various trials: "difficulties of various kinds," "trials of different sorts." The word translated trials means a test. Here it refers to unpleasant experiences (possibly persecutions) that test the genuineness of the Christian faith which the readers have. By the addition of the adjective various, James is allowing for the possibility of hardship of different kinds.

the testing of your faith: the Greek word translated testing may mean the process itself, or else the result of the process. RSV takes it as the process; TEV takes it as the result, meaning that their faith has successfully stood the test and so is genuine. Faith is the Christian belief in Jesus as Savior and Lord.

steadfastness: "endurance," "constancy," the ability to go through difficult experiences and not give up.

The reader may find abstract terms difficult to understand, and so it may be necessary to use verbal phrases, making actors and actions explicit:

> My dear fellow Christians, when you undergo various difficulties, consider yourselves very fortunate. 3 For you know that when you go through such trials and still continue to believe in Jesus Christ, then you have proved that you are able to endure anything.

In some languages it may be more natural to reverse the order of the clauses in verses 2-3, as follows:

> You know very well, my fellow believers, that when you are subjected to hardships and your faith does not weaken, the result is the capacity to endure. So consider yourselves very fortunate when all sorts of trials come your way (or, ...when you are faced with all sorts of trials).

1.4 RSV	TEV
And let steadfastness have its full effect, that you may be perfect and complete, lacking in nothing.	Make sure that your endurance carries you all the way without failing, so that you may be perfect and complete, lacking nothing.

let: this is a way of expressing a command in English: "Your endurance must do all its work," that is, it must achieve complete results, must manifest itself completely, must remain alive and active at all times.

perfect and complete: this refers to the character of the readers; they must have all the qualities of developed, mature Christians, and not be deficient in any aspect. The adjective translated perfect means "complete, flawless, mature" (see its use in Matt 5.48; 19.21); the adjective translated complete means having all parts, or having all parts in working order.

The verse may be translated as follows:

> Your capacity to endure (or, your ability to go through difficult experiences) must never lessen, but must always be at work, so that you will be Christians who are perfect and complete, who do not lack any Christian virtue.

1.5 RSV	TEV
If any of you lacks wisdom, let him ask God, who gives to all men generously and without reproaching, and it will be given him.	But if any of you lacks wisdom, he should pray to God, who will give it to him; because God gives generously and graciously to all.

wisdom: this is not human good judgment which is based on learning; instead it is the wisdom of which the Old Testament speaks, which is based on reverence for and obedience to God. This wisdom results in a life of righteousness and goodness. The translation may say "If any of you is not wise (or, does not have the wisdom that God gives)."

let him ask God: "he should ask God to give it to him."

who gives to all men: "who gives to everyone," "who gives to all people."

without reproaching: that is, when God gives he does not scold the person for bothering him. God gives ungrudgingly, he does not complain when called upon to help, he is not reluctant to give, he does not have to be begged. "God gives generously and gladly to everyone who asks him."

it will be given him: it is better to use the active form, "God will give it to him."

1.6 RSV	TEV
But let him ask in faith, with no doubting, for he who doubts is like a wave of the sea that is driven and tossed by the wind.	But when you pray, you must believe and not doubt at all. Whoever doubts is like a wave in the sea that is driven and blown about by the wind.

let him ask in faith: "he (or, you) must believe (or, have faith) when he asks (or, you ask)." That is, whoever asks God for wisdom must believe that God will answer the prayer.

with no doubting: "and not doubt that God will do it." The negative form emphasizes what is said positively (as in verses 4,5).

like a wave of the sea that is driven and tossed by the wind: the figure here is that of a person who does not have a firm direction or a constant course. The two passive participles "driven" and "tossed" are synonyms; if there is difficulty in finding two appropriate terms, one will be sufficient: "like a wave of the sea that the wind blows in every (or, any) direction," "like a wave of the ocean that is blown every which way by the wind," "...that the wind blows from one direction to the other." Where sea and wave are unknown the translator can say "like the splashings of a river in a storm."

1.7-8 RSV	TEV
For that person must not suppose that a double-minded man, unstable in all his ways, will receive anything from the Lord.	A person like that, unable to make up his mind and undecided in all he does, must not think that he will receive anything from the Lord.

Both RSV and TEV restructure the various elements in these two verses, in order to have will receive anything from the Lord in its natural place at the end of the sentence, and not at the end of verse 7, as it is in Greek.

a double-minded man: "an undecided person," "a person who never can make up his mind about what he thinks," "who is always changing his mind." See the same phrase in Psalm 119.113.

unstable in all his ways: this refers to conduct: "is not consistent in his behavior," "has unpredictable behavior," "acts one way now, and a different way later." Figurative expressions are sometimes used: "a person with two hearts" or "a person with two stomachs."

the Lord: God.

The two verses may be translated as follows: "Such a person can never make up his mind, and is always changing his way of behaving. That person must not think that the Lord will answer his prayer (or, will give him what he asks for)."

SECTION HEADING

Poverty and Riches: "Advice for Poor Christians and for Rich Christians." It is not certain whether in verse 10 the rich means "the rich Christians," parallel to the poor Christians in verse 9. It may well be that the writer is talking about rich people in general, but this seems unlikely. James' concern is for his fellow Christians, and he is not giving advice to wealthy pagans.

1.9-10 RSV	TEV
Let the lowly brother boast in his exaltation, 10 and the rich in his humiliation, because like the flower of the grass he will pass away.	The Christian who is poor must be glad when God lifts him up, 10 and the rich Christian must be glad when God brings him down. For the rich will pass away like the flower of a wild plant.

the lowly brother: "the poor Christian," "a believer who is deprived," "a believer who owns nothing." The word lowly here refers to the outward circumstances of the person who belongs to the lower classes of society.

boast: "take pride in," "be proud of," "be happy about."

in his exaltation: "when God raises him from his lowly condition," "when God makes him prosper." Some understand the words to mean that a poor Christian should be happy because his lowly condition will bring him improvement in character. In the context this seems most unlikely. It is rather the confidence that God will reward him, either now or hereafter, that should fill him with pride.

and the rich: "and the rich Christian" (TEV). It is fairly certain that this is what the Greek means. This command is directed toward wealthy Christians, not wealthy people in general.

his humiliation: like the phrase his exaltation in verse 9, this means "when God brings him down," "when God causes him to lose his riches." It may be necessary in this clause to repeat the verb, as TEV has done: "the rich Christian must be proud when God brings him down." In the context, this refers to some experience in this life that causes him to lose his status and wealth. (See the related verbs "to be lifted up" and "to be brought low" in Luke 14.11.)

because: what follows is proof that the rich Christian will be brought low, and verse 11 develops this thought. The translation should not make it appear that what follows is the reason for the pride of the rich Christian. In some cases it may be better to begin a new sentence here, as TEV has done, without using a conjunction that might indicate cause.

like the flower of the grass he will pass away: "he will disappear like the bloom of a wild plant," "he will last no longer than a wild flower." The figure is from Isaiah 40.6-7 (see 1 Peter 1.24). The word translated grass means the weeds and plants that grow wild in the fields. The verb will pass away could mean "will die"; in the context, however, the meaning is that the rich man will not remain a rich man for very long. His riches will disappear, and he will no longer be a rich man. As commentators point out, to die is the fate and destiny of the poor no less than of the rich.

1.11

RSV	TEV
For the sun rises with its scorching heat and withers the grass; its flower falls, and its beauty perishes. So will the rich man fade away in the midst of his pursuits.	The sun rises with its blazing heat and burns the plant; its flower falls off, and its beauty is destroyed. In the same way the rich man will be destroyed while he goes about his business.

the sun rises with its scorching heat: "after the sun rises it soon begins to shine very hot." In connection with what follows it may be better to say "After the sun rises and begins to shine brightly, its burning heat causes the (wild) plants to wither."

scorching heat: or "the hot east wind," the sirocco which blows from the desert southeast of Palestine.

its flower falls: "the blossom falls off."

its beauty perishes: "its beauty disappears (or, is destroyed)."

will...fade away: "will lose his wealth," "will become poor." This means the same as will pass away in verse 10.

in the midst of his pursuits: "as he is busy with his affairs," "while he is looking after his business."

SECTION HEADING

Testing and Tempting: "The Purpose of Trials," "God Is the One Who Gives All Good Things."

In verses 12-14 James draws a distinction between outward hardships, which are meant to test the Christian's faith and can be of value, and inward temptations, which are not sent by God and which can lead to death.

This leads James to speak of God as the giver of good gifts in verses 16-18. Since these verses do not properly deal with the subject of testing or of tempting, they may be grouped as a separate section, with the heading "All Good Things Come from God."

1.12 RSV	TEV
Blessed is the man who endures trial, for when he has stood the test he will receive the crown of life which God has promised to those who love him.	Happy is the person who remains faithful under trials, because when he succeeds in passing such a test, he will receive as his reward the life which God has promised to those who love him.

Blessed is the man: "Happy is the person" (TEV), or, in the plural, "Happy are those." The Greek word translated Blessed has the same sense that the Hebrew word in Psalm 1.1 and elsewhere has. It means "happy," "fortunate," "is well off," "is in a truly good state."

endures trial: see steadfastness in verse 3 and trials in verse 2. Here the sense is "remains faithful through difficulties," "does not give up when he experiences hard times."

has stood the test: "has come through without giving up." This may be combined with the preceding clause into one statement: "Happy is the person who (successfully) endures all hardships (or, trials) and does not give up" or "...who succeeds in going through all hardships without losing his faith." In some languages it may be better to have "happy" at the end of the clause: "The person who...is happy" or "...is to be congratulated."

he will receive the crown of life: here life, that is, eternal life, is spoken of as a crown, which here means the laurel wreath that was placed on the head of the winner in an athletic contest (see 1 Cor 9.25; 2 Tim 4.8; Rev 2.10). RSV's literal translation is quite ambiguous, and something like TEV should be used: "he will receive as his reward the (eternal) life which God has promised...." Or else, "God will give him the eternal life which he has promised to those who love him."

God has promised: the Greek text says only "he has promised," but God is the subject and should be named.

In some languages he will receive may be better represented by "God will give him as a reward" or "God will reward him with the life that he has promised...."

1.13 RSV	TEV
Let no one say when he is tempted, "I am tempted by God"; for God cannot be tempted with evil and he himself tempts no one;	If a person is tempted by such trials, he must not say, "This temptation comes from God." For God cannot be tempted by evil, and he himself tempts no one.

Let: see verse 4.

when he is tempted: here the Greek uses a verb which is related to the noun translated trial in verse 12. The noun and the verb may mean "trial, testing" when the purpose is good, or "temptation" when the purpose is evil. As such, a hardship is morally neutral, but its effect can be good or bad. If it is endured, the result is good; if a Christian weakens, or loses his faith, the result is bad. (In verse 14, however, the biblical writer goes on to speak of temptations which come from within a person, and not from without.)

TEV tries to represent the double meaning of the word by translating "If a person is tempted by such trials." Barclay has "If in his ordeal a man is tempted to sin."

is tempted: "is tempted to sin" or "is tempted to do wrong."

I am tempted by God: "God is tempting me," "God is trying to make me sin," "This temptation comes from God."

It may be better to use indirect discourse, as follows: "When someone is being tempted (to do wrong), he must not think that God is the one who is tempting him."

God cannot be tempted with evil: "God is not tempted to do wrong," "God cannot be tempted to sin." The impossibility of God's being tempted arises from his nature; evil or sin holds no attraction for God, and what God himself does not experience he does not inflict upon anyone.

The statement may mean "God has no experience of evil," that is, God has nothing to do with evil." The New English Bible (NEB) translates "God is untouched by evil."

he himself tempts no one: "he does not try to make anyone sin (or, do wrong)."

1.14 RSV	TEV
but each person is tempted when he is lured and enticed by his own desire.	**But a person is tempted when he is drawn away and trapped by his own evil desire.**

lured and enticed: "attracted and drawn." The Greek verb translated enticed (TEV "trapped") comes from the word for "bait" which a hunter or a fisherman places in the trap or on the hook (or, net) to catch an animal or a fish. The two verbs are synonymous, and no precise psychological progression from one verb to the next should be read into the text.

desire: the Greek word usually means "evil desire," and in the present context this is what it means.

It may be difficult to speak of one's own "evil desire" tempting a person; but the translation should not say, or imply, "a person tempts himself." This "evil desire" is seen as a force that leads a person to do wrong: "a person is tempted to sin when his own evil desires attract him and catch (or, overcome) him." Or, "The person wants something so much that he gives in and is trapped by his desire. This is how he is tempted."

1.15 RSV	TEV
Then desire when it has conceived gives birth to sin; and sin when it is full-grown brings forth death.	**Then his evil desire conceives and gives birth to sin; and sin, when it is full-grown, gives birth to death.**

In this verse James uses the language of generation of life: desire is like a woman who becomes pregnant and gives birth to a child; that child, when grown up, in turn gives birth to another child. All three verbs, has conceived, gives birth to and brings forth, refer to the woman's role of childbearing.

It may not be possible or desirable to use this figurative language, and something like the following may serve: "When someone yields to an evil desire, the result is sin; and sin will in due time bring death." Or, if verbal phrases are better than abstract nouns: "When someone obeys his evil desire, then he commits a sin. And when a person keeps on sinning, then he will die spiritually (or, eternally)." Or else similes may be used: "The desire to do evil gives birth to sin, like a woman gives birth to a child."

death is here spiritual, or eternal, death; it is not simply physical death.

1.16 RSV	TEV
Do not be deceived, my beloved brethren.	**Do not be deceived, my dear brothers!**

Do not be deceived: either "Don't fool yourselves" or "Don't let anyone fool you."

my beloved brethren: "my dear fellow Christians," "my dear brothers and sisters" (see verse 2).

The writer adds this sharp warning in order to keep his readers from wrong ideas about the source of temptation, sin, and death. God is not the one responsible for them; God gives only good gifts to humankind.

1.17 RSV	TEV
Every good endowment and every perfect gift is from above, coming down from the Father of lights with whom there is no variation or shadow due to change.[a]	**Every good gift and every perfect present comes from heaven; it comes down from God, the Creator of the heavenly lights, who does not change or cause darkness by turning.**

[a]Other ancient authorities read *variation due to a shadow of turning*

good endowment...perfect gift: these are synonymous expressions. The English word endowment, as normally used, is unnatural in this context. "All good and perfect gifts," "Everything we receive that is good and perfect" or "Everything good and perfect that we have is a gift from..." or "...has been given us by...." Sometimes perfect may be represented by an expression such as "without any fault," "could not be better."

from above: "from heaven," where God lives.

from the Father of lights: "from God, who created the sun, moon, and stars" or "who created the heavenly bodies." Father here refers to

God's creation of the heavenly bodies; it is better to use the word "Creator" (TEV) or "Maker," or the phrase "who created" or "who made." Or else, "from God the Father, who created...."

For "heavenly lights" it may be necessary to say "the sun and the moon" or "the sun, moon, and stars." It is not very likely that the phrase means "the source of all light" in the sense of intellectual and moral enlightenment.

no variation or shadow due to change: both the form of the Greek text and its meaning are uncertain. As to the form, the RSV footnote indicates that another text, which is given by two of the oldest and best Greek manuscripts, has: "there is no variation due to a shadow of turning," that is, "there is no change caused by a turning (or, moving) shadow." Most modern translations follow the Greek text represented in the RSV and TEV texts.

with whom there is no variation: "who does not change" or "who is always the same."

with whom there is no...shadow due to change: the heavenly bodies, the sun and the moon, change their position: they "go up" and "go down," and so leave the world in darkness. God, however, never ceases to cause his light to shine, which is to say, he always pours forth life and spiritual knowledge. He does not move or turn, and so he never causes darkness to come over his creatures, that is, he does not leave them in ignorance and death. So the translation of the whole clause can be "God never changes (or, is always the same), and he never turns away from us and leaves us in darkness," or "With him there is no change, no darkness," or "In him there is never any change which causes darkness."

1.18 RSV	TEV
Of his own will he brought us forth by the word of truth that we should be a kind of first fruits of his creatures.	By his own will he brought us into being through the word of truth, so that we should have first place among all his creatures.

Of his own will: "Because he wanted (or, decided) to"; or else "With good will," "Because he was kind (or, good)."

he brought us forth: this translates the same verb brings forth used in verse 15. Here a maternal function is ascribed to God: "he bore us," "he gave us birth," "he brought us into being" (TEV). Or else, "he gave us spiritual life."

by the word of truth: the means by which God brought us into spiritual being is the Christian message, the gospel, which reveals the truth about God and his will for humanity.

that we should be: "so that we should be," "in order for us to be"; or, as result rather than purpose, "as a result, we are."

a kind of first fruits: by the use of a kind of ("so to speak") James indicates that first fruits is not a very adequate figure for what he wants to say. In Hebrew society the first part of the harvest of grain or of fruit was dedicated to God: it was special and, in a sense, better than the rest of the harvest (see the same figure in Rev 14.4; translated first converts in 1 Cor 16.15). It will be a rather unusual situation in which the literal a kind of first fruits of his creatures will make any sense, or any more sense than it does in English. The meaning may be expressed by "that we might be the best of all his creatures" or "and so we occupy first place among all his creatures." It is also possible to take it as meaning "that we might be the first specimens of his new creatures," that is, Christians are the first new creatures in the new world that God is creating.

Verse 18 may be translated as follows:

God himself, by means of the message of salvation, brought us into (spiritual) being (or, gave us spiritual life). He did it because he decided to, and because he wanted us to have the first place among all his creatures.

SECTION HEADING

Hearing and Doing: "We Should Hear and Obey the Gospel," "True Religion."

In this section, verses 19-27, James dwells on the need of believers not only to listen to the gospel but to put it into practice. The first three verses (19-21) deal with the need for self-control and may be handled as a separate section, with the heading, "Practice Self-Control."

1.19 RSV	TEV
Know this, my beloved brethren. Let every man be quick to hear, slow to speak, slow to anger,	Remember this, my dear brothers! Everyone must be quick to listen, but slow to speak and slow to become angry.

Know this: as in verse 16, James is emphasizing a truth his readers should already know; see also verse 3. The Greek may be understood as an indicative instead of an imperative, "You know this," which would refer backward to what James has just written; or else it may be understood as meaning "You have knowledge," "You are wise."

my beloved brethren: see verses 2,16.

every man: "everyone," "every person," "all of you."

quick to hear, slow to speak: "ready to listen (and learn), but slow to speak (and teach)." Both the listening and the speaking have to do with the Christian message.

slow to anger: "slow to get angry." In the next verse James explains why Christians should not get angry quickly.

1.20 RSV	TEV
for the anger of man does not work the righteousness of God.	Man's anger does not achieve God's righteous purpose.

the anger of man: "human anger," "a person's anger." Instead of the abstract phrase "human anger," it may be better to speak in concrete terms, "an angry person."

righteousness of God: here the phrase is used in the general sense of God's purpose and plan for his people. In the Old Testament that purpose and plan are revealed in the Law of Moses; in the New Testament, in the person and teachings of Jesus.

does not work the righteousness of God: "does not accomplish God's purpose for his people." Or "an angry person cannot do (or, obey) God's will" or "...cannot do what pleases God."

1.21 RSV	TEV
Therefore put away all filthiness and rank growth of wickedness and receive with meekness the implanted word, which is able to save your souls.	So get rid of every filthy habit and all wicked conduct. Submit to God and accept the word that he plants in your hearts, which is able to save you.

put away: "get rid of," "take off," "discard" like a garment.

all filthiness: "every filthy (or, sinful) habit."

rank growth of wickedness: "the evil which is so abundant." The Greek phrase does not mean "too much wickedness," as though a small amount were all right; it means that in any person, including Christians, there is a lot of wickedness.

receive with meekness the implanted word: the word is the gospel, the message of salvation; and the passive participle implanted indicates that God "plants" this message in the believer's heart. So James urges his readers to submit humbly, that is, willingly and obediently, to what God does. (See Luke 8.13 "receive the message gladly.") The process of salvation is here described as God's putting, or planting, his message into human hearts (see Deut 30.14; Jer 31.33).

able to save your souls: "has the power to save you." By the use of the word souls James is not limiting salvation to the immaterial part of the person, that is, the person's spirit, as the phrase your souls suggests. The use of "soul" for "person" is thoroughly biblical, and here it is better to translate "able to save you," as TEV and others do.

1.22 RSV	TEV
But be doers of the word, and not hearers only, deceiving yourselves.	Do not deceive yourselves by just listening to his word; instead, put it into practice.

be doers of the word: "put the gospel into practice," "live your Christian faith."

not hearers only: "don't just listen to it." It may be better to place deceiving yourselves at the beginning, as TEV does: "But do not fool yourselves by...." That is, they should not fool themselves that they are good Christians simply because they listen to the gospel message.

The verse may be translated as follows: "But don't fool yourselves into thinking that all you must do is listen to the message of salvation; you must put it into practice." Or, "It is not enough just to listen to the gospel; you must put it into practice. If you don't, you are only fooling yourselves." Or else, "You must live as your faith in the gospel teaches you to. If you don't, you are fooling yourselves."

1.23-24 RSV	TEV
For if any one is a hearer of the word and not a doer, he is like a man who observes his natural face in a mirror; 24 for he observes himself and goes away and at once forgets what he was like.	Whoever listens to the word but does not put it into practice is like a man who looks in a mirror and sees himself as he is. 24 He takes a good look at himself and then goes away and at once forgets what he looks like.

The figure used by James to describe a Christian who only listens to the gospel but does not live it is not very clear. In verse 25 the contrast is drawn between a quick look in a mirror, and a prolonged observation of the law that sets a person free. The main point of the figure seems to be a hasty, careless glance as opposed to a patient study of the gospel. In the first instance, the man quickly forgets what he looks like; in the same way the Christian who only listens but does not practice is not the least benefited by his exposure to the gospel message. In the second instance, the man persists in paying attention to the gospel, and puts it into practice; this man profits from his knowledge of the gospel message.

a man who observes his natural face in a mirror: here natural face translates "the face he was born with," "the face that nature gave him." It is better simply to say "looks at himself (or, at his face) in a mirror."

At that time a mirror was made of polished metal.

he observes himself: "he takes a look at himself," "he glances at himself." The same verb is used here that is used in verse 23.

forgets what he was like: "forgets what he (or, his face) looks like."

1.25 RSV	TEV
But he who looks into the perfect law, the law of liberty, and perseveres, being no hearer that forgets but a doer that acts, he shall be blessed in his doing.	But whoever looks closely into the perfect law that sets people free, who keeps on paying attention to it and does not simply listen and then forget it, but puts it into practice—that person will be blessed by God in what he does.

looks into: here a different verb is used (literally "bend down"), one that indicates a determined effort, not just a passing glance.

the perfect law: "the law that is best." This means the gospel, the Christian message of salvation. It is called perfect because it reveals God's full will for humanity. It may seem strange that James should use the word law to refer to his gospel. But the word in the Bible, both in Hebrew and in Greek, which is used to refer to the Hebrew religion, has a wider range of meaning than the English word law has. It means God's revelation to his people, his teachings, his whole plan for their lives as individuals and as a community. In James' thinking the gospel is the perfect revelation of God's will for his people, and so he calls it the perfect law, the law "that sets people free" (TEV).

the law of liberty: "the law that is the source of liberty," "the law that sets us free."

perseveres: "continues to examine it" or "keeps on studying it." Here the figure of a mirror is dropped, and James talks about a close and persistent study of and obedience to the gospel message.

being no hearer that forgets but a doer that acts: this awkward English clause is an attempt to follow the form of the Greek. "He is not a person who hears and then forgets (what he heard), but is one who puts into practice what he hears."

shall be blessed: for the adjective blessed see 1.12. Here it means either "he will be happy (or, fortunate) in all he does," that is, "he will prosper in everything he does," or else "he will be blessed by God in all that he does" (or, "God will bless everything he does"). Probably the first suggestion is to be preferred.

The following may serve as a model for the translation of this verse:

> But if a person examines closely the teaching of the gospel, which is the perfect law of God that sets people free, and keeps on paying attention to it, and if that person does not forget what he is taught but puts it into practice, then he will prosper in everything he does.

It may be necessary to have a simpler structure, as follows:

> The gospel is the perfect law of God and it sets people free. If a person studies the teachings of the gospel closely, and if that person does not forget what the gospel teaches but puts it into practice, then that person will prosper in everything he does.

1.26 RSV	TEV
If any one thinks he is religious, and does not bridle his tongue but deceives his heart, this man's religion is vain.	Does anyone think he is religious? If he does not control his tongue, his religion is worthless and he deceives himself.

If any one thinks he is religious: "If a person believes that he is a good Christian," "If a person believes he obeys God's will in everything." TEV restructures the first part of the verse, phrasing it as a question: "Does anyone think he is religious?" This could well be put into the second person: "Do you think that you are religious (or, a good Christian)?"

does not bridle his tongue: "doesn't control his talking," "talks without restraint."

deceives his heart: "fools himself"; see similar statements in verses 16,22.

vain: "worthless" (TEV), "of no use," "has no value."

The verse may be translated as follows:

> A person may think he is a good Christian. But he is fooling himself (or, he is mistaken) if he does not control his talking. His religion is of no value.

1.27 RSV	TEV
Religion that is pure and undefiled before God and the Father is this: to visit orphans and widows in their affliction, and to keep oneself unstained from the world.	What God the Father considers to be pure and genuine religion is this: to take care of orphans and widows in their suffering and to keep oneself from being corrupted by the world.

pure and undefiled: two synonyms, which may be translated "pure and genuine" or "completely pure." It may be necessary to translate pure by thc expression "is all good" or "has nothing bad in it."

before God and the Father: in English this means two beings. What James is saying is "in the sight of God, the Father" or "...of God, our Father."

to visit: this is too weak for the Greek verb: "to take care of" (TEV), "to help," "to look after."

affliction: "need," "suffering" (TEV), "difficulties." Orphans and widows are the special object of God's concern (Deut 10.18; Psa 68.5; 146.9).

unstained from the world: here sin is seen as a blot, a stain, that defiles a person, that is, makes a person unfit to worship God. The source of this defilement is the world, that is, sinful and wicked humanity, disobedient to God's commands.

Instead of nouns such as religion and affliction, it may be better to use verbal phrases, as follows: "God our Father considers that a person who is truly religious, without any defects, does this: he takes care of (or, helps) orphans and widows who are in need, and he keeps himself from being corrupted by the evil in the world."

Chapter 2

SECTION HEADING

Warning against Prejudice: "Warning against Discrimination," "Treat All People Alike."

In this section, verses 1-13, James warns his readers not to give the rich any special treatment; they are to treat rich and poor in the same way. Discrimination, he says, is against the Christian law, and all Christians should be aware of the fact that they will be judged according to the demands of the Christian law.

2.1

RSV	TEV
My brethren, show no partiality as you hold the faith of our Lord Jesus Christ, the Lord of glory.	My brothers, as believers in our Lord Jesus Christ, the Lord of glory, you must never treat people in different ways according to their outward appearance.

My brethren: see 1.2.

show no partiality: "do not discriminate," "do not treat people differently," or "treat everyone the same way." The Greek phrase means to judge someone based on that person's outward appearance (see Rom 2.11; Eph 6.9; Col 3.25). Here it applies specifically to differences in social position and wealth.

as you hold the faith of our Lord Jesus Christ: "as people who believe in our Lord Jesus Christ." This can be combined with the preceding as follows: "My fellow Christians, you are (firm) believers in our Lord Jesus Christ, the Lord of glory, and so you must not show favoritism in your treatment of people," or "...you must not treat people differently because of their different social standing."

the Lord of glory: "our glorious Lord," "our majestic (or, divine) Lord," "the Lord whom we honor." In the Bible, glory, when used of God, refers to the bright light which reveals his saving presence with his people. This glory is considered the revelation of the very nature of God, especially in his activity as savior of his people. Jesus Christ not only reveals God's saving power but is himself that saving power.

2.2

RSV	TEV
For if a man with gold rings and in fine clothing comes into your assembly, and a poor man in shabby clothing also comes in,	Suppose a rich man wearing a gold ring and fine clothes comes to your meeting, and a poor man in ragged clothes also comes.

RSV, following the form of the Greek text, has verses 2-4 as one long and complex question. It is better to restructure the material and divide it into smaller units, for easier understanding. (See below, at the end of verse 4, for a possible restructuring.)

with gold rings and in fine clothing: "dressed in expensive clothes and wearing gold rings." It seems that the rich man and the poor man James talks about are considered visitors, not members of the Christian group.

your assembly: "your gathering," "your meeting" (TEV), "your worship meeting." The Greek noun used here is the one that in a Jewish context means "synagogue."

shabby clothing: "poorly dressed," "in ragged clothes" (TEV).

2.3 RSV	TEV
and you pay attention to the one who wears the fine clothing and say, "Have a seat here, please," while you say to the poor man, "Stand there," or, "Sit at my feet,"	If you show more respect to the well-dressed man and say to him, "Have this best seat here," but say to the poor man, "Stand over there, or sit here on the floor by my feet,"

you pay attention to: "you treat with respect," "you receive him well," "you give him a courteous welcome."

Have a seat here, please: "Will you please sit down here." The Greek word that RSV translates please is translated by TEV "best (seat)." Either is possible; most modern translations are like TEV: "a good place to sit," "a seat of honor." For "the best seats in the synagogues" see Mark 12.39; Matthew 23.6; Luke 11.43; 20.46.

"Stand there," or, "Sit at my feet": RSV takes the Greek text to mean that a Christian in the meeting will tell the poor man "You stand over there," or else say to him "You sit here by my feet." TEV takes the text to mean that the Christian in the meeting is giving the poor man a choice either to stand over there or else to sit at his feet. There is not much practical difference between the two, and a translator should feel free to choose either one. It is to be noticed that with regard to what is said to the poor man, the Greek text says "you (plural) say to the poor man...'Sit here at my feet.'" Naturally not all the assembled believers would speak either to the rich man or to the poor man, but only one of them, who would speak in the name of the whole group. If the switch from the second plural "you say" to the first singular "my feet" must be avoided, the translation can say "one of you says...."

2.4 RSV	TEV
have you not made distinctions among yourselves, and become judges with evil thoughts?	then you are guilty of creating distinctions among yourselves and of making judgments based on evil motives.

have you not made distinctions among yourselves: "aren't you guilty of introducing (or, causing) divisions in your group...?" These "divisions," of course, are those based on social standing and wealth. Some take the Greek verb to mean "to have doubts, to waver," that is, to depart from Christian conduct. Most commentators and translators, however, take the sense to be "divide, separate."

become judges with evil thoughts: RSV sounds like "dirty-minded judges." The meaning is "have made judgments (of others) from evil motives," "have used wrong standards in judging people." Here the function of "judging" is precisely that of passing judgment on people on the basis of their social standing. This standard for judging others is evil, sinful, unchristian.

The rhetorical question have you not...? is a way of saying "you have indeed."

> Verses 2-4 may be restructured and divided as follows:
> Suppose you are meeting (for worship) and two men come in. One of them is dressed in expensive clothes and wears a gold ring; the other man is poor, and he is dressed in rags (or, shabby clothes). 3 You welcome the rich man respectfully, and one of you says to him, "Sit here in this good seat (or, seat of honor)." And someone else says to the poor man, "Stand over there, or else sit here on the floor by my feet." 4 Don't you see what you are doing? You are creating divisions among yourselves, and you are using evil standards to judge people (or, your judgment of people is based on evil motives).

2.5 RSV	TEV
Listen, my beloved brethren. Has not God chosen those who are poor in the world to be rich in faith and heirs of the kingdom which he has promised to those who love him?	**Listen, my dear brothers! God chose the poor people of this world to be rich in faith and to possess the kingdom which he promised to those who love him.**

my beloved brethren: see 1.2.

Has not God chosen...?: another rhetorical question, an effective way of making a strong statement: "God has indeed chosen" or "You know that God has chosen." The verb "to choose" is frequently used in the Bible to indicate God's initiative and his activity in saving his people.

poor in the world: "poor in this life," "people the world considers poor," "poor by the world's standard." As in 1.27, the world means the unbelievers, the non-Christians. For this thought see 1 Corinthians 1.26-28.

rich in faith: in Christian terms these people are rich; their faith makes them rich spiritually. Here "in faith" is contrasted with "to the world" and means, in effect, "rich by God's standards," "rich because of what God has done for them."

heirs of the kingdom: here the kingdom is God's kingdom, the situation in which God's authority is acknowledged and his commands are obeyed. The use of heirs shows that God's kingdom is spoken of here as a future reality. The language of "to inherit" should be used with care, so as to avoid giving the impression that only at the death of the donor (God) will people "inherit" what he has promised to give them. See Matthew 25.34; and see "inherit eternal life" in Mark 10.17 and parallels.

It may not be possible, like TEV, to say "to possess the kingdom"; so it may be necessary to say "to belong to the kingdom," or "to have part in the kingdom," or "to be citizens of the kingdom."

he has promised to those who love him: the same as in 1.12.

The verse may be translated as follows:

Now pay attention, my dear brothers and sisters! You know very well that God has chosen (to be his people) those whom non-Christians consider poor (or, those who according to the world's standard are poor). But because of their faith in Jesus Christ, such people are spiritually rich, and will belong to the Kingdom which God has promised to those who love him.

2.6

RSV	TEV
But you have dishonored the poor man. Is it not the rich who oppress you, is it not they who drag you into court?	But you dishonor the poor! Who are the ones who oppress you and drag you before the judges? The rich!

dishonored: "treated with disrespect," "insulted," "humiliated."

the poor man: it is better to use a plural, "those who are poor," "poor people."

Is it not...?: another rhetorical question. "The rich people are the very ones who...."

oppress: "exploit," "lord over," "grind down."

drag you into court: "take you to be condemned by the judge." The implication is that the rich were able to get the judges to rule in their favor against the poor Christians; so the poor Christians did not receive justice in court. It is not necessary to use a verb that means to drag physically; it means "to compel against one's will," "to force to go." It should not appear that a rich man would be actually dragging a poor man into court.

2.7

RSV	TEV
Is it not they who blaspheme the honorable name which was invoked over you?	They are the ones who speak evil of that good name which has been given to you.

Is it not they...?: another rhetorical question. "They are the ones who..." (TEV). Or the question form may be used, together with the answer: "Is it not they who...? Yes, they are the very ones who do that."

blaspheme: "insult," "speak evil of" (TEV), "slander," "use with contempt."

the honorable name which was invoked over you: this refers either to the name "Christian," or else to "Jesus Christ," or else to the confession "Jesus is Lord." The passive verbal phrase was invoked over you seems to refer to baptism, when they were baptized "in the name of Jesus Christ" (see Acts 2.38). The whole phrase may be translated, "the noble (or, honored) name which was given you (or, which you received; or, which you confessed) when you became a Christian."

2.8 RSV	TEV
If you really fulfil the royal law, according to the scripture, "You shall love your neighbor as yourself," you do well.	You will be doing the right thing if you obey the law of the Kingdom, which is found in the scripture, "Love your neighbor as you love yourself."

really fulfil: "obey perfectly," "follow completely," "truly put into practice."

the royal law: "God's law," "the law of the Kingdom" (TEV), or "the supreme law" (see perfect law 1.25).

according to the scripture: "which is found in the passage of scripture." The passage quoted is from Leviticus 19.18; it was quoted also by Jesus (Mark 12.31; Matt 19.19; 22.39; Luke 10.27) and by Paul (Gal 5.14; Rom 13.9). In the Old Testament setting your neighbor refers to fellow Jews. In English neighbor means a person who lives near one's home. Here the most inclusive sense possible is intended, "Your fellow human beings" or "others." "Love others as (much as) you love yourself." The command is given in the second person singular ("you" in Lev 19.18 is the people of Israel); but it may be better here to use the plural (as in you...fulfil and you do well).

you do well: it may be better to place this at the beginning of the verse, as follows: "You will all be doing the right thing if you faithfully obey the supreme law found in the scripture: 'Love others as (much as) you love yourselves.'"

2.9 RSV	TEV
But if you show partiality, you commit sin, and are convicted by the law as transgressors.	But if you treat people according to their outward appearance, you are guilty of sin, and the Law condemns you as a lawbreaker.

show partiality: as in verse 1.

you commit sin: "you are guilty of sin" (TEV). The "law of the Kingdom" requires that a Christian love all people and so treat them all alike. Whoever shows more love for some people than for others is guilty of breaking that law.

and convicted by the law as transgressors: "and the Law condemns you as a lawbreaker" (TEV). It may not be natural to speak of the law functioning as a judge, so it may be necessary to say "and, according to the law, you are a lawbreaker" or, more simply, "and you are guilty of breaking the law."

2.10 RSV	TEV
For whoever keeps the whole law but fails in one point has become guilty of all of it.	Whoever breaks one commandment is guilty of breaking them all.

The point of James' statement in this verse is that the Law of God is indivisible; it does not consist of different laws that are simply brought together in a group, but each individual law expresses one aspect of the supreme law to love others as we love ourselves. "Anyone who obeys all the laws except one is guilty of disobeying all of them" or "...it is as though he had broken all of them." For a similar thought see Matthew 5.18-19; Galatians 3.10.

fails in one point: that is, disobeys one law, or one part of a law.

2.11 RSV	TEV
For he who said, "Do not commit adultery," said also, "Do not kill." If you do not commit adultery but do kill, you have become a transgressor of the law.	For the same one who said, "Do not commit adultery," also said, "Do not commit murder." Even if you do not commit adultery, you have become a lawbreaker if you commit murder.

he who said: a reference to God (not to Moses).

Do not commit adultery: Exodus 20.14. The singular "you" is all Israel. "Do not sleep with another person's spouse," "Do not have intercourse with another man's wife (or, another woman's husband)." The command applies to men and women.

Do not kill: Exodus 20.13. In Exodus this is a prohibition against unauthorized killing of a fellow Jew. Here it prohibits a Christian from killing anyone.

a transgressor of the law: as in verse 9.

The verse may be translated as follows:

God commanded, "Do not commit adultery." He also commanded, "Do not commit murder." So if you do not commit adultery but you do commit murder, then you are guilty of breaking the whole law.

2.12 RSV	TEV
So speak and so act as those who are to be judged under the law of liberty.	Speak and act as people who will be judged by the law that sets us free.

So speak and so act: "Speak and act in the way that people should who...."

who are to be judged under the law of liberty: it is God who judges, and he judges according to the gospel, the law of liberty (see 1.25). "Who will be judged by God in accordance with the law that sets us free."

2.13 RSV

For judgment is without mercy to one who has shown no mercy; yet mercy triumphs over judgment.

TEV

For God will not show mercy when he judges the person who has not been merciful; but mercy triumphs over judgment.

For judgment is without mercy: it is better to use personal terms: "For God shows no mercy when he judges," "For when God judges, he is not merciful."

to one who has shown no mercy: "to the person who has not been merciful to others." See Matthew 5.7 and the parable of the unmerciful servant (Matt 18.21-35).

yet mercy triumphs over judgment: "mercy will win over judgment." The question is whose mercy, and whose judgment? It is quite certain that it is God's judgment of people. Mercy may also be God's mercy; that is, when God judges us he should condemn us, yet his mercy will prevail. If this meaning is preferred, a translation can be "God's mercy will succeed (or, God will be merciful) when he judges people." But in this context it is more likely that mercy is a human quality, and that the sense is "but a merciful person will not be condemned by God." This meaning contrasts well with the preceding, "a merciless person will not be shown mercy when God judges him."

SECTION HEADING

Faith and Actions: "Christians Must Not Only Believe but Must Also Act," "Faith Without Actions Is Worthless."

In this section, verses 14-26, James discusses at length the relation between Christian faith and Christian acts. This is a response to those who wished to divorce faith from actions and who claimed that faith alone, apart from actions, is all that is needed to save a person. James is concerned to show that faith and actions cannot be separated: genuine Christian faith results in actions. No person can claim to have faith if his or her actions do not prove it. It is not a case of *either* faith *or* actions but of *both* faith *and* actions.

2.14 RSV

What does it profit, my brethren, if a man says he has faith but has not works? Can his faith save him?

TEV

My brothers, what good is it for someone to say that he has faith if his actions do not prove it? Can that faith save him?

What does it profit: this is a rhetorical question meaning "It doesn't profit," "It does no good," "Nothing is accomplished."

my brethren: see 1.2.

if a man says: "if someone says," "or else, "if someone claims." Or, better, "if a Christian (or, believer) claims."

but has not works: in RSV, this can be misunderstood to be part of what the unidentified person (a man) says. So in some cases it may be well to use the direct form of address: "...if a believer says, 'I have faith,' but he doesn't have actions?" (Another way of handling this is proposed below.)

has not works: "does not do the things that a Christian should do," "does not live as a Christian should." It is clear from the context (verses 15-16) that these are good works motivated by Christian love. TEV "if his actions do not prove it" brings out more clearly the relation between faith and works (see also the Spanish common language translation [SpCL] "if his actions do not demonstrate it"; NEB "when he does nothing to show it").

Can his faith save him?: "Can that (kind of) faith save him?" (TEV). The implied answer is "No": "That (kind of) faith cannot save him."

The verse may be translated as follows:

> My (dear) fellow believers: it is worthless for a Christian to claim that he has faith (or, he believes in Jesus Christ) if he doesn't put his faith into practice. That kind of faith cannot save him.

2.15-16 RSV	TEV
If a brother or sister is ill-clad and in lack of daily food, 16 and one of you says to them, "Go in peace, be warmed and filled," without giving them the things needed for the body, what does it profit?	Suppose there are brothers or sisters who need clothes and don't have enough to eat. 16 What good is there in your saying to them, "God bless you! Keep warm and eat well!"—if you don't give them the necessities of life?

If: James is using an imaginary case as an example. As in 2.2, a normal way of expressing this in English is "Suppose...."

is ill-clad: "is poorly clothed," "has no decent clothes," "is dressed in rags." The Greek says "are naked," but the meaning is "are without necessary clothing."

in lack of daily food: "does not have enough food for each day" or "doesn't have enough to eat that day."

one of you: as in 2.3 the one person speaks for the whole group; the following Greek verbal clause "but you do not give" is plural, referring to the congregation as a whole.

Go in peace: this represents the normal Jewish greeting; "Good-bye" (that is, "God be with you"); "God bless you," "May everything go well for you"—or any other expression of good will used in saying good-bye to a person. "Go, and God be with you." In Greek the verbs are plural.

be warmed and filled: in terms of clothes and food. "Dress warmly (or, Keep warmly dressed) and eat enough." Or, in more informal speech, "Don't forget to dress warmly and eat plenty!"

the things needed for the body: there will be different expressions for what are called the basic necessities of life: food, clothing, and shelter. "Their physical needs," "the things they need in order to live."

what does it profit: as at the beginning of verse 14.

James 2.15-16

Verses 15-16 may be translated as follows:
Suppose there are some fellow Christians who don't have enough clothes to wear or food to eat. 16 If you don't give them what they need (or, the clothes and food they need), it does no good (or, it is worthless) for you to say to them, "Go, and may God be with you! Be sure to dress warmly and eat plenty!"

2.17 RSV	TEV
So faith by itself, if it has no works, is dead.	So it is with faith: if it is alone and includes no actions, then it is dead.

faith by itself, if it has no works: it may be better to use verbal phrases instead of the nouns faith and works. "A person who (only) believes but does not put his faith into practice" or "A person who believes but does nothing to show it."

Instead of TEV "and includes no actions" it may be better to say "and is not accompanied by actions" or "and does not result in action."

is dead: as in verse 26, below, the word means "ineffective," "impotent," "powerless," "can do nothing."

2.18 RSV	TEV
But some one will say, "You have faith and I have works." Show me your faith apart from your works, and I by my works will show you my faith.	But someone will say, "One person has faith, another has actions." My answer is, "Show me how anyone can have faith without actions. I will show you my faith by my actions."

But some one will say: James now takes up what must have been a fairly common statement made by Christians whose views James is condemning. Most commentaries and translations agree that the unnamed opponents's words are limited to the first statement, as RSV and TEV indicate: "You have faith and I have works." The pronouns You and I, however, do not indicate that only James (You) and the speaker (I) are meant; this is a way of speaking in a general sense: "One person...another" (TEV). What this unnamed Christian opponent means is that the two, faith and works, are separate gifts, and a believer may have one or the other, but not necessarily both. James' reply is that the two are inseparable: there is no faith without works. TEV puts James' reply within quotation marks, as a direct answer to the opponent's statement.

Show me...I...will show you: this can be understood to mean visible proof ("reveal, demonstrate") or a convincing argument ("prove, convince"). TEV adds "My answer is" in order to make clear to the hearer (and to the reader as well) that what follows is not part of the first statement, that of the opponent.

The verse may be translated as follows:

But someone may say, "Some Christians believe, other Christians perform good deeds." I say (to that person),

"Prove to me, if you can, that a Christian can believe and not perform good deeds. But I, by means of my good deeds, will prove to you that I believe."

2.19 RSV	TEV
You believe that God is one; you do well. Even the demons believe—and shudder.	Do you believe that there is only one God? Good! The demons also believe—and tremble with fear.

James is still talking to the opponent: through verse 23 the verbs of address are all second person singular; in verse 24 You see is plural. In languages where quotation marks or their equivalents are used, a translation may extend the quoted reply to the end of verse 23 instead of closing the quotation at the end of verse 18 as TEV does.

You believe that God is one: as RSV translates it, the statement has to do with the unity, or oneness, of God. According to TEV, it has to do with the uniqueness of God: "there is only one God." The statement is an obvious allusion to the basic affirmation of the Hebrew religion in Deuteronomy 6.4. Most translations are like TEV: "there is (only) one God."

This part of the verse may be punctuated as a statement (RSV) or as a question (TEV). The difference is not great, for the question is rhetorical, equivalent to a strong affirmation: "I know you believe there is one God."

you do well: as the comment that follows makes clear, this is slightly ironical: "That's fine!" "Good for you!" "Excellent!" "Congratulations!"

Even the demons believe: by this remark James is pointing out that a belief in the one God does not of itself indicate that a person has true Christian faith.

demons: or "evil spirits." These are regarded as spiritual evil beings.

and shudder: "and (they) tremble" (TEV), "and they are afraid," that is, of God. Their "faith" does them no good.

The verse may be translated as follows:

> Of course you believe that there is only the one God. That's fine! But remember that even the demons believe that—and it makes them tremble with fear.

2.20 RSV	TEV
Do you want to be shown, you shallow man, that faith apart from works is barren?	You fool! Do you want to be shown that faith without actions is useless?[a]

[a]useless; *some manuscripts have* dead.

Do you want to be shown...?: or "Do you want me to prove to you ...?" The question is rhetorical, and the meaning may be represented in the form of a statement. "I will now prove to you...."

you shallow man: "foolish man" or "you fool." See similar expressions in Matthew 5.22; Luke 12.20; 1 Corinthians 15.36.

faith apart from works: as in verse 18.

barren: "unproductive," "ineffective," "useless," "worthless." As the TEV footnote shows, instead of "useless" many Greek manuscripts and early versions have (as in 2.26) "dead." It is clear that "useless" and not "dead" is the original text here.

2.21 RSV	TEV
Was not Abraham our father justified by works, when he offered his son Isaac upon the altar?	How was our ancestor Abraham put right with God? It was through his actions, when he offered his son Isaac on the altar.

Was not...?: another rhetorical question. TEV breaks up the whole question into a question and an answer.

Abraham our father: "our ancestor Abraham"; the our includes all believers. See the same expression in Romans 4.1,16.

justified: the Greek verb may mean "be acquitted (or, forgiven)," "be declared innocent," in the context of a law court, with God as Judge, pronouncing sentence on a person. In a more general sense the verb "to justify" can mean "to be pleased with," "to accept (as righteous)," or, as Paul uses it, "to put into a right relationship." Here the general sense "approve" seems adequate: "Our ancestor Abraham was approved by God" or, in the active voice, "God approved of our ancestor Abraham."

justified by works: "approved because of what he did," "approved for his actions." The one "work" of Abraham which James cites was Abraham's willingness to offer his son Isaac as a sacrifice (Gen 22.1-14).

offered: as James and the people he wrote to knew, Isaac was not slain as a sacrifice on the altar; but Abraham was ready to do so.

The verse may be translated as follows:

> Why did God approve of Abraham? Because of what Abraham did: he offered his son Isaac on the altar as a sacrifice to God.

2.22-23 RSV	TEV
You see that faith was active along with his works, and faith was completed by works, 23 and the scripture was fulfilled which says, "Abraham believed God, and it was reckoned to him as righteousness"; and he was called the friend of God.	Can't you see? His faith and his actions worked together; his faith was made perfect through his actions. 23 And the scripture came true that said, "Abraham believed God, and because of his faith God accepted him as righteous." And so Abraham was called God's friend.

You see: "You understand." This is the answer to the question in verse 20, Do you want to be shown...?

faith was active along with his works: the argument here is that Abraham believed God's promise (as the quotation of Gen 15.6 in verse 23 makes clear). Not only did he believe, he also acted: "his faith was cooperating with (or, working together with) his actions."

faith was completed by works: "his faith was made perfect by means of his actions," "his actions made his faith perfect (or, complete)." For perfect see 1.4. It may be easier in verse 22 to use verbal phrases instead of the nouns faith and works: "So you see that Abraham believed and acted (or, Abraham had faith and he also did what God demanded); and so, because of what he did, Abraham was able to believe (in God) completely (or, Abraham's faith became perfect)."

the scripture: see 2.8.

was fulfilled: "came true"; or "it happened as the scripture had said" or "what the scripture had said did happen."

The quotation is from the Septuagint, the Greek translation of Genesis 15.6.

it was reckoned to him as righteousness: in Greek the noun translated righteousness is related to the verb which RSV translates "to justify" in verse 21. The verb translated reckoned is a commercial term and means "to place to one's credit," "to add to one's (bank) account." The whole verbal clause may be translated "God considered (or, treated) him (as) a righteous person."

Abraham believed God: in the context of Genesis 15.6, Abraham's belief had to do with God's promise to him that he would have many descendants. "Because Abraham believed God's promise, God accepted him (or, approved of him) as a righteous (or, good) man."

he was called the friend of God: or "God said that Abraham was his friend," or "God said, 'Abraham is my friend.'" The statement is found in Isaiah 41.8; see also 2 Chronicles 20.7.

2.24 RSV	TEV
You see that a man is justified by works and not by faith alone.	You see, then, that it is by his actions that a person is put right with God, and not by his faith alone.

You see: this is plural (whereas in verse 22 it is singular); here James is speaking to his readers and not, as in verses 18b-23, to the Christian opponent. In some languages it may be more natural and effective to say, "We see," the "We" being inclusive.

a man is justified by works and not by faith alone: "God approves of a person not only because that person believes, but also because that person puts faith into practice"; or "God approves of a person because of what that person does, and not just because that person believes."

2.25 RSV	TEV
And in the same way was not also Rahab the harlot justified by works when she received the	It was the same with the prostitute Rahab. She was put right with God through her actions,

RSV	TEV
messengers and sent them out another way?	**by welcoming the Israelite spies and helping them to escape by a different road.**

Like verse 21, the case of Rahab the harlot is presented in the form of a rhetorical question. "The same thing happened with the prostitute Rahab." For her story see Joshua 2.1-21; 6.17,25. Care must be taken to avoid a vulgar term to refer to a prostitute.

justified by works: as in verse 21, Rahab's "work" was to welcome the Israelite spies, hide them from the king of Jericho's officials, and then send the two spies away from the city by a different road so they would not be captured by the king's officials.

received: "welcomed" or "welcomed secretly."

the messengers: "the (two) Israelite spies," "the spies sent by Joshua." Although the Greek word means "messengers," the task of the two Israelites was not to carry a message to anyone in Jericho but to spy out the city and the surrounding country. This was a military expedition.

2.26 RSV	TEV
For as the body apart from the spirit is dead, so faith apart from works is dead.	**So then, as the body without the spirit is dead, also faith without actions is dead.**

In conclusion James compares faith without works to a body without the living spirit in it. "Faith without works is dead, just like a body without spirit (or, breath)." Care must be taken to use a word for spirit which will indicate the vital principle of life in a person, not a ghost or a disembodied (evil) spirit. It may be better to use verbal phrases, as follows: "If a Christian only believes, but does not have actions to show it, his faith is useless: it is just like a dead body." A body cannot live without life-giving spirit: Christian faith is not alive without works.

Chapter 3

SECTION HEADING

The Tongue: "Controlling the Tongue," "A Christian Must Be Careful about Talking."

James has already made reference to the matter of uncontrolled talk (1.19,26). In this section he develops the subject more fully. The amount of space he devotes to it indicates that this was a real problem, and James wanted his readers to be aware of the disastrous consequences of loose talk. He speaks first of the power of the tongue (verses 1-5a) and then goes on to describe the destructive effect of loose talk (verses 5b-8). In the last four verses (verses 9-12) he deals specifically with the matter of inconsistency.

3.1

RSV	TEV
Let not many of you become teachers, my brethren, for you know that we who teach shall be judged with greater strictness.	My brothers, not many of you should become teachers. As you know, we teachers will be judged with greater strictness than others.

teachers: a recognized office in the Church (see Acts 13.1; 1 Cor 12.28; Eph 4.11). They taught the responsibilities and duties of the Christian life, and this Letter of James itself is an example of the kind of lessons that a Christian teacher would give.

If the negative expression not many of you is difficult to represent, the positive form may be useful: "Only a few of you should want (or, try) to be teachers."

my brethren: see 1.2.

you know: see 1.3.

we who teach: "we who are teachers," "we teachers" (TEV), or "we Christian teachers."

shall be judged: by God. The active form may be preferable: "God will judge us who are teachers."

greater strictness: that is, more strictly than he will judge others. The last part of the verse may be translated as follows: "God will be stricter when he judges us (who are) teachers than when he judges other people." Or, "God will judge us teachers more carefully (or, severely) then he will judge others."

3.2 RSV	TEV
For we all make many mistakes, and if any one makes no mistakes in what he says he is a perfect man, able to bridle the whole body also.	All of us often make mistakes. But if a person never makes a mistake in what he says, he is perfect and is also able to control his whole being.

we all: not just teachers, but all believers.

if any one: "if any believer (or, Christian)."

a perfect man: although the Greek word is the specific one for a male human being, a man, it should not be inferred that what James says applies only to men. It should be noted that in 1.7-8 and 1.19-20 he shifts from the generic word "person" to the specific word "man." Here it is better to say "a perfect person (or, Christian)." For perfect see 1.4.

bridle: the same verb used in 1.26.

the whole body also: "his whole being" (TEV), "every part of himself," "control himself completely."

3.3 RSV	TEV
If we put bits into the mouths of horses that they may obey us, we guide their whole bodies.	We put a bit into the mouth of a horse to make it obey us, and we are able to make it go where we want.

If we put bits: "When we place bits" or "We place bits...in order to."

bits into the mouths of horses: "a bit in a horse's mouth." The bit is the metal mouthpiece of a bridle, which is used to control and direct the horse. Where this is not used, a cultural equivalent may be employed such as "a bridle on the horse's head." In some places it may be necessary to use a phrase such as "animal guide rope" or even "a rope thing put in the horse's mouth to guide it." Where horses are not used in this fashion, any animal that is used to do work or to be ridden may be referred to. The main point of this example, as of the one in verse 4, is the small size of the controlling device compared with the large size of what is being controlled.

guide their whole bodies: "make them go where we want them to," "make them take whatever direction we wish." It may be better to imitate TEV and speak of "a horse" and not of horses.

The verse may be translated as follows:

When we want to make a horse obey us, we put a bit in its mouth, and in this way we make the horse go anywhere we wish.

3.4 RSV	TEV
Look at the ships also; though they are so great and are driven by strong winds, they are guided by a very small rudder wherever the will of the pilot directs.	Or think of a ship: big as it is and driven by such strong winds, it can be steered by a very small rudder, and it goes wherever the pilot wants it to go.

Look at the ships: "Think about ships (or, a ship)."

great: "large," "immense," "huge."

driven by strong winds: this is an obvious reference to sailing ships. Where ships are not known, a translator faces many problems in translating passages in the Gospels and in Acts. By the time this Letter is translated, such problems should have been solved. It may be necessary to use such descriptive phrases as "big boats that travel far" or "big boats that go out into the great waters."

a small rudder: "a small steering oar" (see Acts 27.40) or "a small oar at the back of the ship used for steering."

wherever the will of the pilot directs: "in whatever direction the pilot wants it to go." The pilot was the man who held and moved the rudder. If the specialized term pilot is not available, one may translate "wherever the man who moves the rudder wants the ship to go."

3.5

RSV	TEV
So the tongue is a little member and boasts of great things. How great a forest is set ablaze by a small fire!	So it is with the tongue: small as it is, it can boast about great things. Just think how large a forest can be set on fire by a tiny flame.

a little member: "a small member (or, part) of the body."

boasts of great things: "brags a lot," "claims that it can do extraordinary things," or "brags of the great things it can do."

Throughout this whole passage the physical organ the tongue is spoken of as though it had the will, the power, and the ability to determine what a person says. If this is a natural usage in other languages, then the Greek should be imitated. In some instances "lips" or "mouth" will be more natural. But in some cases it will be better to say "A person uses his tongue, which is little, to boast about very big things."

It is to be noticed that TEV begins a new paragraph at verse 5b. This is done since the figure changes to a fire, which is used through verse 6.

How great...!: this kind of exclamation in English requires no main verb; but it may be better in some languages to do something like TEV: "Just think..." (as in verse 4). The order of the Greek may be reversed: "Just think how a tiny flame can set a huge forest on fire."

3.6

RSV	TEV
And the tongue is a fire. The tongue is an unrighteous world among our members, staining the whole body, setting on fire the cycle of nature,[b] and set on fire by hell.[c]	And the tongue is like a fire. It is a world of wrong, occupying its place in our bodies and spreading evil through our whole being. It sets on fire the entire course of our existence with the fire that comes to it from hell itself.

[b]Or *wheel of birth*
[c]Greek *Gehenna*

the tongue is a fire: or, as a simile, "the tongue is like a fire," or, as a descriptive comparison, "the tongue is able to destroy, as a fire does."

an unrighteous world: this is another figure, which compares the tongue to an organized system of evil, a "universe" controlled by wrong. "It is like a world ruled by evil."

among our members: "set in its place in our bodies."

staining the whole body: "corrupting our whole being," "making the whole person to become evil"; see unstained in 1.27. In many languages the use of the word body would indicate that the effects of evil talk are physical.

setting on fire: "the tongue sets on fire." The language is figurative, that is, the author is not talking about an actual fire, but uses fire as a figure of destruction.

the cycle of nature: the precise meaning of the Greek phrase is uncertain (see the RSV footnote "Or *wheel of birth*"), but the general sense seems clear enough. It means "the entire course of existence," "the whole life," or perhaps "all of creation," "the whole realm of nature."

set on fire by hell: Gehenna was the name given to the place of final punishment for the wicked, which was thought of as a place where fire burned all the time (see Mark 9.47-48).

3.7-8 RSV	TEV
For every kind of beast and bird, of reptile and sea creature, can be tamed and has been tamed by humankind, 8 but no human being can tame the tongue—a restless evil, full of deadly poison.	Man is able to tame and has tamed all other creatures—wild animals and birds, reptiles and fish. 8 But no one has ever been able to tame the tongue. It is evil and uncontrollable, full of deadly poison.

beast...bird...reptile...sea creature: with these four words James includes all living creatures other than human beings. Beast is properly "wild animals" (TEV); as for sea creature it is better to say "fish" (TEV; the Greek word is literally "[what lives] in the sea").

All animals on earth can be tamed and actually have been tamed by human beings; the tongue is the only "animal" that cannot be tamed.

restless evil: "an evil thing that never rests (or, stops)," "an uncontrollable evil."

full of deadly poison: the tongue is here compared to a poisonous snake. It may not be possible to keep the metaphor, and so it may be necessary to say "the tongue can kill, as though it were a poisonous substance (or, a poisonous snake)."

Verses 7-8 may be translated as follows:

> We human beings can tame all the wild animals, the birds, the reptiles, and the fish; as a matter of fact we have tamed them all. 8 But no one can tame the tongue. It is an evil thing that cannot be controlled, and it can kill just like a poisonous snake.

3.9 RSV	TEV
With it we bless the Lord and Father, and with it we curse men, who are made in the likeness of God.	We use it to give thanks to our Lord and Father and also to curse our fellow-man, who is created in the likeness of God.

we bless: "we praise," "we give thanks to" (TEV), "we offer grateful prayers to."

the Lord and Father: "our Lord and Father" (TEV), or "God, who is our Lord (or, Master) and Father." In languages in which God cannot be possessed ("our God"), one may say "we thank God, who rules over us and is the Father of us all."

curse: "say bad things about," "revile," "wish (or, call) evil upon."

men: "other people," "others," "our fellow human beings."

made in the likeness of God: "whom God created (to be) like himself." This is an allusion to the creation account in Genesis 1.26-27 (see also 9.6).

3.10 RSV	TEV
From the same mouth come blessing and cursing. My brethren, this ought not to be so.	Words of thanksgiving and cursing pour out from the same mouth. My brothers, this should not happen!

blessing and cursing: "praise and curses," "Words of thanksgiving and of cursing" (TEV). The two contrast with each other: good and bad, attractive and ugly.

come: "come out." It may be necessary to say something like "The same mouth speaks" or "A person speaks both good words and bad words."

My brethren: see 1.2.

ought not to be so: "should not happen" (TEV), "it is wrong to happen." Or, in more personal terms, "a believer shouldn't talk like this."

3.11 RSV	TEV
Does a spring pour forth from the same opening fresh water and brackish?	No spring of water pours out sweet water and bitter water from the same opening.

The rhetorical question expresses something that is impossible: "A spring (of water) cannot send sweet water and bitter water from the same opening"; or, more simply, "Fresh water and salty water don't flow from the same spring."

brackish: salty water, not fit to drink.

If a spring of water is unknown, a pool of water can be a substitute: "A pool of water (or, A well) doesn't have fresh water and salty water in it."

3.12 RSV	TEV
Can a fig tree, my brethren, yield olives, or a grapevine figs? No more can salt water yield fresh.	A fig tree, my brothers, cannot bear olives; a grapevine cannot bear figs, nor can a salty spring produce sweet water.

Two more impossible things: "A fig tree does not bear olives; a grapevine does not produce figs." Where figs, olives, and grapes are not known, appropriate cultural substitutes may be used: "A banana tree does not bear mangoes."

salt water yield fresh: it is better to say "a spring of salt water (or a salt spring) cannot produce fresh water." In some instances "Fresh (or, sweet) water" will be translated "water that people can drink" or "water that is good to drink."

SECTION HEADING

The Wisdom from Above: "True Wisdom," "Good Wisdom and Evil Wisdom."

In verses 13-18 James turns his attention to wisdom, of which he had spoken in 1.5-6. He may still be speaking primarily to those who would like to be teachers, but what he says applies to all believers. There is earthly wisdom and there is heavenly wisdom, and a believer should choose the wisdom that God gives.

3.13 RSV	TEV
Who is wise and understanding among you? By his good life let him show his works in the meekness of wisdom.	Is there anyone among you who is wise and understanding? He is to prove it by his good life, by his good deeds performed with humility and wisdom.

Who is wise...?: by means of the question form, James addresses himself to the readers who considered themselves wise and understanding. No difference of meaning is to be seen between the two adjectives: "wise and intelligent" or "truly wise."

The meaning may be expressed with a statement instead of a question: "Those among you who are wise and intelligent must...."

By his good life let him show his works: this obscure statement is an attempt to translate the Greek text literally. To "show his works by his good life" makes no sense in English. The meaning may be expressed as follows: "He must prove that he is wise and intelligent by his good conduct, by the actions he performs with humility and wisdom (or, with the humility that comes from wisdom)." The last part may be translated, "by living the way a humble and wise person should live."

the meekness of wisdom: this is either "humility that comes from wisdom" or "wise humility," that is, humility that a truly wise person has. Instead of meekness, something like "humility" (TEV) or "gentleness" seems better. In some languages meekness is spoken of as "a person who speaks softly."

3.14 RSV	TEV
But if you have bitter jealousy and selfish ambition in your hearts, do not boast and be false to the truth.	But if in your heart you are jealous, bitter, and selfish, don't sin against the truth by boasting of your wisdom.

bitter jealousy: or "fanatical zeal." The word translated jealousy may mean "zeal," according to the context. The context here allows either meaning, but perhaps jealousy, "envy," is more probable as the opposite of "humility" in verse 13. In translating jealousy care should be taken to avoid the idea of sexual rivalry and antagonism. The adjective bitter may be represented by "strong," "intense" (see its use in verse 11).

selfish ambition: this translates a Greek noun which means an intense desire to gain one's ends with little regard for the rights of others. This promotes rivalry and leads to divisions in a group.

in your hearts: by the use of this phrase, James is speaking of feelings which Christians might have but which they cover up; they are hidden qualities.

do not boast: either in the general sense of "don't boast that you are better than others," or in the more restricted sense (which the context seems to favor), "don't boast that you are wise" (see TEV).

and be false to the truth: this is probably not an additional matter but describes the boasting: such boasting would be a lie. So TEV "don't sin against the truth by boasting of your wisdom." Another possibility is "You have no reason for boasting, and you are not being truthful" (see SpCL). Or it could be that by the truth James means the gospel, the Christian faith.

3.15 RSV	TEV
This wisdom is not such as comes down from above, but is earthly, unspiritual, devilish.	Such wisdom does not come down from heaven; it belongs to the world, it is unspiritual and demonic.

This wisdom: it is not the real wisdom, which comes from God; so it may be better to say "This kind of wisdom."

comes down from above: "comes from heaven," or "is given by God," or "which God gives."

earthly, unspiritual, devilish: these three adjectives describe such wisdom as being from this world, of sinful human origin, of demonic origin, as the opposite of wisdom that is heavenly, spiritual, divine. The first one may be translated "of this world"; the second one, "of sinful human nature" (as opposed to God's spiritual, sinless nature); the third one, "demonic," "of evil spirits."

3.16 RSV	TEV
For where jealousy and selfish ambition exist, there will be disorder and every vile practice.	Where there is jealousy and selfishness, there is also disorder and every kind of evil.

jealousy and selfish ambition: as in verse 14.

disorder: "anarchy." This is sometimes described as "people disobeying all the rules." James is obviously thinking about the fellowship in the church; selfish ambition leads inevitably to the formation of rival groups in the congregation.

every vile practice: "all kinds of evil deeds," "every kind of sin."

It may be better to use verbal phrases instead of abstract nouns: "For when there are people in the church who are jealous and selfish, there is disorder in the fellowship and people do all kinds of bad things."

3.17 RSV	TEV
But the wisdom from above is first pure, then peaceable, gentle, open to reason, full of mercy and good fruits, without uncertainty or insincerity.	But the wisdom from above is pure first of all; it is also peaceful, gentle, and friendly; it is full of compassion and produces a harvest of good deeds; it is free from prejudice and hypocrisy.

the wisdom from above: as in verse 15.

pure: "without any faults in it."

peaceable, gentle, open to reason: it is quite obvious that these are human qualities, not abstract virtues. So it may be much better to speak in personal terms: "Believers who have the wisdom that comes from God are pure (or, lead a pure life); they are also peaceful, gentle, and reasonable."

full of mercy and good fruits: "they are always compassionate (or, merciful) and perform all kinds of good deeds."

without uncertainty: the Greek word means "impartial," "unprejudiced."

without insincerity: "not hypocritical," "sincere."

3.18 RSV	TEV
And the harvest of righteousness is sown in peace by those who make peace.	And goodness is the harvest that is produced from the seeds the peacemakers plant in peace.

the harvest of righteousness: James continues to use abstract virtues to speak of personal qualities and actions. Here he uses the metaphors of sowing, or planting, of those who sow, and of a harvest. In some instances similes may be used, such as "like a harvest of righteousness." The phrase the harvest of righteousness means that righteousness is the harvest that is gathered in. It seems that here righteousness is a personal quality, "goodness," "right living," that is, true Christian character and conduct. In this context it does not seem to mean "justice" in human relationships, or the operation of God's will in human affairs.

is sown in peace: there is a slight misuse of the figure; a harvest, strictly speaking, is not sown. Seeds are sown, which later produce a harvest. So TEV has "goodness is the harvest that is produced from the seeds the peacemakers plant in peace."

in peace may describe the manner of sowing, "peaceably," or else the purpose of sowing, "for peaceful purposes." The second is probably the meaning intended.

by those who make peace: "by peacemakers" (see Matt 5.9). These are not just peaceful persons, but persons who actively promote peace between others, who reconcile people who are enemies. In this context it is peacemaking in the church.

It is possible, however, that the Greek phrase means "*for* the peacemakers," as follows: "And goodness is the harvest that is reaped by peacemakers from seeds planted (or, seeds they planted) in a spirit of peace." This interpretation of the Greek has much to recommend it, and it may be followed by the translator.

Chapter 4

SECTION HEADING

Friendship with the World: "Christians Must Always Obey God," "The Desire for Worldly Pleasures is Displeasing to God."

The main theme of this section, verses 1-10, is the need for believers not to be governed by worldly desires. James is writing to a Christian group that is divided by people who quarrel and fight because of their desire for pleasures. They must repent of their sins and turn to God, and he will be with them.

4.1

RSV	TEV
What causes wars, and what causes fightings among you? Is it not your passions that are at war in your members?	Where do all the fights and quarrels among you come from? They come from your desires for pleasure, which are constantly fighting within you.

What causes wars, and...fightings...?: it seems better to retain the question form, since James himself provides the answer. But a statement may be used: "You know what causes fights and quarrels among you." In this context there is no difference between wars and fightings: "conflicts and quarrels," "arguments and fights." "Why are there arguments and quarrels" or "Why do you argue and quarrel."

Is it not...?: this represents an affirmative statement: "It is ...."

your passions: the Greek word may mean desire for an innocent pleasure, but in the New Testament it is always used for pleasures which conflict with Christian conduct (see Luke 8.14; Titus 3.3; 2 Peter 2.13). So here the translation may be "selfish desires" or "lusts." The idea of complete self-indulgence is uppermost, which is contrary to the demands of the Christain faith. In 2 Timothy 3.4 there is a wordplay: "lovers of pleasure rather than lovers of God." James may be thinking primarily of physical desires, as implied by the following that are at war among your members (see 3.6 "in our members"); so RSV and TEV. But it is possible to understand this to mean "that are fighting among you," that is, in the fellowship of the church. Because of their selfish desires church people are fighting one another.

4.2

RSV	TEV
You desire and do not have; so you kill. And you covet[d] and cannot	You want things, but you cannot have them, so you are ready to

obtain; so you fight and wage war. You do not have, because you do not ask.

[d]Or *you kill and you covet*

kill; you strongly desire things, but you cannot get them, so you quarrel and fight. You do not have what you want because you do not ask God for it.

You desire and do not have; so you kill: there are different ways of punctuating this verse in Greek (see the RSV footnote); RSV and TEV punctuate alike. (For a different punctuation see the end of the verse, below.)

You desire: the text does not say what it is they desire, but the implication is that material things are meant; in a general way, "You want something."

and do not have: "and you don't get it," "and you are unable to have it."

so you kill: this seems impossibly harsh, for it accuses Christians of murder. Commentators give various explanations for the language. TEV, like some other translations, has "so you are ready to kill." But it is impossible to deny that the verb means simply "you commit murder," "you assassinate," and a translator is justified in so translating.

you covet and cannot obtain: this repeats the idea already expressed.

you fight and wage war: the two verbs are related to the two nouns wars and fightings in verse 1. Here, as in the case of you kill, the readers are accused of attacking people in order to get what they want.

because you do not ask: that is, you don't ask God for it; so "you don't pray for it."

Instead of the punctuation followed by RSV and TEV, another punctuation is given in the United Bible Societies' (UBS) Greek New Testament "You desire (things), but you don't get (them); you kill, and you covet (things), but you can't have (them); you quarrel and fight." Some take the verb translated "you covet" to mean "you are fanatics (or, zealots)," and connect it closely to you kill, as follows: "Your fanaticism makes you kill others" or "Your fanaticism drives other Christians to murder." This is possible; it reflects the understanding that the Christians being addressed were living at a time when religious uprisings caused by fanatic Christians and Jews were happening.

4.3 RSV

You ask and do not receive, because you ask wrongly, to spend it on your passions.

TEV

And when you ask, you do not receive it, because your motives are bad; you ask for things to use for your own pleasures.

You ask: again, "You ask God (for things)."

ask wrongly: "ask from wrong motives," "ask for bad purposes."

to spend it: that is, the material blessings, the wealth they are asking God to give them.

passions: as in verse 1.

The verse may be translated as follows: "You ask God for material wealth, but he doesn't give it to you because your motives are bad. All you want to do is to use that wealth to satisfy your pleasures (or, to please yourselves)."

4.4

RSV	TEV
Unfaithful creatures! Do you not know that friendship with the world is enmity with God? Therefore whoever wishes to be a friend of the world makes himself an enemy of God.	Unfaithful people! Don't you know that to be the world's friend means to be God's enemy? Whoever wants to be the world's friend makes himself God's enemy.

Unfaithful creatures!: this translates the Greek word "adulteresses," which reflects the Old Testament use of the word to refer to the people of Israel when they worshiped idols instead of Yahweh. By doing so they were unfaithful to him, like a wife who is unfaithful to her husband. A translation may say "You are people that worship other gods."

It is to be noted that some copyists of the Greek manuscripts thought the word was meant literally, and so they added "adulterers" (see the King James Version [KJV]). The original text, however, had only "adulteresses," used figuratively.

Do you not know...?: "Of course you know" (see 1.3; 3.1).

friendship with the world: as the context makes clear, James is saying that the desire for the things of this world—wealth, honor, power—is directly contrary to God's will. It means to be God's enemy, not his friend. It may be necessary to represent the world by "people who do not want to obey God."

Therefore: James draws out the consequence of the statement he has just made.

The verse may be translated as follows:

> You are unfaithful to God! Surely you know that to be in love with the (things of this) world means to be against God. So a person who decides to make this world his friend becomes an enemy of God.

4.5

RSV	TEV
Or do you suppose it is in vain that the scripture says, "He yearns jealously over the spirit which he has made to dwell in us"?	Don't think that there is no truth in the scripture that says, "The spirit that God placed in us is filled with fierce desires."[b]

[b]The spirit...fierce desires; *or* God yearns jealously over the spirit that he placed in us.

do you suppose...?: another rhetorical question. James is saying that his readers know very well that the scripture he quotes means exactly what it says.

The opening statement may be translated "You know that the scripture is true that says."

the scripture: see 2.8. There is no Old Testament passage that says what is here quoted. There are two main interpretations, represented by RSV (see also TEV margin) and TEV:

(1) He yearns jealously over the spirit he has made to dwell in us. This refers to God, and the translation should be "God yearns jealously...." As for the verbal phrase, the meaning is "extremely concerned with." "is zealously devoted to," as an expression of God's great love and care for the human spirit. Exodus 20.5 speaks of Yahweh as "a jealous God," that is, a God who tolerates no rivals (see RSV and TEV); God demands total and undivided loyalty from his people.

(2) "The spirit that God placed in us is filled with fierce desires" (TEV). This assumes that "the spirit" is the subject of the verb, not the object. The "fierce (or, strong) desires" could be directed to something good (for example, "the spirit longs earnestly for God") or to something bad. This is what TEV intends to say, and this seems to fit more logically with what follows in verse 6.

(3) There is another possible interpretation, and that is to take "the spirit" to mean "the Holy Spirit," in which case the meaning would be "The Spirit that God placed in us loves us deeply (or, passionately)" or "...longs deeply for our love." There is no certain way to decide dogmatically which is the correct interpretation. It is suggested that the translator choose either the RSV or the TEV interpretation for the text, and place the other interpretation as an alternative in a footnote.

4.6 RSV	TEV
But he gives more grace; therefore it says, "God opposes the proud, but gives grace to the humble."	**But the grace that God gives is even stronger. As the scripture says, "God resists the proud, but gives grace to the humble."**

But he gives more grace: "But God gives even greater grace." Following the RSV interpretation of the scripture quoted in verse 5, But goes back to verse 4; it cannot stand in contrast with what is said in verse 5. The TEV interpretation takes "But" to refer to the quotation; the evil desires of the human spirit are indeed strong, but God's grace is even stronger.

grace is God's great love for his people, manifested in the blessings he gives them.

therefore it says: "that is why the scripture says." The quotation that follows is from Proverbs 3.34, according to the text of the Septuagint, the ancient Greek translation of the Old Testament.

God opposes the proud, but gives grace to the humble: "God is against proud (or, arrogant) people, but is good to humble people." The "proud people" are those who make pleasure their god and reject God's claims over them.

opposes: "resists" (TEV), "sets himself against," "is opposed to."

4.7 RSV	TEV
Submit yourselves therefore to God. Resist the devil and he will flee from you.	So then, submit yourselves to God. Resist the Devil, and he will run away from you.

Submit yourselves...to God: here James begins his advice to the readers, which goes through verse 10. He tells them what they must do in order to return to a total allegiance to God: "Be obedient to God," "Accept God's authority over you," "Let God tell you what to do."

Resist the devil: "Fight against the devil," "Oppose the devil." In the context, the Devil is seen as the source of the temptations the readers feel to make pleasure their chief aim in life. James says they can successfully resist the temptations: the Devil is not invincible, and he will run away if they fight him (see Eph 6.11; 1 Peter 5.8). The powers of evil are ruled by the Devil, who tries to make people sin.

4.8 RSV	TEV
Draw near to God and he will draw near to you. Cleanse your hands, you sinners, and purify your hearts, you men of double mind.	Come near to God, and he will come near to you. Wash your hands, you sinners! Purify your hearts, you hypocrites!

Draw near to God: James takes for granted that his readers know how to get near to God, that is, to have a close relation with him.

he will draw near to you: God responds to human initiative and will come to meet those who are trying to go to him (see Luke 15.20, the father's action as his son returns).

Cleanse your hands: the ritual washing of the hands was required before certain actions (see Mark 7.3), in order to remove any ceremonial defilement. The language is figurative and stands for outward behavior (see Psa 24.4; Isa 1.16); the following purify your hearts refers to inner motives and desires.

you sinners...you men of double mind: these are Christian people who are warned to repent and reform. For double mind see 1.8; here, in parallel with sinners, it means people whose loyalty is divided, who want to be friends of the world and of God at the same time. So something like the following may be said: "you people who are not completely loyal to God," "you people who want to love both the world and God."

4.9 RSV	TEV
Be wretched and mourn and weep. Let your laughter be turned to mourning and your joy to dejection.	Be sorrowful, cry, and weep; change your laughter into crying, your joy into gloom!

Be wretched and mourn and weep: the three verbs are synonyms, and it is not necessary for a translator to have three different verbs. "Be miserable, cry, and mourn," or "You should be sorry, and cry bitterly." Instead of indulging in worldly pleasures, they should repent of their sins.

Let your laughter be turned to mourning: "Instead of laughing you should mourn," "Stop your laughing and start crying."
and your joy to dejection: the command is repeated. "Stop being happy and be sad."

4.10 RSV	TEV
Humble yourselves before the Lord and he will exalt you.	Humble yourselves before the Lord, and he will lift you up.

Humble yourselves: "Make yourselves humble," "Adopt a humble attitude" (see humble in verse 6). As the opposite of pride, this means to confess to God that one is a sinner and does not deserve God's love and care.
before the Lord: in prayer. The translation can be "where you pray to the Lord" or "where you worship the Lord." Here the Lord is God.
exalt you: "lift you up" (TEV), "honor you," "make you great" (see Matt 23.12; 1 Peter 5.6).

SECTION HEADING

Warning against Judging a Christian Brother: "Do Not Judge Your Fellow Believer," "Do Not Say Evil Things about Your Fellow Believers."

In these two verses, 11-12, James takes up the matter of harsh criticism and judgment. Only God has the right to pass judgment on people, and so believers should not condemn one another.

4.11 RSV	TEV
Do not speak evil against one another, brethren. He that speaks evil against a brother or judges his brother, speaks evil against the law and judges the law. But if you judge the law, you are not a doer of the law but a judge.	Do not criticize one another, my brothers. Whoever criticizes a Christian brother or judges him, criticizes the Law and judges it. If you judge the Law, then you are no longer one who obeys the Law, but one who judges it.

Do not speak evil against: "Stop saying bad things about," "Do not slander," "Don't criticize."
brethren: "my fellow believers" (see 1.2).
judges: here in the sense of condemning: "condemns," "says is bad (or, no good)."
speaks evil against the law and judges the law: for the law see 1.25; 2.8-12. James speaks here in personal terms of the law, that is, the biblical code of conduct. The Law demands that a believer love his fellow believer (see 2.8); to slander and condemn a fellow believer, then, is to break the Law, and thus to set oneself above the Law, as though one were God.
if you judge the law: "when you pass judgment on the law," "any time that you judge the Law." Or, "If you say the Law is no good." The

whole sentence may be translated as follows: "Whenever you pass judgment on the Law you have stopped obeying it and have started judging it."

4.12 RSV	TEV
There is one lawgiver and judge, he who is able to save and to destroy. But who are you that you judge your neighbor?	God is the only lawgiver and judge. He alone can save and destroy. Who do you think you are, to judge your fellow-man?

There is one lawgiver and judge: it may be better, like TEV, to say explicitly "God is the only lawgiver and judge," "God is the only one who can make laws and judge people."

he who is able to save and to destroy: "the only one who can save people or destroy them" (see Matt 10.28). James is talking about God's power to determine a person's final destiny—salvation or condemnation.

who are you...?: another rhetorical question, which may be represented by "You have no right to...."

your neighbor: see 2.8. Here the more general sense may be intended, "to judge others," "to judge your fellow human being," or the more restricted sense "to judge your fellow believer." The latter is probably meant.

SECTION HEADING

Warning against Boasting: "Do Not Boast," "Life Is Uncertain," "We Cannot Be Sure of the Future."

It is to be noticed that neither in this section (verses 13-17) nor in the following one (5.1-6) does James say "my fellow believers." This has led some to conclude that the warnings in these two sections are general, not limited specifically to Christians. This may well be true, but it seems unlikely.

In this section James condemns those who feel quite self-sufficient and presume to make their plans as though their future were certain. Instead, they should always confess that God is the one who determines the future of all people. So believers should always acknowledge God's will before making their plans.

4.13 RSV	TEV
Come now, you who say, "Today or tomorrow we will go into such and such a town and spend a year there and trade and get gain";	Now listen to me, you that say, "Today or tomorrow we will travel to a certain city, where we will stay a year and go into business and make a lot of money."

Come now: this is a strong attention getter: "Listen to me" (TEV), "Now hear this," "Pay attention to what I'm going to say."

Today or tomorrow: the plans are indefinite; a decision has not been made yet.

we will go: the plural is required by the fact that James is talking to a number of people; but in translation it may be preferable to use the singular form, to avoid giving the idea that James is talking about a group of people traveling together.

such and such: this is an idiomatic way in English of referring to something (or, some place) as yet undetermined. Most languages have ways of saying this; or else the translation can be "to a certain city" (TEV), "to this or that place."

and trade: "and start a business," "and buy and sell things."

get gain: "make a profit," "make money," "get rich."

The verse may be translated as follows:

> Some of you are in the habit of saying, "Today or tomorrow I plan to go to a certain city and live there a year. I will start a business and make money." Now you pay attention to what I say!

4.14 RSV	TEV
whereas you do not know about tomorrow. What is your life? For you are a mist that appears for a little time and then vanishes.	You don't even know what your life tomorrow will be! You are like a puff of smoke, which appears for a moment and then disappears.

you do not know about tomorrow: "you don't know what will happen tomorrow" or "...what tomorrow will bring" (see Prov 27.1).

What is your life?: this is a rhetorical question, designed to make the readers think about the answer James is about to give. TEV follows a different punctuation of the Greek text from that followed by RSV. TEV joins "what is your life" to the preceding words as part of one statement: "You do not know about tomorrow, what your life (then) will be."

you are a mist: this may be better represented by a simile: "you are like a bit of mist," or "like a small cloud," or "like a puff of smoke" (TEV).

appears for a little time and then vanishes: "appears and soon afterward disappears." "Smoke," "vapor," or "thin fog" is quickly dispersed by a breeze or by the heat of the sun. The main idea of the figure is the quickness with which it disappears.

4.15 RSV	TEV
Instead you ought to say, "If the Lord wills, we shall live and we shall do this or that."	What you should say is this: "If the Lord is willing, we will live and do this or that."

Instead you ought to say: instead of confidently affirming what they will do in the near future, believers should say "If the Lord wills." Here the Lord is God: "If God allows," "If it is God's will" (see Acts 18.21; 1 Cor 4.19; Heb 6.3).

we shall live: "we will still be alive" or, in a negative form, "we will not die."

do this or that: a way of referring to a plan without being specific.

4.16 RSV	TEV
As it is, you boast in your arrogance. All such boasting is evil.	But now you are proud, and you boast; all such boasting is wrong.

As it is: "As things are," "Actually," "But to tell the truth."

you boast in your arrogance: "you talk proudly," "you boast and brag," "you boast about what you will do." The "boasting" here is not about something that has already been done; it is a matter of being presumptuous, of confidently supposing that one can make plans for the future without taking God into account.

is evil: "is wrong" (TEV); or "You (or, Believers) should not brag like that."

4.17 RSV	TEV
Whoever knows what is right to do and fails to do it, for him it is sin.	So then, the person who does not do the good he knows he should do is guilty of sin.

Whoever knows: RSV fails to represent the Greek conjunction which TEV translates "So then." The connection between verse 17 and verse 16 is not at all clear; verse 17 serves to end this section and allow the beginning of a new section. Instead of Whoever it may be well to say "The person who" (TEV) or "The believer who."

for him it is sin: "that person is sinning." It may be better to use a different structure: "If someone knows the right thing to do but doesn't do it, then that person is committing a sin." Or "It is a sin for a believer not to do the good thing he knows he ought to do."

Chapter 5

SECTION HEADING

Warning to the Rich: "James Warns Rich People," "James Tells Rich People What They Should Not Do."

In this section, verses 1-6, James warns rich people about their sins. It must be assumed that he is talking to Christians. The language he uses seems highly inappropriate for Christians, but here he accuses them of things no worse than what in 4.1-3 he accuses his readers of doing.

5.1

RSV	TEV
Come now, you rich, weep and howl for the miseries that are coming upon you.	And now, you rich people, listen to me! Weep and wail over the miseries that are coming upon you!

Come now: as in 4.13.

weep and howl: "cry aloud in misery," "weep in pain," "mourn and cry."

the miseries: "the terrible things," "the sufferings."

are coming upon you: it may be unnatural to speak of miseries as coming upon someone, and it may be better to say "the miseries (or, sufferings) that you will have (or, experience)."

5.2

RSV	TEV
Your riches have rotted and your garments are moth-eaten.	Your riches have rotted away, and your clothes have been eaten by moths.

Your riches have rotted: it is to be noticed that here and in verse 3 James speaks as though these things have already happened. In the style of a Hebrew prophet, he is speaking of future events as though they have already taken place. In order to avoid misleading the readers, a translator may wish to use the future tense: "Your riches will all rot." The verb "to rot," if meant literally, applies to crops, such as grains and fruit. But if it is used figuratively, it means generally "Your riches will become worthless" or "Your wealth will disappear."

your garments are moth-eaten: "your clothes will be eaten by moths." At that time rich and expensive clothing was one important form of wealth. See Matthew 6.19 for reference to moths and rust.

5.3

RSV	TEV
Your gold and silver have rusted, and their rust will be evidence against you and will eat your flesh like fire. You have laid up treasure[e] for the last days.	Your gold and silver are covered with rust, and this rust will be a witness against you and will eat up your flesh like fire. You have piled up riches in these last days.

[e]Or *will eat your flesh, since you have stored up fire*

Your gold and silver have rusted: this refers either to gold and silver coins, or else to gold and silver bowls and plates. In either case, says James, "they will be covered (or, eaten) by rust," "they will be destroyed by rust." It is a fact that gold and silver do not rust; silver can become tarnished, but it is not destroyed by the tarnish. James' language should be faithfully represented, however, since the figure of rust is used in what follows.

their rust will be evidence against you: on the Day of Judgment the rusted silverware and goldware will be evidence of how worthless all this material wealth is. Or, as TEV translates, "this rust will be a witness against you," that is, will testify to the fact that these people have nothing to show for their lives except worthless possessions.

will eat up your flesh like fire: James extends the figure even further. The rust will not only destroy their possessions but will destroy them as well. So to speak, that rust will be like the flames of hell.

This part of the verse may be translated as follows:

> The gold and silver that you have saved up will be covered with rust, and on the Day of Judgment this will show (or, prove) that you have been selfish and corrupt. And that same rust will be like fire, and will destroy you.

You have laid up treasure for the last days: as RSV interprets it, the wealth of these rich people will condemn them at the Judgment Day. So the irony is that what seems valuable now will be not merely worthless but will condemn the rich. TEV, however, translates "in these last days," which takes the last days to be the time in which they were living then. If the translator follows this interpretation, it will be better to say "in these days, which are the last days"; or, as some do, "you have accumulated riches in a world that will soon end" or "...in this world, which is coming to an end."

As the RSV footnote shows, the Greek text may be punctuated in such a way as to join the phrase like fire with what follows and not with what precedes. In TEV language the meaning would be "...and this rust will consume your flesh. What you have stored up in these last days is like fire." Another possible interpretation of the alternative punctuation is "...and the rust will eat up your flesh, since you have stored up fire in these last days." However, most translations punctuate the Greek text as RSV and TEV do.

5.4 RSV	TEV
Behold, the wages of the laborers who mowed your fields, which you kept back by fraud, cry out; and the cries of the harvesters have reached the ears of the Lord of hosts.	You have not paid any wages to the men who work in your fields. Listen to their complaints! The cries of those who gather in your crops have reached the ears of God, the Lord Almighty.

Behold: "Listen," "Remember," "Don't forget."

the wages...cry out: it may not be possible to use this kind of language in translation, and so it may be necessary, like TEV, to speak of the workers crying out, that is, loudly complaining.

the laborers who mowed your fields: "the workers who reaped your crops." In current English the verb "to mow" connotes machinery that did not exist at that time. The Greek verb means "to reap," "to harvest."

which you kept back by fraud: "which you did not pay," "which you stole from them." The use of the verb "to rob" indicates that these rich men were illegally withholding the pay of their field workers. See Deuteronomy 24.15.

the harvesters: "those who gather in your harvests."

the Lord of hosts: an Old Testament expression which portrays God as the commander of the heavenly armies.

This verse may be translated as follows:

You have not paid the wages of the workers who gather in your crops. Listen to their loud complaints! Their cries have been heard by the Lord Almighty.

5.5 RSV	TEV
You have lived on the earth in luxury and in pleasure, you have fattened your hearts in a day of slaughter.	Your life here on earth has been full of luxury and pleasure. You have made yourselves fat for the day of slaughter.

in luxury and pleasure: "spending money to satisfy your desire for pleasure."

fattened your hearts: a literal translation of this makes little if any sense in English. James says that their lives of pleasure and ease have made them "fat" (TEV)—just like calves or sheep that are fattened up before being slaughtered.

in a day of slaughter: it seems best to translate "for the day of slaughter" (TEV), that is, the Judgment Day, the day when God will judge all people.

5.6 RSV	TEV
You have condemned, you have killed the righteous man; he does not resist you.	You have condemned and murdered innocent people, and they do not resist you.[c]

[c]people, and they do not resist you; *or* people. Will God not resist you?

You have condemned, you have killed: "You have condemned and put to death."

the righteous man: this is used generically (as the poor man in 2.6); "good people," "innocent people" (TEV).

he does not resist you: "and they do not resist you" (TEV) or "even though they had not been opposed to you."

The Greek text of the last part of the verse may be punctuated as a question: "Does he not resist you?" which is a rhetorical question meaning "He resists you." This may be interpreted in two different ways: (1) The unnamed subject is "the righteous man," that is, the innocent people: "They will oppose you (on the Day of Judgment)." (2) The unnamed subject is God, "God will resist you" (as in 4.6). This interpretation is assumed in the Greek text edited by Westcott and Hort, and appears in at least one translation in English. See also the TEV footnote.

SECTION HEADING

Patience and Prayer: "Concluding Words of Advice."

There are several different matters in this section, verses 7-20, and a translator may wish to divide the material into several sections. In verses 7-11 James encourages his readers to be patient and to endure their difficulties, for the Lord will come soon.

In verse 12 James instructs his readers not to use any oaths when making a promise. James' instructions are like the teaching of Jesus on the subject (see Matt 5.34-37).

In verses 13-18 the subject is mainly prayer, not just personal prayer, but prayer as a church practice.

The last two verses (verses 19-20) deal with the matter of church discipline.

5.7

RSV

Be patient, therefore, brethren, until the coming of the Lord. Behold, the farmer waits for the precious fruit of the earth, being patient over it until it receives the early and the late rain.

TEV

Be patient, then, my brothers, until the Lord comes. See how patient a farmer is as he waits for his land to produce precious crops. He waits patiently for the autumn and spring rains.

Be patient: "Endure patiently." The verb occurs again in verse 8, and the related noun is used in verse 10. The two words are very similar in meaning to the verb "to endure" and the noun "endurance" (see 1.3), both of which appear in verse 11. Because of difficulties and of persecutions from rich and powerful people, believers must learn to endure patiently, confident of the Lord's help.

brethren: "my brothers and sisters" (see 1.2).

the coming of the Lord: "the Lord's return." Here the Lord is Jesus Christ.

the farmer waits: an example of patience. The farmer waits for the seasonal rains, confident that they will come in time. Until it is the right time for his fields to produce a rich harvest, he must wait patiently.

the precious fruit: "the valuable harvest."

it receives: that is, the land, or the farmer's field.

the early and the late rain: the fall rains (the early rain), in late October and early November; and the spring rains (the late rain), in April and May (see Deut 11.14).

5.8 RSV	TEV
You also be patient. Establish your hearts, for the coming of the Lord is at hand.	You also must be patient. Keep your hopes high, for the day of the Lord's coming is near.

Establish your hearts: "Stand firm," "Keep up your courage"; or "Don't give up," "Don't lose heart."

is at hand: "is near" (TEV), "will soon be here."

5.9 RSV	TEV
Do not grumble, brethren, against one another, that you may not be judged; behold, the Judge is standing at the doors.	Do not complain against one another, my brothers, so that God will not judge you. The Judge is near, ready to appear.

grumble...against one another: times of hardship and difficulty create stress in the fellowship and make it easy for members of the group to start bickering and fighting. "Don't blame one another for the troubles you are having," "Don't complain against one another."

that you may not be judged: "so that God will not judge you"(TEV). Complaining against a fellow believer involves passing judgment on that person (see 4.11-12), which is not permitted by the teaching of the gospel.

the Judge is standing at the doors: this is another way of speaking of the imminent coming of the Lord. "The time of final Judgment is near." It may be impossible to keep the figure of standing at the doors; so it may be better to say "will soon come (or, arrive)" or "God will soon judge all people."

5.10 RSV	TEV
As an example of suffering and patience, brethren, take the prophets who spoke in the name of the Lord.	My brothers, remember the prophets who spoke in the name of the Lord. Take them as examples of patient endurance under suffering.

<u>As an example...take the prophets</u>: "The prophets are a good example," "Consider how the prophets were patient," "Think how patient the prophets were."

<u>of suffering and patience</u>: "of patient enduring of suffering," "of remaining patient while suffering."

<u>the prophets</u>: James is talking about the Hebrew prophets, those <u>who spoke in the name of the Lord</u>, that is, "who proclaimed the Lord's message," "who were sent by God to proclaim his message." Here <u>the Lord</u> is God.

The verse may be translated as follows:

> My fellow believers: The prophets, who proclaimed the Lord's message, are good examples of people who patiently endured suffering (or, persecution).

5.11

RSV	TEV
Behold, we call those happy who were steadfast. You have heard of the steadfastness of Job, and you have seen the purpose of the Lord, how the Lord is compassionate and merciful.	We call them happy because they endured. You have heard of Job's patience, and you know how the Lord provided for him in the end. For the Lord is full of mercy and compassion.

<u>we call those happy</u>: here <u>we</u> means "we believers," "we Christians." The verbal phrase <u>call...happy</u> translates the Greek verb that is related to the adjective in 1.12 translated "happy" by TEV. "We consider them happy," that is, "fortunate," "well-off." "We think highly of them," "we praise them."

<u>who were steadfast</u>: "who did not give up" (see the same verb in 1.12).

<u>the steadfastness of Job</u>: "Job's patient endurance," "how Job remained patient while suffering." See Job 1.21-22; 2.10.

<u>you have seen the purpose of the Lord</u>: this is not a separate matter, as the RSV translation implies, but is still a reference to Job: "and you know how the Lord finally dealt with him (or, dealt with him in the end)." This refers to the conclusion of the story of Job. See Job 42.10-17. <u>The Lord</u> here is God.

<u>how the Lord is compassionate and merciful</u>: or "because the Lord is merciful and kind" (see Psa 103.8; 111.4).

The verse may be translated as follows:

> We say that the people who patiently endured suffering are to be praised (or, admired)....

Or:

> We say, "Happy are those who endure suffering patiently." And you remember how patient Job was, and you recall how the Lord rewarded (or, blessed) him in the end. For the Lord is merciful and kind.

5.12

RSV	TEV
But above all, my brethren, do not swear, either by heaven or	Above all, my brothers, do not use an oath when you make a

RSV	TEV
by earth or with any other oath, but let your yes be yes and your no be no, that you may not fall under condemnation.	promise. Do not swear by heaven or by earth or by anything else. Say only "Yes" when you mean yes, and "No" when you mean no, and then you will not come under God's judgment.

But above all: "This is very important," "Remember especially this."

do not swear: as in Matthew 5.34, "to swear" means to make a solemn promise or to state an important truth, and in order to make it even more impressive, to use the name of God, or a substitute for the name of God. In this way the hearers would be convinced that the promise would be kept, or that the truth was really being spoken.

by heaven or by earth: as in Matthew 5.34-35. To avoid using the sacred name of God, pious Jews would say "by heaven" or "by earth" to confirm their vows.

or with any other oath: "or by anything else" (TEV), "or in any other way."

let your yes be yes and your no be no: it is better to begin a new sentence here. "Instead, say only 'Yes' when you mean yes, and say only 'No' when you mean no." Since yes and no refer here specifically to a promise to do something or not to do something, it may be better to translate "When you promise to do something, don't use any vows with the promise; and when you promise not to do something, don't use any vows either. Just say 'I will' or 'I will not.'"

that you may not fall under condemnation: "so that God will not condemn you."

The following may serve as a model for translating this verse:

> My dear fellow believers: this is very important. When you make a solemn promise, do not add to your promise the words "By heaven" or "By earth" or any other words. Just say "I promise to do it" or "I promise not to do it," and keep your promise. In this way God will not condemn you.

5.13 RSV	TEV
Is any one among you suffering? Let him pray. Is any cheerful? Let him sing praise.	Is anyone among you in trouble? He should pray. Is anyone happy? He should sing praises.

suffering: "in trouble" (TEV), "experiencing difficulties."

Let him pray: "Pray that God will help you."

cheerful: "happy" (TEV), "pleased."

sing praise: that is, sing songs of thanksgiving to God.

It may be more forceful to abandon the question and answer form and to use conditional statements: "If someone in your group is in trouble, he should pray (to God) about it. If someone is happy, he should sing praises."

5.14 RSV	TEV
Is any among you sick? Let him call for the elders of the church, and let them pray over him, anointing him with oil in the name of the Lord;	Is there anyone who is sick? He should send for the church elders, who will pray for him and rub olive oil on him in the name of the Lord.

Is any among you sick?: or "If someone in your group is sick...."

call for the elders of the church: "ask the church elders to come." The elders were church officers who at that time had general charge of the affairs of the church. See Titus 1.5-9

pray over him: or "pray that God will restore him to health." The over him means "standing at his bedside."

anointing him with oil: the only other reference in the New Testament to this as a religious practice is in Mark 6.13. Olive oil was used as a medicine (see Luke 10.34), and here it is part of a religious rite intended to restore a sick believer to health.

in the name of the Lord: "asking the Lord to help" or "as representatives of the Lord Jesus Christ."

5.15 RSV	TEV
and the prayer of faith will save the sick man, and the Lord will raise him up; and if he has committed sins, he will be forgiven.	This prayer made in faith will heal the sick person; the Lord will restore him to health, and the sins he has committed will be forgiven.

the prayer of faith: "the prayer that is offered by people who believe (that God will answer the prayer)."

save the sick man: here in the sense of "make that sick person well."

the Lord will raise him up: that is, from bed. "God will make him healthy again," "God will restore that person to health."

if he has committed sins, he will be forgiven: "and any sins he may have committed will be forgiven" or "and God will forgive any sins he committed." The conditional form if is used in this context because James is talking about the sins which may have been the reason for the person's illness.

The verse may be translated as follows:

If the church elders believe that God will answer their prayer, the sick person will be healed. God will restore that person to health, and he will also forgive any sins that the person committed.

5.16 RSV	TEV
Therefore confess your sins to one another, and pray for one another, that you may be healed. The prayer of a righteous man has great power in its effects.	So then, confess your sins to one another and pray for one another, so that you will be healed. The prayer of a good person has a powerful effect.

Therefore: "Because God answers prayer," "Because God heals."

confess your sins to one another: "tell one another the bad things you have done." This is still in the context of the sick being healed (as the end of the verse makes clear). The confession is made by the sick, since without a person's confession, that is, the admission of sins, God cannot forgive. Here, as elsewhere in the New Testament, confession is the oral expression of repentance.

pray for one another: not just the elders of the church should pray, but all believers.

that you may be healed: this goes both with confession and with prayer: "in order for you to be healed," "so that God will heal you."

a righteous man:"a good person" (TEV), "a person who does God's will."

has great power in its effects: "is able to accomplish great things," "has powerful results." Or "the fervent prayer of a good person is very effective" or "...has much power."

5.17

RSV	TEV
Elijah was a man of like nature with ourselves and he prayed fervently that it might not rain, and for three years and six months it did not rain on the earth.	Elijah was the same kind of person as we are. He prayed earnestly that there would be no rain, and no rain fell on the land for three and a half years.

James refers to Elijah as a man of prayer (see 1 Kgs 17.1; 18.1, 42-45).

a man of like nature with ourselves: "an ordinary person just like us" is the meaning. Elijah was not superhuman; he was a sinful person, just like everyone else. The meaning may be put in a negative form: "Elijah was not different from us," "Elijah's nature was no different from ours."

prayed fervently: "prayed very hard," "kept on praying."

three years and six months: see the same length of time in Luke 4.25. 1 Kings 18.1 says only that it started raining again "in the third year of the drought."

on the earth: or "in the land of Israel"; or, more simply, "no rain fell," "it did not rain for three and a half years."

5.18

RSV	TEV
Then he prayed again and the heaven gave rain, and the earth brought forth its fruit.	Once again he prayed, and the sky poured out its rain and the earth produced its crops.

he prayed again: this should not be translated "the next time he prayed," as though Elijah did not pray for three and a half years.

the heaven gave rain: "rain began to fall," "it began to rain." It may not always be natural to say "the rain came down from the sky."

the earth brought forth its fruit: "the fields produced crops," "once more there were crops in the land."

5.19-20 RSV	TEV
My brethren, if any one among you wanders from the truth and some one brings him back, 20 let him know that whoever brings back a sinner from the error of his way will save his soul from death and will cover a multitude of sins.	My brothers, if one of you wanders away from the truth and another one brings him back again, 20 remember this: whoever turns a sinner back from his wrong way will save that sinner's soul[d] from death and bring about the forgiveness of many sins.

[d]that sinner's soul; *or* his own soul.

My brethren: see 1.2.

any one among you wanders from the truth: "any of you leaves the way of truth" or "...the right way." Here the truth stands for the gospel, and by use of the verb "to wander" James is comparing it to a road that the believer follows. So it has to do with conduct and not just with belief.

some one brings him back: "a fellow believer leads that person back to the right way."

let him know: in English this is an imperative, meaning "that person must (or, is to) know." Him refers to the believer who brings the fellow believer back to the right way.

brings back a sinner from the error of his way: "stops a person from continuing to do wrong things" or "makes a person quit his sinful way."

will save his soul from death: that is, the soul of the sinner who is brought back from the error of his way. It is better to translate "will save that person from eternal death."

It is possible, but does not seem likely, that the text means that the person who turns back an erring fellow believer to the true way will thereby save himself from spiritual death (see the TEV footnote).

will cover a multitude of sins: this is the language of forgiveness (see Psa 32.1; Rom 4.7): "and many sins will be forgiven," "and God will forgive many sins." The question which the Greek text does not answer (nor do RSV, TEV, and most other translations) is, Whose sins will be forgiven? It is generally assumed that the text means the erring fellow believer's sins; he will be saved from spiritual death and his many sins will be forgiven. It is recommended that the translator follow this interpretation.

But it is possible that the text refers to the believer who brings his erring brother back; his many sins will be forgiven.

Another possibility is that the vague language means the sins of the whole group to which both believers belong.

An Outline of 1 Peter

1. Introduction 1.1-2
2. The Christian Joy 1.3-12
3. The Holy Life 1.13—2.10
4. Practical Aspects of Christian Living 2.11—3.12
5. The Christian Attitude toward Persecution 3.13—4.19
6. Exhortation to Church Leaders and to All Christians 5.1-11
7. Closing Words 5.12-14

Title

THE FIRST LETTER FROM PETER

It may be better to have "The First Letter that Peter Wrote" as the title of this Book. Peter may be referred to as "the Apostle Peter." If helpful, the readers may be included in the title as follows: "...Wrote to His Fellow Christians" (see remarks on the title of James).

Chapter 1

1.1-2

RSV	TEV
Peter, an apostle of Jesus Christ, To the exiles of the Dispersion in Pontus, Galatia, Cappadocia, Asia, and Bithynia, 2 chosen and destined by God the Father and sanctified by the Spirit for obedience to Jesus Christ and for sprinkling with his blood: May grace and peace be multiplied to you.	From Peter, apostle of Jesus Christ— To God's chosen people who live as refugees scattered throughout the provinces of Pontus, Galatia, Cappadocia, Asia, and Bithynia. 2 You were chosen according to the purpose of God the Father and were made a holy people by his Spirit, to obey Jesus Christ and be purified by his blood. May grace and peace be yours in full measure.

The beginning of this Letter follows the usual pattern: the name of the writer, the people to whom the Letter is being written, and a greeting. TEV does not have a heading for this section. If one is desired, something like "Introduction" or "Opening Greeting" will be appropriate.

Peter, an apostle of Jesus Christ: the third person address may not be natural in some languages, and so it may be better to translate "I, Peter, an apostle of Jesus Christ, write this letter...." An apostle is one who is sent to speak and act in the name and with the authority of the one who sends him. He is not just a messenger but an authorized representative.

the exiles of the Dispersion: the author uses Old Testament language to speak of Christians. The Jewish people had been deported from their country and were living in communities all over the Roman Empire. They were known as the Diaspora, or Dispersion, that is, people who were "scattered" (see James 1.1). The word exiles stresses the fact that this world is not the real home of the readers; while here they are away from their heavenly homeland (see 2.11; Gal 4.26; Phil 3.20; James 1.1). Believers are away from their real home, scattered throughout the world.

If a translation keeps the figure, the translator must be certain that the readers understand it. If not, it may be better to say "I write this letter to God's people who live scattered throughout the (Roman) provinces of...." But if the passive "scattered" is a problem, it may be necessary to say "who are living away from their true home."

Pontus, Galatia, Cappadocia, Asia, and Bithynia were Roman provinces in what is now Turkey. It may be better to specify, as TEV does, "the provinces of" or "the Roman provinces of." A word such as "area" or "region" may be more easily understood. The word "country," as understood today in the sense of "nation," should not be used. Care should be taken in translating these place names to avoid words that may have some other meaning, and also avoid words that may sound like vulgar terms. If there is some way to indicate that these are foreign place names, this should be done.

chosen and destined by God the Father: in the Greek text the word meaning "To the chosen," which RSV translates chosen, comes right after Jesus Christ, and destined translates a phrase that comes at the beginning of verse 2, literally, "according to his foreknowledge." It seems better to place "To God's chosen people" (TEV) or "To the people whom God has chosen" at the beginning of this paragraph, in verse 1. The verb "to choose" reflects the Old Testament concept of the Israelites as the people whom God picked out from all other peoples to belong to him. In the same way, Christians are the people of God.

The adverbial phrase "according to the foreknowledge of God the Father" indicates not only that God knew about it ahead of time, but that he determined or decided what would happen. So RSV destined expresses this idea; or else "predestined," or phrases using the nouns "purpose" (TEV), "will," or "intention" of God. This emphasizes that their status as God's people is due to God's decision and initiative, not to their own efforts.

God the Father: "God, who is our Father." Here our is inclusive.

sanctified by the Spirit: "made a holy people by God's Spirit." The biblical concept of holiness is not so much that of moral purity or sinlessness as that of being dedicated to the worship and service of God. The readers are "saints," that is, they belong to God. So here the translation may say "the (Holy) Spirit has made you God's people" or "God's Spirit has dedicated you to the service of God."

for obedience to Jesus Christ: "to obey Jesus Christ" (TEV), "so that you will obey Jesus Christ."

and for sprinkling with his blood: "and to be purified by his blood." The expression refers to the forgiveness of sins (see Heb 9.11-12) and also seems to reflect the Christian rite of baptism. It would not be advisable to introduce the subject of baptism into the text, but the literal expression sprinkling may be misunderstood by many readers. The blood of Jesus Christ is a way of speaking of Christ's sacrificial death on the cross. So the translation can be "and to have your sins forgiven by Christ's sacrificial death" or "and to have your sins forgiven because Christ died on the cross."

It is possible that the Greek phrase "obedience and sprinkling of the blood" is a way of referring to the covenant which Christ makes with his people, a covenant sealed by his death (see the words of the Lord's Supper in Mark 14.23-24), and which calls for obedience on the part of the people (see the covenant at Mount Sinai, Exo 24.7-8). So the meaning could be "to obey Jesus Christ, as required by his covenant with us, which he sealed (or, ratified) by his sacrificial death."

May grace and peace be multiplied to you: grace is God's saving love, manifested to all people through Jesus Christ; peace is spiritual well-being, which is a gift from God. The prayer is that the readers may have both in ever increasing measure.

The following may serve as a model for translating verses 1-2:

> I, Peter, an apostle of Jesus Christ, write this letter to God's chosen people, who live away from their true home and are scattered throughout the (Roman) provinces of Pontus, Galatia, Cappadocia, Asia and Bithynia. 2 By his own decision, God, our Father, made you his people. The Holy Spirit dedicated you to God's service, so that you would obey God and have your sins forgiven through the sacrificial death of Jesus Christ.
>
> I pray that God will bless you more and more, and that your spiritual well-being will keep on growing.

SECTION HEADING

A Living Hope: "Christian Hope," "We Have a Hope That Never Fails."

In this section, verses 3-12, the writer praises God for his goodness, and in a long, skillfully constructed sentence, deals with some of the main features of the Christian faith and life. There are many technical theological terms in this section, and often it will be necessary to represent abstract nouns by verbal phrases or even whole sentences which specify the actors and the goals of the action expressed by the verb.

The exposition of the material will follow the RSV verse division; at regular intervals alternative reconstructions of the material will be proposed.

1.3

RSV	TEV
Blessed be the God and Father of our Lord Jesus Christ! By his great mercy we have been born anew to a living hope through the resurrection of Jesus Christ from the dead,	Let us give thanks to the God and Father of our Lord Jesus Christ! Because of his great mercy he gave us new life by raising Jesus Christ from death. This fills us with a living hope,

Blessed be: this is the regular form used in Jewish prayer, and means "Let us praise," "We must give thanks to," "We must confess that God is very wonderful."

the God and Father of our Lord Jesus Christ: care must be taken not to make it appear that the God and Father are two different beings. The one God is the God of Jesus Christ and is also his Father. "Let us praise our God, who is the God of our Lord Jesus Christ (or, the God whom Jesus Christ worships) and is also his Father." In some languages our Lord must be expressed as "the Lord whom we serve" or "the Lord who rules over us."

By his great mercy: "Because he had great mercy on us." Mercy should not be thought of simply as pity, but as tender, loving care: "Because he cares deeply for us."

we have been born anew: "we have been given new life." This is spiritual life, and God is the one who gives it. The Greek is literally "who begot us again." The we is inclusive: the writer is talking about all believers.

a living hope: "a hope that never dies." The word living here means that the believer's hope that God will keep his promise will never disappear. Here, as elsewhere in the New Testament, hope is almost the same as "confidence," "assurance." The preposition to in the expression born...to a living hope expresses either the result of the new birth, or else the quality of the new life: "he has given us new life, and so we have a strong (or, indestructible) hope." Or else, "...and so we have complete confidence in him."

through the resurrection of Jesus Christ from the dead: this modifies "God gave us new life." The new life that believers have is made possible through Christ's resurrection. "God gave us new life by raising Jesus Christ from death" or "...by causing Jesus Christ to live again." Or "Because Jesus Christ rose from death (or, Because God made Jesus Christ come back to life). God gave us new life."

1.4-5 RSV	TEV
and to an inheritance which is imperishable, undefiled, and unfading, kept in heaven for you, 5 who by God's power are guarded through faith for a salvation ready to be revealed in the last time.	and so we look forward to possessing the rich blessings that God keeps for his people. He keeps them for you in heaven, where they cannot decay or spoil or fade away. 5 They are for you, who through faith are kept safe by God's power for the salvation which is ready to be revealed at the end of time.

and to an inheritance: in RSV this phrase is governed by we have been born anew in verse 3: we have been born anew...to an inheritance. The inheritance is the goal or the consequence of the new birth: "and so we have (or, possess) an inheritance" or else "and so we look forward to receiving an inheritance." In the Bible the verb "to inherit" and the noun "inheritance" in this kind of context refer to the blessings that God has for his people, either in terms of the future Kingdom of God or of life eternal. Here it is defined in verse 5 as a salvation ready to be revealed in the last time. In most languages "to inherit" and "inheritance" always imply the death of someone, and it is usually better to abandon the figure. So TEV has "and so we look forward to possessing the rich blessings that God keeps for his people."

imperishable, undefiled, and unfading: the translation of these three adjectives will depend on the way inheritance is translated. If it is translated "gift," then the adjectives may be translated by "(a gift that) does not disappear or lose its beauty or its value." Or "a gift that nothing can destroy or defile or spoil." If the word "life" is used (as some translations do), the translation can be "a life eternal, forever beautiful and precious." Or if, like TEV, the expression "rich (or, precious) blessings" is used, the adjectives can be translated "(rich blessings which) cannot be destroyed or ruined or damaged." The two main components of the three adjectives are "never ceasing to exist" and "never losing its value." So any two words or expressions that effectively represent those two ideas, either in a positive or a negative form, will be satisfactory.

kept in heaven for you: "God keeps it (or, them) safe in heaven for you."

you, who...are guarded: RSV continues verse 5 without a break from verse 4. It may be better to end verse 4 with a full stop and begin verse 5 as a new sentence, as TEV does: "You are protected (or, kept safe)."

by God's power...through faith: these two phrases express the source of the believer's protection (God's power) and the means whereby it works (faith). These two may be expressed by verbal phrases: "By his power God protects you" or "God is powerful, and he protects you"; and, "through your faith in Christ you have God's protection" or "you believe in Christ, and so God protects you." The two may be combined as follows: "because you believe in Christ, God protects you by means of his power."

for: again, as in the case of to an inheritance in verse 4, this is the result or goal of the protection that believers enjoy. "So you will possess the salvation that is now ready for us, and which God will reveal (or, make known) at the end of time." In this statement, salvation is both a situation into which believers will enter, and a completed plan which God will put into effect at the end of the age. So it may be difficult to use a verbal phrase for salvation unless something like the following is said: "And so God will save you (or, will set you free). He is always ready to do it, and will finally do so on the last day."

ready to be revealed expresses not just the idea that God will make known what he has planned; it is a way of saying that God will put it into effect. Here salvation is seen as a future event.

The following may serve as a model for translating verses 3-5:

3-5 We must always praise God, who is the God and Father of our Lord Jesus Christ. Because of God's great compassion for us (or, Because God loves us very much), he gave us new life, spiritual life. He did this by raising Jesus Christ from death. And so we have a hope that will never disappear (or, weaken). We look forward to receiving the rich blessings that God will give his people. He keeps them safe in heaven for you; there they will not be destroyed, or be ruined, or lose their value. By his power God protects you, and because of your faith in him (or, in Christ) you have that protection. And so you look forward to the salvation that God has prepared, and which he will put into effect (or, make known) at the end of time.

1.6 RSV	TEV
In this you rejoice,[a] though now for a little while you may have to suffer various trials,	Be glad about this, even though it may now be necessary for you to be sad for a while because of the many kinds of trials you suffer.

[a]Or *Rejoice in this*

In this you rejoice: it is probable that this refers back to the description in verses 3-5 of the Christians' situation, and not to any particular item in that situation."Because all of this is true," "Because all these things have happened to you." As the RSV footnote shows, the Greek can be understood as imperative: "Be glad about this" (TEV). Most modern translations understand the Greek to be imperative.

though now for a little while: this modifies somewhat the command to rejoice. The writer says that suffering seems inevitable, but in spite of the suffering (which will not last very long) they should rejoice. It may be better in some languages to reverse the clauses: "At this time you are having to endure hardships (or, trials). But still you must rejoice, because God has done all these things for you" (in which "these things" refers back to verses 3-5).

you may have to: this is stated as a possibility, not a certainty. But it seems evident, from the Letter as a whole, that the readers were being persecuted—or at least some of them were.

1.7 RSV	TEV
so that the genuineness of your faith, more precious than gold which though perishable is tested by fire, may redound to praise and glory and honor at the revelation of Jesus Christ.	Their purpose is to prove that your faith is genuine. Even gold, which can be destroyed, is tested by fire; and so your faith, which is much more precious than gold, must also be tested, so that it may endure. Then you will receive praise and glory and honor on the Day when Jesus Christ is revealed.

so that: this refers back to the suffering the readers are experiencing. TEV begins a new sentence and makes the relationship with what precedes clear by saying "Their purpose is...."

the genuineness of your faith: the Greek word translated genuineness may be taken to mean the process by which the quality of the faith is shown, and not only the result; so TEV "prove that your faith is genuine." Or the translation may be "to determine (or, find out) whether your faith is genuine" or "to test your faith and prove whether or not it is real." Here faith is probably best understood as saving faith in Jesus Christ; but it can be taken to mean "faithfulness," "loyalty."

more precious than gold which though perishable is tested by fire: Christian faith is compared with gold in two ways: (1) its value and (2) the process of refining. As for value, faith is much more valuable than gold, which is perishable, that is, it belongs to the material world and so does not have eternal value, as faith has. The word used to translate gold should be one that refers to it as precious metal, not gold bars (bullion) or coins. As for the "testing" of gold, this is a reference to the process of refining the gold ore, which burns away the impurities and leaves only the gold itself. And even though gold is perishable, it must undergo this process in order to rid it of impure substances. Faith, which is eternal, is much more valuable than gold. Therefore it must also be "tested," that is, cleansed of its impurities by means of the "fires" of hardship and persecution. So the writer sees a positive value in the difficulties the readers are experiencing.

may redound to praise and glory and honor: this phrase goes back to the first part of the sentence, so that the genuineness of your faith. The verb in Greek is "may be found," which TEV represents by "that it may endure." The praise and glory and honor may refer either to the believers' faith, or to the believers themselves. "Your faith will be praised, acclaimed and honored" or "You will receive praise and glory and honor" (TEV). The actor is God: "God will praise you (or, your faith)...." Or, "God will speak well of you because you believe him."

at the revelation of Jesus Christ: "when Jesus Christ is revealed" (TEV) or "when Jesus Christ appears." This refers to the coming of Jesus Christ on the last day. The noun revelation may be represented by the passive verbal phrase "is revealed"; or, better, "when Jesus Christ comes."

One model for translating verse 7 is found in TEV. Another model may be the following:

> Even gold, which can be destroyed, is placed in the fire so that its impurities will be burned away. And so your faith, which is so much more valuable than gold, is being put to the test by the hardships you are suffering. If your faith endures, you will receive praise and honor and glory from God on the day that Jesus Christ comes.

1.8

RSV	TEV
Without having seen[b] him you[c] love him; though you do not now see him you[c] believe in him and rejoice with unutterable and exalted joy.	You love him, although you have not seen him, and you believe in him, although you do not now see him. So you rejoice with a great and glorious joy which words cannot express,

[b]Other ancient authorities read *known*
[c]Or omit *you*

Without having seen him you love him: "You have never seen him, but you love him" or "Although you have never seen him you love him" or "You love him even though you have not seen him."

1 Peter 1.8

As the RSV footnote shows, instead of seen, many Greek manuscripts and ancient versions have "known," a wording which does not fit the context. In Greek the two are quite similar (*idontes* and *eidotes*). The second footnote shows that instead of the indicatives you love him and you believe in him, the verbs may be understood as imperatives: "love him" and "believe in him." This is possible but seems quite improbable.

A similar contrast is drawn: the readers do not see Jesus Christ now, that is, his presence is spiritual, not bodily. Even so they do believe in him or "are faithful to him." Or "you continue to believe in him (or, to be faithful to him)."

rejoice with unutterable and exalted joy: unutterable...joy means joy which cannot be expressed or described with words. Human language is not adequate to express this kind of happiness (see similar statement in 2 Cor 12.4); exalted joy means "very great (or, wonderful) joy."

1.9 RSV	TEV
As the outcome of your faith you obtain the salvation of your souls.	because you are receiving the salvation of your souls, which is the purpose of your faith in him.

TEV and RSV differ in their understanding of the force of the Greek participle "obtaining." RSV takes it to represent a separate thought and so begins verse 9 as a new sentence; TEV takes it to be related to verse 8, expressing the reason for the great joy of the believers: "because you are receiving" or "because you have received." Or else the participle may express the circumstances surrounding the readers' great joy: "as you receive." Any one of these is possible, and a translator must make a choice. If the choice is to follow TEV, then it may be better to begin verse 9 as a new sentence, as follows: "You rejoice like this because you are receiving...."

the outcome of your faith: the word translated outcome may mean "result," "purpose" (TEV), "goal." Faith is faith in Christ, and this should be made explicit.

the salvation of your souls: the Greek word for souls appears also in 1.22; 2.25; 3.20; 4.19; and soul in 2.11. It is possible that by souls the writer means the spiritual part of the believers, in contrast with their physical bodies. It seems more probable, however, that here, as in most places where the word is used, the biblical writer means "yourselves." For salvation see 1.5.

The verse may be translated as follows:

> You rejoice so greatly because you are being given your salvation (or, because God is now saving you), which is the result (or, goal) of your faith in Jesus Christ.

1.10 RSV	TEV
The prophets who prophesied of the grace that was to be yours	It was concerning this salvation that the prophets made

searched and inquired about this salvation;	**careful search and investigation, and they prophesied about this gift which God would give you.**

In verses 10-12 the writer talks about the Old Testament prophets, who had proclaimed the coming of the Messiah and the salvation he would bring. These three verses may appear as a separate section, with the section heading "The Prophets and the Gospel" or "The Message of the (Hebrew) Prophets."

The prophets who prophesied: "God's messengers in the past who spoke about." If "messenger" is the normal word for angel, it will be necessary to translate "people who proclaimed God's message." In the Bible a prophet is a person who proclaims God's message to his people. Sometimes the message had to do with future events, and New Testament writers found in the books of the Old Testament predictions of Jesus Christ and his message and mission. Here the writer declares that the Hebrew prophets had predicted the grace that was to be yours. The verb translated prophesied may be translated "predicted," or "spoke about," "announced," "proclaimed." Here grace refers specifically to this salvation which the readers possess, and describes it as a gift (TEV); or else grace could be here God's love, as in Paul's writings, and so some translate "what God, in his love, was going to give you."

searched and inquired: the two verbs are synonymous, expressing the same idea: "They tried to discover," "they investigated carefully." This kind of investigation is not exploration, as one explores a terrain or a forest; nor is it to be understood as the examination of books; it is rather thinking and reflecting upon God's message, and attempting to discover God's plans for his people (see Hab 2.1).

1.11 RSV	TEV
they inquired what person or time was indicated by the Spirit of Christ within them when predicting the sufferings of Christ and the subsequent glory.	**They tried to find out when the time would be and how it would come.[a] This was the time to which Christ's Spirit in them was pointing, in predicting the sufferings that Christ would have to endure and the glory that would follow.**
	[a]when the time would be and how it would come; *or* who the person would be and when he would come.

inquired: this translates the same Greek verb translated inquired in verse 10.

what person or time was indicated: here the TEV text differs from RSV (the TEV alternative in the footnote agrees with RSV). The Greek test is ambiguous: the indefinite pronoun "what" may be read in an absolute sense, "what person," or as modifying the following time, "what...time," meaning "when the time (or, occasion) would come." Either interpretation makes sense, and a translator should feel free to choose. If the translator follows RSV, the translation can be, "who the person would be and when the time would come." If the translator prefers TEV: "the (precise) time and the circumstances."

indicated by the Spirit of Christ within them: "revealed by the Spirit of Christ which was in them" or "which the Spirit of Christ in them revealed (or, told them)." The phrase the Spirit of Christ is found only here with reference to Old Testament prophets; it appears once more in the New Testament (Rom 8.9), where it refers to Christians (see also "the Spirit of Jesus" in Acts 16.7; "the Spirit of his Son" in Gal 4.6; and "the Spirit of Jesus Christ" in Phil 1.19). By the use of the phrase here, the writer is expressing the view that it was Christ's Spirit acting in the Hebrew prophets, implying thereby Christ's existence with God. The translation of Spirit here should be the same as the translation of "the Spirit of God" or "the Holy Spirit" elsewhere.

when predicting: "when speaking about it before it happened." The Spirit of Christ in the prophets was predicting what would happen.

the sufferings of Christ and the subsequent glory: "the sufferings that Christ would have to endure and the glory that would come afterward." The form of the Greek phrase translated the sufferings of Christ indicates that these were inevitable, that is, they were according to God's will. The glory here is Christ's resurrection and ascension (see verse 21; Luke 24.26); the word may be represented by "victory" or "honor," or even "wonderful events" (in Greek the word is plural).

The following may serve as a model for translating the verse:

> The Spirit of Christ was in the prophets, and the Spirit was predicting that Christ would have to suffer, but after suffering he would have triumphs (or, honor). The prophets tried to discover when this would happen and how it would take place.

If the RSV exegesis is preferred (what person or time), then the last sentence may be "The prophets tried to discover who the person would be and when these things would happen."

1.12 RSV	TEV
It was revealed to them that they were serving not themselves but you, in the things which have now been announced to you by those who preached the good news to you through the Holy Spirit sent from heaven, things into which angels long to look.	God revealed to these prophets that their work was not for their own benefit, but for yours, as they spoke about those things which you have now heard from the messengers who announced the Good News by the power of the Holy Spirit sent from heaven. These are things which even the angels would like to understand.

It was revealed to them: "God revealed (or, explained) to them."

they were serving not themselves but you: this "service" (TEV "their work") was the prophets' predictions, which were not for their own benefit but for the benefit of all Christians. The writer says you, but he does not mean to exclude other Christians. The prophets' messages about the Messiah's suffering and glory were for the benefit of all Christian believers.

in the things which have now been announced to you: the content of the prophets' messages was the same as the gospel message which was proclaimed to the readers of this Letter. The gospel is the fulfillment of the prophets' messages about the Messiah.

those who preached the good news to you: these are the apostles, or the early evangelists of the Church, as they spread the gospel everywhere.

through the Holy Spirit sent from heaven: that is, the Holy Spirit was directing and empowering the Christian messengers as they proclaimed the gospel to the readers of this Letter. The passive sent from heaven stands for God's action, "the Holy Spirit, sent from heaven by God" or "the Holy Spirit, whom God sent from heaven."

things into which angels long to look: the things are the truths proclaimed by the Christian messengers. The statement long to look means that the angels very much want to know the matters, or events, of the Christian faith, but they cannot. Christians have knowledge and experience that angels would like to have, but cannot.

The verse may be translated as follows:

> God revealed (or, made known) to the prophets that what they were doing was not (or, the messages they were proclaiming were not) for their own benefit, but for yours. What they said has now been told you by those who proclaimed the gospel to you. As they announced the Good News, the Holy Spirit, who was sent from heaven by God, inspired (or, guided) them. And these are matters that the angels themselves would very much like to know.

SECTION HEADING

A Call to Holy Living: "Believers Should Live Holy Lives," "How Believers Should Live."

As a result of what Christ has done, Christians must live lives that reflect God's will. They must not behave as they did before becoming Christians, but should strive to be the kind of people who are like the God they worship (verses 13-16). Christ's own sacrifice makes it possible for them to live Christian lives (verses 17-21), and so they should be ruled by Christ's love in their relationships with their fellow believers (verses 22-25).

1.13 RSV	TEV
Therefore gird up your minds, be sober, set your hope fully upon the grace that is coming to you at the revelation of Jesus Christ.	So then, have your minds ready for action. Keep alert and set your hope completely on the blessing which will be given you when Jesus Christ is revealed.

Therefore: this refers back to what was said in verses 3-9, that is, what God has done for them; it does not refer immediately back to verses 10-12.

gird up your minds: "be mentally prepared for action." They must be alert; they must think clearly and sensibly. The verb gird up, used here in a figurative sense, means to tighten the loose-fitting outer tunic at the waist in order to be able to work or move about quickly.

be sober: "be self-controlled," "use good judgment."

set your hope fully upon: "base all your hope on," "keep your hope fixed on." For hope see verse 3.

the grace that is coming to you at the revelation of Jesus Christ: this refers to the salvation that will take place when Jesus Christ comes in power (see verse 5; and see grace in verse 10). Here grace may be translated "the gift of salvation." For the revelation of Jesus Christ see verse 7.

1.14 RSV	TEV
As obedient children, do not be conformed to the passions of your former ignorance,	Be obedient to God, and do not allow your lives to be shaped by those desires you had when you were still ignorant.

As obedient children: the literal translation of the Greek expression fails to represent the meaning. Here the word children refers to the kind of people that the readers are: "Because you (want to) obey God." This is stated as the reason for the command that follows. Or else, as TEV and others translate, "Be obedient to God," "Obey God."

do not be conformed: "do not be controlled by" or "don't let your conduct be shaped (or, determined) by." See the same verb in Romans 12.2.

the passions of your former ignorance: "the evil desires you had before you knew Christ (or, God)." The word translated passions means "desires" (TEV) or, as here, "evil desires," that is, desires for evil things. The translation could be "sinful desires." These are not primarily sexual, as the word passions might imply. The readers' ignorance was during the time before they knew the gospel or Jesus Christ. The translation could be "before you accepted the gospel," "before you became believers (or, Christians)."

1.15 RSV	TEV
but as he who called you is holy, be holy yourselves in all your conduct;	Instead, be holy in all that you do, just as God who called you is holy.

he who called you: "God, the one who called you." God's "call" is his appeal in the gospel for human beings to worship and obey him.

holy: this is the essence of God in terms of moral qualities, his perfect goodness, his moral perfection. He is the standard to which his people are commanded to measure up: they are to be perfectly good, completely virtuous, as he is (see Matt 5.48). This is achieved, of course, only through being completely dedicated to God, the basic qualifications for human holiness.

in all your conduct: "in everything you do."

1.16 RSV	TEV
since it is written, "You shall be holy, for I am holy."	**The scripture says, "Be holy because I am holy."**

The quotation in verse 16 is from Leviticus 19.2 (see also 11.45).

it is written: "the Scriptures say" or "it is written in the (Hebrew) Scriptures." A word that means the whole Bible, that is, the Old Testament and the New Testament, should not be used. Since You shall be holy in Leviticus 19.2 was not addressed to the readers of this Letter, it may be necessary to say "in the Scriptures it is written that God said to his people, 'Be holy because I am holy.'"

Verses 14-16 may be translated as follows:

> Obey God, and do not let your conduct (or, behavior) be determined by the sinful desires you had before you knew Jesus Christ (or, became believers). 15 Instead, try to be completely good (or, pure) in all you do, just as God, who called you to be his own people, is himself completely good. 16 In the Scriptures it is written that God said to his people, "You must be holy, because I am holy."

1.17 RSV	TEV
And if you invoke as Father him who judges each one impartially according to his deeds, conduct yourselves with fear throughout the time of your exile.	**You call him Father, when you pray to God, who judges all people by the same standard, according to what each one has done; so then, spend the rest of your lives here on earth in reverence for him.**

if: although this is formally a condition, it is actually a way of making a statement: "You pray to him as your Father...." Or, "Since you pray...."

invoke: "call upon," "pray to" (TEV). This is prayer and refers to the Christian habit of addressing God as Father when praying to him. "You say 'Father' (or, 'our Father') when you pray to God, who judges ...."

who judges each one impartially according to his deeds: this truth is often stated in the New Testament (see Acts 10.34; Rom 2.6,11; Col 3.25; Rev 22.12). The adverb impartially means that God applies the same standards to all; everyone is judged on the same basis. The same rules apply to all. In some languages this will be stated negatively: "God doesn't show (or, give) special favors to anyone." Each person is responsible for his or her sentence, for God judges "according to what each one has done" (TEV).

Since God is an impartial judge, the believers should conduct themselves with fear, that is, with respect and reverence for God and his law.

throughout the time of your exile: "for the rest of your lives here on earth." For exile see 1.1. At the end of this earthly life believers go to their true home.

Verse 17 may be translated as follows:

You say "Our Father" when you pray to God. So remember that he judges each person according to what that person has done, and does not show special favor for anyone. So then, you must have reverence (or, respect) for God in all you do, for the rest of your lives here on earth.

1.18

RSV	TEV
You know that you were ransomed from the futile ways inherited from your fathers, not with perishable things such as silver or gold,	For you know what was paid to set you free from the worthless manner of life handed down by your ancestors. It was not something that can be destroyed, such as silver or gold;

You know: "You realize," "You are fully aware of." The writer is appealing to a belief held by all Christians.

ransomed: "set free," "liberated," "saved from." The actor is God, and so the translation may say "God set you free" or "God saved you." In a narrow sense "to ransom" means to pay a price for someone's release. In this particular passage that meaning is reflected in the words that follow, as the writer says that it was not money that was used to set the readers free, but the death of Christ on the cross. So in some languages it may be necessary to use a verb such as "to pay," but extreme care should be used in order not to lead the reader to ask "To whom was the price paid?" So it may be better to say "set free" or "saved."

the futile ways inherited from your fathers: by futile ways the writer means "useless manner of life," "a way of living that is not worthwhile." This is, in essence, the pagan way of life which the readers had inherited from their ancestors. "God set you free from a useless way of life, the kind of life that your (pagan) ancestors had."

not with perishable things such as silver or gold: the writer is talking about the means used by God to save the readers of the Letter. TEV has "what was paid to set you free"; as noted above, this may cause difficulties by raising the question, To whom was the payment made? So here it may be better to say "what was the means God used" or "what made it possible (for God to set you free)." So the translation can be "No silver or gold was used (or, paid) when God set you free" or "God set you free, but he did not use silver or gold to do it." Here silver or gold may be translated "silver or gold money" or "money made of silver or gold." Or, more simply, "money."

perishable: "which loses its value," "which can be destroyed" (see 1.7).

1.19 RSV	TEV
but with the precious blood of Christ, like that of a lamb without blemish or spot.	**it was the costly sacrifice of Christ, who was like a lamb without defect or flaw.**

the precious blood of Christ: "the costly sacrifice of Christ" (TEV). For blood see 1.2. Christ's death on the cross was the means whereby God set them free from their pagan way of life.

like that of a lamb without blemish or spot: "like a lamb that is perfect (or, that has no defects)." In the Hebrew sacrificial rites the animal to be sacrificed had to be perfect, without any physical flaw or defect. Christ had no moral or spiritual flaws or defects; he was sinless and pure, and so the sacrifice of his life on the cross was effective in redemption.

Verses 18-19 may be translated as follows:

Always remember how God set you free from your old way of life, the useless way of life that your ancestors had. God did not save you by using something that can lose its value, like silver or gold. 19 He saved you by means of the costly sacrifice of Christ, who was like a lamb that has no flaws or defects.

1.20 RSV	TEV
He was destined before the foundation of the world but was made manifest at the end of the times for your sake.	**He had been chosen by God before the creation of the world and was revealed in these last days for your sake.**

destined: see 1.2.

before the foundation of the world: "before the world was made," "before God created the world."

was made manifest: this refers to Christ's coming the first time, as a human being; the writer is not talking about the Second Coming. Christ's coming began the end of the age, and the translation here may be "in these last times," "now that the end of the age is near," or "now when this age will not last much longer."

for your sake: "for your good (or, benefit)" or "for your salvation."

The verse may be translated as follows:

Before God created the world, he chose Christ as the one through whom he would save you. And so Christ came to save you, now that this age is coming to a close.

1.21 RSV	TEV
Through him you have confidence in God, who raised him from the dead and gave him glory, so that your faith and hope are in God.[d]	**Through him you believe in God, who raised him from death and gave him glory; and so your faith and hope are fixed on God.**

[d]Or *so that your faith is hope in God*

Through him: this indicates how it was possible for the believers to have confidence in God. This idea of a causative agent may be expressed by saying "Because you believe in him (or, Christ)" or "He caused you (or, made it possible for you) to have confidence in God."

have confidence in God: the text may mean, as TEV translates, "believe in God." Or one may say "you trust in God," "you have faith in God."

raised him from the dead and gave him great glory: as in verse 11, Christ's glory is his exaltation to the place of power at God's right side (see Eph 1.20). Here the translation can be "he made Christ very great (or, powerful)." The equivalent of "he honored him" does not seem adequate.

so that your faith and hope are in God: "so that you have your faith and your hope securely fixed in God" or "so that God is the one you believe in and are sure of" or "so that you believe in God and are certain that he will keep his promises." Here faith is trust in God, and hope, as often in the New Testament, is confidence or assurance that God will keep his promises.

As the RSV footnote shows, it is possible that the Greek text means "so that your faith is hope in God," but this does not seem very likely.

1.22

RSV	TEV
Having purified your souls by your obedience to the truth for a sincere love of the brethren, love one another earnestly from the heart.	**Now that by your obedience to the truth you have purified yourselves and have come to have a sincere love for your fellow believers, love one another earnestly with all your heart.**[b]
	[b]**with all your heart;** *some manuscripts have* **with a pure heart.**

In verses 22-25 the writer tells his readers how they are to show their love for one another as brothers and sisters in Christ. The three verses that follow (2.1-3) speak of attitudes and actions they should avoid. So a translation may choose to make a separate section of 1.22—2.3, and have as heading, "How Believers Should Treat One Another."

Having purified your souls: here, as in verse 9, your souls means "yourselves" (TEV). This is spiritual purification and refers to the forgiveness of sins and moral purity (see 1.2 sprinkling with his blood). Here, as in 1.2, the rite of Christian baptism is in the background, but it should not be introduced into the text itself.

The following by your obedience to the truth indicates the means by which their spiritual purification was achieved. Here the truth stands for the gospel message and its demands. The whole statement may be translated, "You have obeyed the demands of the gospel, and so you are spiritually pure" or "Because you have obeyed the commands of Jesus Christ, your sins have been forgiven and you are (spiritually) pure."

for a sincere love of the brethren: the preposition translated for goes back to purified, and it indicates the purpose or the result of the spiritual purification. It is the sincere love that believers have for one another. The phrase love of the brethren translates a word meaning "brotherly love," that is, love for one's fellow believers.

love one another earnestly from the heart: the command love one another in Greek uses a different word for love from the word used for love in the preceding clause. For a similar change see 2 Peter 1.7. In the context, no great difference is intended; love of the brethren could be taken to mean "brotherly affection," "care and concern for fellow believers."

The expression from the heart may be translated "with all your might" or "as much as you can."

As the TEV footnote shows, many Greek manuscripts and ancient versions have "from a pure heart." The translator should feel free to follow this text.

The following may serve as a model for the translation of this verse:

> You have obeyed the commands of the gospel (or, of Christ), and so your sins have been forgiven and you are spiritually pure. This makes it possible for you to have a sincere love for your fellow believers. So you must love one another with all your heart.

If the translation follows the Greek text that includes "pure" (see above), the last sentence may be "So you must love one another with all your heart, and your love must be pure (or, true)." A "pure love" has no hidden motives and is not mixed up with envy or suspicion or fear.

1.23 RSV	TEV
You have been born anew, not of perishable seed but of imperishable, through the living and abiding word of God;	**For through the living and eternal word of God you have been born again as the children of a parent who is immortal, not mortal.**

You have been born anew: see 1.3. Here the source of the new life is the living and abiding word of God. This is God's power to create and save by means of his command. In this context (see verse 25b), the gospel is the means by which God's life-giving word does its work of rebirth: as the readers heard and accepted the gospel, they were given new life by God's power. The two adjectives living and abiding modify word of God; the Greek text can be taken to mean "the word of the living and abiding God." For living...word of God the translation can be "the command (or, word) of God that always works (or, saves)" or, in a negative fashion, "the word of God that never fails." And abiding can be translated "always continues," "never changes," "is always true."

not of perishable seed but of imperishable: here seed is used in the sense of "parentage," that is, the one who begets, the father. In this context God is the spiritual parent, and he is contrasted with human parents, who are mortal; God himself is immortal. God is the spiritual parent, and by means of his living and eternal word he begets children, giving them life.

The following may serve as a model for translating this verse:

> You have been given new life by God, who is your Father. He

is not mortal, but immortal, and he gave you life by means of his word, which lives and which will exist forever.

1.24-25 RSV

for
"All flesh is like grass
and all its glory like the flower of grass.
The grass withers, and the flower falls,
25 but the word of the Lord abides for ever."
That word is the good news which was preached to you.

TEV

As the scripture says,
"All mankind are like grass,
and all their glory is like wild flowers.
The grass withers, and the flowers fall,
25 but the word of the Lord remains forever."
This word is the Good News that was proclaimed to you.

The scripture quoted is from Isaiah 40.6-8.

for: in most cases it will be better to have "for (or, as) the scripture says," in order to make clear to the reader that what follows is a quotation.

All flesh: "All human beings" or "All living creatures."

like grass: here grass means uncultivated, wild plants that grow without human labor. So "like wild plants" or even "like weeds" may serve as a translation. As the whole quotation makes clear, the point of the comparison is that human beings and wild plants are short-lived; they do not last long, but quickly die and disappear, in contrast with the word of the Lord.

glory: "beauty" or "honor," "fame," "greatness." The word applies to human beings, not to wild plants.

the flower of grass: "wild bloom," "the blooms of wild plants," "wild flowers" (TEV).

withers...falls: "dries up...falls off," "dies...drops off."

the word of the Lord: here Lord stands for God; abides for ever describes God's word as always existing, always true, always active.

The Christian writer explains to his readers the meaning of the word of the Lord in Isaiah 40.8: it is the gospel. The translator must make it clear to the readers and, if possible, to the hearers, that this is not part of the quotation from the Old Testament.

was preached to you: "was proclaimed (or, announced) to you" or "which you heard." The passive may best be translated by an active form: "the messengers of the gospel proclaimed to you" (see verse 12).

Chapter 2

SECTION HEADING

The Living Stone and the Holy Nation: The TEV section heading is composed of two figures: Christ as the living stone (verse 4) and believers as a holy nation (verse 9). In most languages it will be better to use another phrase or statement as a heading here: "Christ is the Cornerstone of the Church" or "Believers Are God's Holy People."

As suggested above (1.22), the first three verses of chapter 2 may be combined with 1.22-25 into a separate section.

After telling his readers the attitudes and actions they should avoid as Christians (verses 1-3), the writer speaks about Christ in terms of the biblical figure of a stone, which has both a constructive function and a destructive function (verses 4-8). Then, in a series of biblical figures, the writer speaks of the status and function of believers as God's people (verses 9-10).

2.1 RSV	TEV
So put away all malice and all guile and insincerity and envy and all slander.	Rid yourselves, then, of all evil; no more lying or hypocrisy or jealousy or insulting language.

So: as a result of their new birth (1.23), the readers are urged to get rid of those feelings which create dissension and conflict in the Christian fellowship.

put away: "get rid of." The verb in Greek is the one used for taking off a garment; the sins listed are like old, dirty garments that must be taken off and discarded.

all malice: "every kind of evil (or, wickedness)." Or, in a more restricted sense, "all feelings of ill will," "every form of hatred."

guile: "lying" (TEV), "deceit."

insincerity: "hypocrisy" (TEV), "pretense."

envy: "jealousy" (TEV).

slander: "insults," "abusive language."

It may be better to use verbs or verbal phrases instead of nouns, as follows: "You must not commit any wrong (or, do anything wicked): do not lie to people or deceive them; do not be jealous, and do not say bad things about others."

2.2 RSV	TEV
Like newborn babes, long for the pure spiritual milk, that by it	Be like newborn babies, always thirsty for the pure spiritual

you may grow up to salvation;	**milk, so that by drinking it you may grow up and be saved.**

Like newborn babes: this figure follows naturally from the language of new birth in 1.3,23. The point of comparison is the constant craving that babies have for milk; in the same way, believers must always desire the pure spiritual milk. It may be necessary to make this comparison explicit, as follows: "As newborn babies want their mother's milk, in the same way you...." In some languages the literal translation of newborn babes will be redundant, and "babies," or "infants," or "young children" will be more natural. Some believe the adjective newborn indicates that only recently had the readers of the Letter heard of and accepted the gospel. This may be so, but it seems more natural to assume that the language reflects the rite of baptism and entrance into the Christian fellowship.

the pure spiritual milk: here milk is the food that babies are nourished on. And the phrase spiritual milk refers to the gospel message, on which Christians are nourished. The figure may be difficult for some readers, and the figure "spiritual food" might not be quite so difficult. The adjective pure means that this "milk" does not have any other foreign substances mixed in it; it is undiluted. It may be more desirable to say "Desire pure spiritual nourishment (or, food)." Or else, in an expanded form, "Always desire the kind of pure food that will nourish your spirit." Or else, "Always crave for the pure (or, wholesome) food (or, drink) that God's Spirit gives."

that by it: "so that by drinking (or, eating) it."

may grow up to salvation: the figure of a baby being well-nourished and growing up is continued. Here salvation is seen as the end of a process of growth: "so that you will grow up and be saved (or, and attain salvation)," "so that you will grow up and become spiritually mature."

The verse may be translated as follows:

Just as newly born babies want their mother's milk, you must always desire pure spiritual food (or, pure food that will nourish your spirits). If you eat that (spiritual) food, you will grow up and be saved.

2.3 RSV	TEV
for you have tasted the kindness of the Lord.	**As the scripture says, "You have found out for yourselves how kind the Lord is."**

for you have tasted: TEV makes it clear that this is a quotation from Psalm 34.8: "As the scripture says" (see comment on 1.24). Here tasted means "experienced," "discovered," "learned through experience."

the kindness of the Lord: "that the Lord is kind (or, good)." In the psalm the Lord is God; here, however, it refers to Jesus Christ, as the next verse makes clear.

2.4 RSV

Come to him, to that living stone, rejected by men but in God's sight chosen and precious;

TEV

Come to the Lord, the living stone rejected by man as worthless but chosen by God as valuable.

Come to him: "Come to the Lord (Jesus Christ)," "Draw near to the Lord." This is a continuous process, and believers must always keep close to their Lord.

that living stone: this looks ahead to the three Old Testament quotations (verses 6-8) that use the figure of stone. The writer uses the figure to speak of Jesus Christ as a living stone and the believers as living stones (verse 5). The metaphor living stone may be difficult to represent, and it may be easier to use a simile: "Christ is like a stone that is alive." Of course, even this is strange, but in this context it is not quite so difficult.

rejected by men: "which people rejected," "which people did not want (to use)." The Greek verb translated rejected has in it the idea of unfavorable judgment: "the stone which people considered worthless." It may seem strange to speak of a stone that people have rejected but that God has chosen, so it may be helpful to indicate here that this is a stone that is used in putting up a building (as the following verses make clear.

in God's sight chosen and precious: "which God considers useful and valuable." Or else the two adjectives may be translated, "God considered it valuable and so he chose it."

The following may serve as a model for translating this verse:

> Keep drawing close to the Lord (Jesus Christ). He is like a building stone that builders considered worthless; but God, the builder of a spiritual (or, living) temple, considers him valuable, and so he chose (or, used) him.

2.5 RSV

and like living stones be yourselves built into a spiritual house, to be a holy priesthood, to offer spiritual sacrifices acceptable to God through Jesus Christ.

TEV

Come as living stones, and let yourselves be used in building the spiritual temple, where you will serve as holy priests to offer spiritual and acceptable sacrifices to God through Jesus Christ.

like living stones: here the figure of a living stone is applied to believers. They must allow themselves to be used by God, the builder of the spiritual temple. It may be possible to translate living stones as "stones that God has caused to live."

be yourselves built into: the passive form may not be easily understood, and so it may be better to translate "and let God build you (or, make you)" or "and God will build you." "You are like living stones that God uses (or, will use) to build a spiritual temple." Here house is clearly "temple" (TEV) and should be so translated (see Eph 2.20-22 for a similar figure).

to be a holy priesthood: here the figure changes, and believers are not stones used for building God's temple but are priests serving in the temple. Holy describes their character as priests: all believers, because they are dedicated to God's service, are priests. In many languages holy will be translated "dedicated to God (or, to God's service)."

offer spiritual sacrifices: as the gospel is spiritual food (verse 2), and as the church is a spiritual temple, so Christian worship and praise are spiritual offerings that believers present to God (see Rom 12.1; Phil 4.18; Heb 13.15-16).

acceptable to God: "pleasing to God," "which pleases God," "which God accepts."

through Jesus Christ: this probably goes with the verb to offer. It is as followers of Jesus Christ that believers offer spiritual sacrifices to God; or they do so in the name of Jesus Christ. Or, in a more general sense, "because of what Jesus Christ has done you are able to offer...." It is true that through Jesus Christ may modify acceptable to God, but this seems less likely.

2.6 RSV	TEV
For it stands in scripture: **"Behold, I am laying in Zion** **a stone, a cornerstone** **chosen and precious,** **and he who believes in him** **will not be put to shame."**	**For the scripture says,** **"I chose a valuable stone,** **which I am placing as the** **cornerstone in Zion;** **and whoever believes in** **him will never be disap-** **pointed."**

For it stands in scripture: "For it is written in the Scriptures" or "For the Scriptures say." The quotation is from Isaiah 28.16, according to the text of the ancient Greek translation of the Old Testament, the Septuagint. Since the speaker is God, it may be well to make that explicit: "For it is written in the Scriptures that God said."

I am laying in Zion a stone: here Zion means Jerusalem and must be so translated in many languages. The stone, which God uses as a cornerstone, is used either in the construction of the city itself or, more probably, the temple. Here the stone is Jesus Christ himself, who is the cornerstone of the spiritual temple of God, the church.

cornerstone: a stone at the corner of a building where two walls meet. If in a given culture the use of cornerstone is unknown, something like "the most important stone" can be said.

chosen and precious: as in verse 4, above, TEV has distributed the components differently: "I chose a valuable stone, which I am placing as the cornerstone in Zion." Or else, "I am placing in Zion a valuable stone which I chose to use as the most important stone (in the building)."

he who believes in him: "whoever believes in him" (TEV), "anyone who trusts him." In Greek the personal pronoun may refer to the stone or to a person. In this context it refers to Christ, and it may be necessary to make this explicit: "and whoever believes in Christ, who is the cornerstone of God's temple, will not be disappointed." The only trouble with this is that it introduces into the Old Testament passage a distinctively Christian concept. So it may be more satisfactory to translate "and whoever believes in the one I choose to be the cornerstone...."

will not be put to shame: "will not be defeated." "will not be disappointed (or, disillusioned)." Or, in a positive fashion, "will always be confident (or, safe)."

2.7 RSV

To you therefore who believe, he is precious, but for those who do not believe,
"The very stone which the builders rejected
has become the head of the corner,"

TEV

This stone is of great value for you that believe; but for those who do not believe:
"The stone which the builders rejected as worthless
turned out to be the most important of all."

you...who believe: "you...who believe in him," that is, in Jesus Christ.

he is precious: this translates what is literally "(is) the honor (or, price)," which some take to mean that believers share in Christ's honor. But most, like RSV and TEV, take it to refer to the adjective precious of the quotation from Isaiah 28.16 in verse 6.

In contrast with what Jesus Christ means to believers, the writer now refers to unbelievers and cites two passages which also use the word stone. The first one is from Psalm 118.22, which is quoted also in Matthew 21.42; Mark 12.10; Luke 20.17; Acts 4.11.

The very stone which the builders rejected: as in verse 4, except that here the word builders is used, whereas in verse 4 it is men.

has become the head of the corner: this is another way of saying "the cornerstone" or "chief cornerstone." Here, as in verse 6, the phrase "most important stone" or "principal stone" may be used. The translation of has become should not imply that the stone was somehow changed; it means that it was later used as the cornerstone, after its initial rejection by the builders.

2.8 RSV

and
"A stone that will make men stumble,
a rock that will make them fall";
for they stumble because they disobey the word, as they were destined to do.

TEV

And another scripture says,
"This is the stone that will make people stumble,
the rock that will make them fall."
They stumbled because they did not believe in the word; such was God's will for them.

RSV shows that another passage is being quoted here, by the use of the conjunction and and the opening quotation marks. It may be better to do as TEV does: "And another scripture says." This passage is from Isaiah 8.14-15.

The two lines are parallel and mean the same thing. A stone is the same as a rock, and make men stumble is the same as make them fall.

In some languages the repetition may seem odd or may be confusing. A translation may choose to say "This is the stone that will make people stumble and fall." If it is unnatural to speak of a stone causing people to fall down, it may be better to say "People will trip on (or, over) this stone and will fall down."

Why do they stumble and fall? Because they disobey the word, that is, they do not accept the gospel. As in 1.25, the word is the gospel.

as they were destined to do: for the idea expressed by destined, see 1.2,20. "God had decided that this would happen to them." See the same thought in Jude 4.

2.9 RSV	TEV
But you are a chosen race, a royal priesthood, a holy nation, God's own people,[e] that you may declare the wonderful deeds of him who called you out of darkness into his marvelous light.	But you are the chosen race, the King's priests, the holy nation, God's own people, chosen to proclaim the wonderful acts of God, who called you out of darkness into his own marvelous light.

[e]Greek *a people for his possession*

The writer uses a number of phrases which in the Old Testament apply to Israel; here he applies them to the church. See Exodus 19.5-6; 23.22; Isaiah 43.20-21.

a chosen race: "the people that God chose for his own."

a royal priesthood: "priests who serve the king," that is, who serve God, who is the King. It may be necessary to go beyond TEV ("the King's priests") and say "priests who serve God, the (or, our) King."

a holy nation: "a nation dedicated to God's service" (see comments on holy in 2.5).

God's own people: this essentially repeats the thought of a chosen race; the translation can be "people who belong only to God."

The task of believers is to declare the wonderful deeds of God. This is also Old Testament language; see Isaiah 43.21 (also 42.12). This may be expressed as "to proclaim to all people the wonderful things that God has done."

God is described as the one who called you out of the darkness into his marvelous light. In the Bible darkness stands for ignorance, sin, and death, while light stands for saving knowledge, salvation, and life. It may be necessary to say "the darkness of sin" and "the light of salvation." This will make it easier to represent the meaning of marvelous as a modifier of "salvation" or "life" instead of light.

The verse may be translated as follows:

> But you are the race (of people) that God chose; you are priests who serve God, the King; you are a nation dedicated to God's service; you are people who belong exclusively to God. He is the one who called you out of the darkness of sin into the glorious light of salvation. He chose you to proclaim the wonderful things that he has done.

2.10 RSV

Once you were no people but now you are God's people; once you had not received mercy but now you have received mercy.

TEV

At one time you were not God's people, but now you are his people; at one time you did not know God's mercy, but now you have received his mercy.

This verse draws its language from Hosea 2.23 (see also 1.6,9; 2.1).

Once...now: "In the past...at the present time," "Formerly...now."

no people...God's people: "not God's people...God's own people."

had not received mercy...have received mercy: "God did not have mercy on you...God has mercy on you." Here mercy is not just pity or compassion; it is more like "tender care" or "love" (see 1.3).

SECTION HEADING

Slaves of God: "Live as Servants of God," "Obey God in All You Do."

In this section, verses 11-17, the writer is especially concerned with believers' relations with non-Christians. In verses 11-12 he speaks of the need to live a moral, virtuous life, and in verses 13-17 he shows the necessity of their being law-abiding citizens.

2.11 RSV

Beloved, I beseech you as aliens and exiles to abstain from the passions of the flesh that wage war against your soul.

TEV

I appeal to you, my friends, as strangers and refugees in this world! Do not give in to bodily passions, which are always at war against the soul.

Beloved: "My dear friends," "My dear fellow believers."

I beseech you: "I appeal to you" (TEV), "I ask you," "I urge you." This is more of a request than a demand.

as aliens and exiles: this takes up the thought expressed in 1.1 (exiles) and 1.17 (the time of your exile). For Christians this world is not a permanent home but a temporary dwelling place, as a refugee camp is meant to be. The translation can be "foreigners and exiles," "aliens and temporary residents," "people who live in this world for only a short time."

abstain from the passions of the flesh: "do not allow bodily desires to control you." For passions see 1.14. In contrast with the following your soul, here flesh is the physical or bodily part of a person; or else, in a broader sense, the word refers to what is specifically human, as contrasted with God's demands. Either "human desires" or "physical desires" may serve as a translation of the Greek phrase.

wage war against your soul: "are in opposition to your souls," "fight against the soul," or "put the soul in danger." It may be difficult to speak of passions fighting the soul, and a simile may be preferable: "the desires of the body, which are like enemies fighting against your soul." Here soul represents the higher, spiritual part of human nature.

2.12 RSV	TEV
Maintain good conduct among the Gentiles, so that in case they speak against you as wrongdoers, they may see your good deeds and glorify God on the day of visitation.	Your conduct among the heathen should be so good that when they accuse you of being evildoers, they will have to recognize your good deeds and so praise God on the Day of his coming.

Maintain good conduct: "Behave well," "Conduct yourselves well," "Live good lives." This is moral, ethical behavior.

the Gentiles: "the pagans," "the heathen." This term reflects the Old Testament classification of Jews, the people of God, in contrast with Gentiles, all other people.

in case they speak against you as wrongdoers: "whenever they accuse you of doing wrong," "if they denounce you as evildoers." As the rest of the verse shows, the accusation will be false, and this may be said or implied in the translation: "if they falsely accuse you of breaking the law." In some instances it may be better to use a form of direct address: "If they say, 'These Christians are evildoers.'"

they may see your good deeds: the Greek verb translated see means not just to observe or witness the good things that Christians do, but to be convinced by them that believers are indeed good, law-abiding people, not evil or criminals. See the similar idea in Matthew 5.16.

glorify God: "give praise to God."

on the day of visitation: "on the day God comes to judge the world," "on the Day of Judgment."

The verse may be translated as follows:

> Live good lives among non-Christians. They may accuse you of being evildoers, but when they see the good things you do they will have to admit that you are good (or, that they are wrong). And so they will give thanks to God (for you) on the Day of Judgment.

2.13 RSV	TEV
Be subject for the Lord's sake to every human institution,[f] whether it be to the emperor as supreme,	For the sake of the Lord submit yourselves to every human authority: to the Emperor, who is the supreme authority,

[f] Or *every institution ordained for men*

Be subject...to every human institution: "Obey...all human authority," "Submit yourselves...to all legal authority." The phrase translated human institution means, in this context, all legal state authorities. So the translation can be "Be law-abiding citizens" or "Obey all government (or, state) laws" (see Titus 3.1).

In a footnote, RSV gives an alternative translation of the Greek phrase; this is possible, but the meaning given in the text is much more probable.

for the Lord's sake: "because you are followers of the Lord (Jesus Christ)" or "in order to bring honor to the Lord."

the emperor: the Roman Emperor, the highest human authority in that part of the world. If there is no particular word for emperor or king, something like "the most important ruler" or "the most powerful official (or, chief)" can be said. In this case, as supreme does not have to be explicitly represented in translation, since its meaning will be expressed in the title itself.

2.14 RSV	TEV
or to governors as sent by him to punish those who do wrong and to praise those who do right.	**and to the governors, who have been appointed by him to punish the evildoers and to praise those who do good.**

governors: these are the officials appointed by the Emperor to rule the various provinces.

sent by him: "appointed by him" (TEV), "installed in office by him," "authorized by him"; or "whom he has appointed (or, authorized)."

It is assumed that the government officials will carry out their duties in a fair and just manner, punishing the criminals and rewarding the law-abiding citizens. In translation it may be necessary to use a causative form of the verb to punish; "to cause (or, order) to be punished."

who do right: in this context, "law-abiding," "upright (citizens)."

2.15 RSV	TEV
For it is God's will that by doing right you should put to silence the ignorance of foolish men.	**For God wants you to silence the ignorant talk of foolish people by the good things you do.**

it is God's will: "God's purpose is" or "God wants you to" (TEV).

by doing right you should put to silence: "you should do what is right and so put to silence." This "putting to silence" does not mean to restrain people by force from talking; instead it means to take away any reason they might have for slandering Christians.

the ignorance of foolish men: "the ignorant accusations of foolish people" or "the talk of foolish and ignorant people." Here ignorance means not just lack of knowledge but the deliberate disregard of the facts; it is slanderous abuse, false accusation.

The following may serve as a model for translating this verse: "God wants you to do good so that ignorant and foolish people will have no chance of (or, reason for) speaking evil of you."

2.16 RSV	TEV
Live as free men, yet without using your freedom as a pretext for evil; but live as servants of God.	Live as free people; do not, however, use your freedom to cover up any evil, but live as God's slaves.

The writer here shows that the duty to obey government officials is not a restriction of Christian freedom, as some might think.

Live as free men: "Live as free people" (TEV), "Conduct yourselves as people who are free." Here free refers not to their status as citizens in the Roman Empire (many of the readers would be slaves), but to their spiritual freedom as followers of Christ (see especially Gal 5.1). Christ had set them free from the power of sin.

without using your freedom as a pretext for evil: "but you must not think that your freedom gives you the right to do what is wrong." The word translated pretext means "covering" in the sense of an excuse, a "cover-up."

live as servants of God: "live as people who serve (or, obey) God" or "live as people whose master is God." The Greek word may be translated "slaves" (TEV), but in many languages the word has such a bad connotation that it is impossible to use it in a context like this.

2.17 RSV	TEV
Honor all men. Love the brotherhood. Fear God. Honor the emperor.	Respect everyone, love your fellow believers, honor God, and respect the Emperor.

In four short commands the writer tells his readers the attitude they should have toward their fellow Christians, non-Christians, and God.

Honor all men: "Respect everyone" (TEV), "Show the proper attitude toward all people." This is done in action and in language. A negative form may be better: "Do not be disrespectful to anyone" or "Do not treat anyone disrespectfully."

Love the brotherhood: "Love your fellow believers" (see 1.22).

Fear God: "Honor God" (TEV), "Have reverence for God" (see 1.17).

Honor the emperor: "Respect the Emperor" (the same verb used in the first command).

SECTION HEADING

The Example of Christ's Suffering: "Christian Slaves and their Masters." The TEV section heading concentrates on Christ's suffering, which is referred to as the reason why Christian slaves should endure patiently the unjust punishments they might suffer. They should imitate Jesus, their spiritual Shepherd and Guardian. He patiently endured suffering and death on the cross, and by his death he achieved salvation for all.

2.18 RSV

Servants, be submissive to your masters with all respect, not only to the kind and gentle but also to the overbearing.

TEV

You servants must submit yourselves to your masters and show them complete respect, not only to those who are kind and considerate, but also to those who are harsh.

Servants: this translates a word different from the one in 2.16, which TEV translates "slaves." The Greek word here means primarily house slaves, but it is not probable that the writer was addressing only the household servants.

be submissive: this translates the same verb used in 2.13; here, as there, the translation can be "obey."

with all respect: the same Greek word is used here that in 1.17 and 2.17 is translated fear. It means the attitude of accepting the authority of the master without resentment or complaint, even if the master is overbearing, that is, harsh and unfair.

The verse may be translated as follows: "Servants, obey your masters and always be respectful to them. You must do this not only if your master is kind and considerate, but also if he is mean (or, unreasonable)."

2.19 RSV

For one is approved if, mindful of God, he endures pain while suffering unjustly.

TEV

God will bless you for this, if you endure the pain of undeserved suffering because you are conscious of his will.

one is approved: this translates what is literally "this is grace (or, favor)." RSV takes it to mean "a person is approved by God"; this can be translated "God will approve you." TEV also takes the word to represent God's response: "God will bless you for this." (In TEV "this" is meant to refer forward to "if you endure the pain," and not backward to verse 18.) Some take the Greek word to mean human reaction or judgment: "It is a good thing," "You deserve praise," "It's admirable."

mindful of God: "with an awareness of God's will." This phrase indicates that praise, or blessing, is due only when the Christian slave's patient endurance of unjust suffering is motivated by his conscious determination to follow God's will.

he endures pain while suffering unjustly: "he patiently endures pain, even though he does not deserve to suffer (or, to be punished)."

The verse may be translated as follows:

For if you have resolved to follow God's will, and so you patiently endure the pain of punishment you do not deserve, then God will bless you.

2.20 RSV

For what credit is it, if when you do wrong and are beaten for

TEV

For what credit is there if you endure the beatings you deserve it you take it patiently? But if when you do right and suffer for it you take it patiently, you have God's approval.

for having done wrong? But if you endure suffering even when you have done right, God will bless you for it.

In this verse the writer points out, in support of what he said in verse 19, that a Christian slave deserves no praise for patiently enduring well-deserved punishment.

what credit is it: or, in a more personal form, "why should you get credit (or, praise)." This may be either from God or from people; in line with God's approval at the end of the verse, it seems that here this refers also to God.

you do wrong and are beaten for it you take it patiently: "You patiently endure the beating you get for having done wrong." It may be necessary to specify who gives the beating: "you patiently endure the beating your master gives you because you did something bad."

But if...: now the writer presents the other alternative, that is, the patient endurance of undeserved punishment: "If you are punished for having done something good, and patiently endure the pain (or, suffering), then God will bless you for it."

you have God's approval: "God will be pleased with you," "God will bless you" (TEV).

2.21 RSV

For to this you have been called, because Christ also suffered for you, leaving you an example, that you should follow in his steps.

TEV

It was to this that God called you, for Christ himself suffered for you and left you an example, so that you would follow in his steps.

to this you have been called: this refers back to what is said in verse 20 about a Christian patiently enduring the pain of undeserved suffering. You have been called means "God called you" (TEV). God's "call" (see 1.15) is here the particular duty he places on his people. The writer has been speaking directly to Christian slaves, but it seems probable that from here to the end of the section (verse 25) he is addressing all believers and not just the slaves.

Christ also suffered for you: the also should not be taken to imply that someone else besides Christ suffered for the readers of this Letter. So it may be better to say "Christ himself" (TEV) or simply "Christ." Here for you shows that Christ's sufferings was for the salvation of people.

leaving you an example, that you should follow in his steps: the two statements reinforce each other, and the two can be expressed as one: "He gave you an example for you to follow."

follow in his steps means "imitate him," "do as he did," "be like him."

The following may serve as a model for translating the verse: "God has given you the duty of suffering like this, for Christ himself suffered for you, and you must imitate the way in which he endured his sufferings."

2.22 RSV

He committed no sin; no guile was found on his lips.

TEV

He committed no sin, and no one ever heard a lie come from his lips.

This verse uses the language of Isaiah 53.9b but does not label it as a quotation.

He committed no sin: "He did not sin," "He never sinned" (see 1.19).

no guile was found on his lips: "he was never heard to lie," "he never lied," "he never deceived anyone." For guile see 2.1.

2.23 RSV

When he was reviled, he did not revile in return; when he suffered, he did not threaten; but he trusted to him who judges justly.

TEV

When he was insulted, he did not answer back with an insult; when he suffered, he did not threaten, but placed his hopes in God, the righteous Judge.

This verse refers particularly to Christ's behavior during his trial and execution.

reviled: "insulted" (TEV). See the statements in Mark 15.17-20, 29-32. "When others (or, his enemies) insulted him, he did not insult them."

when he suffered, he did not threaten: "when he was punished (or, beaten), he did not threaten those who punished him." Or "when his enemies made him suffer, he did not threaten (to punish) them." The verb "to threaten" means to promise to do evil to someone as a way of getting revenge on that person. For statements about Christ's silence see Mark 14.61; 15.5; Luke 23.9.

he trusted to him who judges justly: it is possible that he trusted to means he left it to God to punish his persecutors. It seems more likely, however, that it means that Jesus gave up all thought of revenge and trusted God to save him. A similar verb is used in Luke 23.46: "In your hands I place my spirit" (TEV). So here the translation can be "he entrusted his life to God," "he placed himself in God's care."

him who judges justly: "God, who judges justly" or "God, the righteous judge" (TEV).

2.24 RSV

He himself bore our sins in his body on the tree,[g] that we might die to sin and live to righteousness. By his wounds you have been healed.

TEV

Christ himself carried our sins in his body to the cross, so that we might die to sin and live for righteousness. It is by his wounds that you have been healed.

[g]Or *carried up...to the tree*

bore our sins in his body on the tree: for the statement bore our sins see Isaiah 53.11,12. Here our includes not only believers but, in keeping with Christian faith, all people everywhere; the tree means "the cross" (TEV).

The RSV footnote shows that instead of bore...on the tree the Greek text may mean "carried up...to the tree." This is how TEV and other modern translations understand the Greek text.

The affirmation describes our sins as a burden, or a load, which was placed on Christ and which he carried to the cross. This figure for Christ's death as the means of achieving the forgiveness of sins reflects the Hebrew sacrificial rites. In these rites the forgiveness of sins was effected by the offering of an animal as a sacrifice on the altar. It may also reflect the rite of "placing" the sins of the community on a goat before sending it off to the desert (see Lev 16.20-22).

If possible, the figurative speech should be retained, since it makes use of Old Testament language and symbols. But if it makes no sense, or makes the wrong sense, something should be done to make the meaning clear, such as "Christ suffered for us, and he died on the cross in order that our sins might be forgiven" or "...and he died on the cross to make it possible for God to forgive our sins."

If the idea of purpose ("in order that" or "to") is introduced here, then the following that we might die to sin and live to righteousness may be stated as an additional purpose ("and in order that") or as a result ("and so we...").

die to sin and live to righteousness: to die to sin means to be free of it (see Rom 6.2,11). The metaphor may not carry the right sense, and so the meaning may be expressed by "we are set free from (the power of) sin" or "we are no longer ruled by sin" (see Rom 6.7).

live to righteousness: "live a righteous life," "live as God wants us to live," "live in obedience to God's law."

By his wounds you have been healed: here the writer directly addresses his readers once more, using the language of Isaiah 53.5. The metaphor is unusual and may need to be made somewhat clearer: "You are given spiritual health (or, salvation) because he was wounded (or, crucified)." It should be noted that in Greek the word translated wounds is singular (as it is in the Greek translation of Isa 53.5 in the Septuagint) and so may be taken to refer here not only to the welts and bruises left by the scourging which Christ received, but to the whole process of punishment and execution. "He was punished (or, crucified), and so you are made spiritually whole." The "healing" is spiritual; if necessary, it is possible to say "you are saved." The following may serve as a model for translating the verse:

> Christ took our sins upon himself and carried them to the cross, where he was put to death. He did this so that we might be set free from the power of sin and live as God wants us to live. Because Christ suffered (or, was crucified) you have spiritual health (or, life).

2.25 RSV	TEV
For you were straying like sheep, but have now returned to the Shepherd and Guardian of your souls.	You were like sheep that had lost their way, but now you have been brought back to follow the Shepherd and Keeper of your souls.

you were straying like sheep: "you were wandering away (or, getting lost) like sheep" or "you were like sheep that wander off and get lost" (see Isa 53.6).

have now returned: or, as TEV has it, "have now been brought back," in which God is the implied actor: "God has brought you back."

the Shepherd and Guardian of your souls: the word translated Guardian is "overseer," "superintendent," and when used of a church leader is usually translated "bishop." The two titles here mean the same thing, and it is not necessary to have two words in translation: "the one who takes care of you, as a shepherd takes care of his sheep." It should be clear that Christ is the one meant, and so it may be necessary to say "to Christ, who is the shepherd and keeper of your souls" or "to Christ, who cares for you and protects you like a shepherd."

For your souls see 1.9.

Chapter 3

SECTION HEADING

Wives and Husbands: "How Christian Wives and Husbands Should Treat Each Other."

The writer speaks at length about the way a Christian wife should act toward her husband (verses 1-6), and then has a brief statement for Christian husbands on how they should treat their wives (verse 7). It seems likely that the reason the section for wives is longer is that there were more Christian women married to non-Christian men than Christian men with non-Christian wives, and also that such marriages would bring greater difficulty for Christian women than for Christian men.

3.1-2 RSV	TEV
Likewise you wives, be submissive to your husbands, so that some, though they do not obey the word, may be won without a word by the behavior of their wives, 2 when they see your reverent and chaste behavior.	In the same way you wives must submit yourselves to your husbands, so that if any of them do not believe God's word, your conduct will win them over to believe. It will not be necessary for you to say a word, 2 because they will see how pure and reverent your conduct is.

Likewise you wives, be submissive: as slaves are to be submissive to their masters (2.18), in the same way Christian wives are to be submissive to their husbands. This seems to be the meaning of the Greek text. But it is possible that here Likewise means "As for you (wives)," as the same expression means in verse 7 (see below). The same verb should be used here (and in verse 5) that is used in 2.18. And since in verse 6 the verb "to obey" is used, it is better, if possible, to have here a different verb or expression: "do what your husbands tell you to do." Care should be taken to avoid a term or an expression that means only, or mainly, submitting to the husband's sexual demands.

so that some, though they do not obey the word: this refers to non-Christian husbands (see they disobey the word in 2.8). It will be necessary to reconstruct the material differently from the RSV, so as to make it easy to understand: "so that those husbands who are non-believers." Although this is presented as a possibility (see TEV "if any of them do not believe God's word"), it addresses a real situation. The writer is not saying that all non-Christian husbands will become believers, but he believes that some of them will. Commentators point out that it is very likely that most Christian wives the Letter addresses had non-Christian husbands.

may be won without a word: "may be led to accept the gospel without your saying anything about it" or "...without your urging them to do so." For the same use of the verb "to win," see 1 Corinthians 9.19-22. The writer sees the behavior of the Christian wives as the means of convincing non-Christian husbands to accept the gospel.

they see: this translates the same verb used in 2.12 and carries the same meaning.

your reverent and chaste behavior: "how respectful and moral you are (or, your behavior is)." Reverent translates the phrase "in fear," which here means a respectful attitude toward the husband (see 2.18), although it could be the attitude of respect and awe toward God (see 1.17; 2.17). Chaste means moral behavior, including sexual fidelity but not limited to it.

Verses 1-2 may be translated as follows:

> Christian wives, submit yourselves to your non-Christian husbands so that they will (be led to) accept the gospel because of the way you behave. You won't have to urge them to do it; they will be convinced by noticing that your behavior is pure and respectful.

3.3 RSV	TEV
Let not yours be the outward adorning with braiding of hair, decoration of gold, and wearing of fine clothing,	You should not use outward aids to make yourselves beautiful, such as the way you fix your hair, or the jewelry you put on, or the dresses you wear.

A woman's beauty, says the writer, should not be an exterior quality, which is gained by artificial means, but an inner disposition.

Let not yours be the outward adornment: "Your beauty should not consist of (or, depend on) outward adornments," "You should not rely on outward (or, artificial) adornments to make yourselves beautiful."

braiding of hair: "exaggerated hairdo," "elaborate coiffure." What is being condemned is not a particular way of fixing the hair, but costly or extravagant hairdos that are intended to attract attention to a woman. In many parts of the world braided hair is the normal and proper way for women to fix their hair, and a translation should not give the impression that this is forbidden.

decoration of gold: "gold ornaments," "jewelry" (TEV), "gold bracelets."

wearing of fine clothing: "expensive clothes," "luxurious dresses."

The following may serve as a model for translating this verse: "You should not try to make yourselves beautiful by means of outward (or, artificial) devices, such as an extravagant hairdo, or gold ornaments, or expensive dresses."

3.4 RSV	TEV
but let it be the hidden person of the heart with the imperishable jewel of a gentle and quiet spirit, which in God's sight is very precious.	Instead, your beauty should consist of your true inner self, the ageless beauty of a gentle and quiet spirit, which is of the greatest value in God's sight.

but let it be: the sentence is not too complex, and some translations may wish to follow RSV in making verses 3-4 one sentence. Others, however, may prefer to imitate TEV and begin a new sentence in verse 4: "Instead of doing this, your beauty should be...."

the hidden person of the heart: "the invisible inner self," "the true self, which is unseen." Here hidden, as a description of the inner being, may be taken to mean "real" or "genuine" (see TEV).

with the imperishable jewel of a gentle and quiet spirit: it is impossible to decide what RSV with means. It is better to take the figure of the imperishable jewel as another way of describing the inner beauty the writer is recommending. There is in Greek no word corresponding to jewel; it seems better to take the Greek "the imperishable (thing)" to refer to "beauty," as TEV does: "the ageless beauty" or "the beauty that never disappears," "the beauty that lasts always."

a gentle and quiet spirit: here spirit is "disposition," "attitude," "manner." A translation should not give the impression that a bodyless spirit is meant. Here quiet means "calm," "peaceable," "serene."

which in God's sight is very precious: "which God regards (or, considers) as very valuable."

The verse may be translated as follows:

> Instead of trying to be beautiful that way, your beauty should consist of your unseen self, which is within you. It should be the enduring beauty of a gentle and calm disposition. This is the kind of beauty that God considers very valuable.

3.5 RSV	TEV
So once the holy women who hoped in God used to adorn themselves and were submissive to their husbands,	For the devout women of the past who placed their hope in God used to make themselves beautiful by submitting themselves to their husbands.

So: "In this way," "This was how."

once: "at one time," "in the past," "in past times."

the holy women who hoped in God: here holy means "devout" (TEV), "pious," "religious." The additional who hoped in God describes them in one particular way: "who trusted in God," "who believed that God would do what he had promised." For hope see 1.3,21.

used to adorn themselves: "had the habit of making themselves beautiful," "would always make themselves beautiful."

and were submissive: RSV takes the Greek participial verbal phrase "being submissive" (or, "submitting themselves") to be an additional item. However, it seems more probable that the participle defines the way in which the religious women of the past used to make themselves beautiful: "by being submissive to their husbands." For submissive see 3.1.

In some instances it may be better to change the order of the clauses, as follows: "In past times religious women who trusted in God would submit themselves to their husbands, and in this way they made themselves (truly) beautiful."

3.6

RSV	TEV
as Sarah obeyed Abraham, calling him lord. And you are now her children if you do right and let nothing terrify you.	Sarah was like that; she obeyed Abraham and called him her master. You are now her daughters if you do good and are not afraid of anything.

as Sarah obeyed Abraham: this is one specific example of the rule given in verse 5. Here the verb "to obey" is synonymous with the verb "be submissive" in verses 1,5. It may be well to end verse 5 with a period and begin a new sentence in verse 6: "Sarah was one of those women," "Sarah was like that" (TEV).

calling him lord: "and called him her master" (TEV). Or "when she spoke to him she called him 'My master.'" See Genesis 18.12, where the Hebrew word translated "my husband" is translated in the Septuagint "my lord (or, master)."

you are now her children: here children, as in 1.14, is used in a figurative sense (TEV "daughters"). But this figure may not be suitable in some languages, and it may be better to say "you will be like her."

if you do right: "by doing what is right (or, good)."

let nothing terrify you: "don't be afraid of anything." It seems fairly certain that the writer is referring to not being afraid of what the unbelieving husband might do to the Christian wife. A pagan husband might threaten his Christian wife with physical abuse if she did not give up her religion. It may be necessary to say this: "and don't be afraid of anything your husband might threaten to do."

3.7

RSV	TEV
Likewise you husbands, live considerately with your wives, bestowing honor on the woman as the weaker sex, since you are joint heirs of the grace of life, in order that your prayers may not be hindered.	In the same way you husbands must live with your wives with the proper understanding that they are the weaker sex. Treat them with respect, because they also will receive, together with you, God's gift of life. Do this so that nothing will interfere with your prayers.

Likewise: as in 3.1, this probably should be "As for you." It cannot mean "In the same way" (TEV), that is, that the same rule applies to husbands.

you husbands: "Christian husbands."

live considerately with your wives: the Greek phrase translated considerately is "according to knowledge." In the context this means a Christian point of view, a Christian understanding of women and how a Christian husband is to treat his wife. So something like TEV may be said, "with the proper understanding that they are the weaker sex." Or else, "with the proper (or, Christian) understanding about married life." It seems clear that the assumption is that the wives, like the husbands, are Christians.

bestowing honor on the woman as the weaker sex: "treating your wives with respect, since they are the weaker sex." The expression "the weaker sex" in English is a proper way to speak of women, but in some languages it may be inappropriate. Something like "because women are not as strong as men" may be required. This assumes that the reference is to physical strength; but it may involve social status also, since at that time women were considered to be men's inferiors.

since you are joint heirs of the grace of life: since refers back to the command to live considerately with your wives; you includes husbands and wives—it does not mean only husbands. For heirs see inheritance in 1.4; "they will receive, together with you," "you and they will receive together."

the grace of life: "the gift of (eternal) life," "God's gift of eternal life."

in order that: this refers back also to live considerately with your wives.

your prayers may not be hindered: the writer seems to be speaking to husbands only, although it is possible that he includes the wives as well. As used here, "to hinder" prayers is to prevent them from achieving their purpose: that is, God cannot or will not answer their prayers.

The verse may be translated as follows:

> As for you, Christian husbands, you must live with your wives with the proper understanding of their needs (or, of married life). Treat them with respect, because they are weaker than you, and also because they, as well as you, will receive God's free gift of eternal life (or, because God has promised to give eternal life to them as well as to you). If you husbands do this, God will answer your prayers.

SECTION HEADING

Suffering for Doing Right: "A Christian's Suffering and Christ's Suffering."

The theme of suffering runs through this fairly long section, verses 8-22. Christians must be prepared to suffer because they obey God's will; their suffering should never be the result of their doing evil. Christ's own suffering is the example and motivation for the suffering of Christians.

3.8 RSV	TEV
Finally, all of you, have unity of spirit, sympathy, love of the brethren, a tender heart and a humble mind.	To conclude: you must all have the same attitude and the same feelings; love one another as brothers, and be kind and humble with one another.

Finally: it seems strange that this should be said when the Letter is barely half finished. Some take the Greek to mean "In summary" or "To sum up." But since what follows is not really a summary of what precedes, the meaning seems to be "To conclude" (TEV) or "And now to finish what I want to say." In this verse the writer lists five Christian qualities he urges all his readers to cultivate.

unity of spirit: "the same attitude (or, opinion)," "the same point of view." This first quality has to do with attitudes and thinking (see Rom 15.5; Phil 2.2).

The next one, sympathy, has to do with feelings, emotion, sentiment, whether of gladness or of sadness (see Rom 12.15). Christians are called upon to share grief and happiness with one another, to feel one another's pain and joy.

love of the brethren: "love your fellow believers" (see 1.22).

a tender heart: "compassion," "pity," "kindness."

a humble mind: "humility," "gentleness." It may be easier to express this quality with a negative expression: "don't be proud," "don't be arrogant."

3.9 RSV	TEV
Do not return evil for evil or reviling for reviling; but on the contrary bless, for to this you have been called, that you may obtain a blessing.	Do not pay back evil with evil or cursing with cursing; instead, pay back with a blessing, because a blessing is what God promised to give you when he called you.

Do not return evil for evil: "Do not do something bad to those who do something bad to you," "Do not mistreat (or, harm) those who mistreat (or, harm) you." Or, as a conditional clause, "If others mistreat you, don't mistreat them."

reviling for reviling: "don't curse (or, speak evil of) those who curse (or, speak evil of) you" (see 2.23; see also Matt 5.44; Luke 6.27-28).

but on the contrary: "instead of speaking evil of them, you should...."

bless: either "say good things to them" or "ask God to bless them." Probably the latter is meant.

to this you have been called: this refers either backward (that is, to the command to ask God to bless others) or forward (as TEV translates). Either interpretation is possible; the quotation in verses 10-12 of Psalm 34.12-16 makes it quite likely that this points backward. For called see 1.15; 2.9. This may be expressed as follows: "Instead, pay back with a blessing, because this is what God wants you to do."

that you may obtain: as translated by RSV, that means "in order that," indicating purpose. It is not clear, however, whether it is connected to the command bless or to the statement you have been called. It seems better to connect it with the statement "you have been called (by God) to obtain...."

obtain translates the verb "to inherit" (see 1.4; 3.7). Believers must pray that God will bless others because they, the believers, have been promised a blessing by God.

a blessing: this means "blessings" in general, not one specific blessing.

3.10 RSV	TEV
For "He that would love life and see good days, let him keep his tongue from evil and his lips from speaking guile;	As the scripture says, "Whoever wants to enjoy life and wishes to see good times, must keep from speaking evil and stop telling lies.

The quotation, from Psalm 34.12-16, follows the text of the ancient Greek translation of the Old Testament, the Septuagint, and not the Hebrew text.

For: as in 1.24, it is better to say "As the scripture says" (TEV).

He that would love life: here love life is used in the sense of "enjoy life" (TEV), "have a good (or, happy) life." In the Old Testament context life is life on this earth; in this context the writer may be thinking of eternal life. But the following and see good days makes this rather unlikely. "Whoever wants to have an enjoyable life," "Those who wish to live happily."

and see good days: here see is used in the sense of "to experience," "to have." So it may be better to translate "and have (or, experience) good days" or "...happy times." In the Old Testament context this would be a reference to prosperity and success. As used in this Letter, love life and see good days both refer to a happy, successful life here on earth.

let him: the third person imperative may be expressed by "he (or, they) must." In some languages it may be easier in verses 10 and 11 to use the second plural form: "If you want to enjoy life, and have a happy time, then do not...."

keep his tongue from evil: "don't say bad things about others."

his lips from speaking guile: "don't tell lies" (see 2.1,22).

3.11 RSV	TEV
let him turn away from evil and do right; let him seek peace and pursue it.	He must turn away from evil and do good; he must strive for peace with all his heart.

turn away from evil: "stop doing evil," "quit doing things that are bad."

do right: "do good things."

seek...and pursue: this is an emphatic way of saying "try hard to have (or, get)," "do everything possible to achieve." Here peace is a harmonious and friendly relationship with others; in this context it is particularly the relationship with fellow believers.

3.12

RSV	TEV
For the eyes of the Lord are upon the righteous, and his ears are open to their prayer. But the face of the Lord is against those that do evil."	For the Lord watches over the righteous and listens to their prayers; but he opposes those who do evil."

the eyes of the Lord are upon: this is a way of expressing God's care and concern for people: "the Lord watches over" (TEV), "the Lord takes care of," or "the Lord is concerned about." Here the Lord is God.

the righteous are God's people; "those who obey him," "those who follow his will" (see righteousness in 2.24).

his ears are open to: "he listens to," "he answers."

the face...is against: this is a way of expressing God's opposition to or disapproval of people. "The Lord is against those who do evil." It may be easier to express this attitude with a negative expression: "The Lord does not help (or, like) those who do evil."

3.13

RSV	TEV
Now who is there to harm you if you are zealous for what is right?	Who will harm you if you are eager to do what is good?

By means of a rhetorical question, the writer says that no real harm will come to those who are dedicated to doing good. In some languages a rhetorical question will be a normal way of expressing this: "Will anyone harm you if you always do what is right?" or "If you try very hard to do what is good, will anyone want to do evil to you?" In other languages, however, a statement may be preferable: "No one is going to harm you if you desire to do good."

zealous: this expresses a deep desire, an enthusiasm, an eagerness always to do what is right (see a similar expression in Titus 2.14).

3.14

RSV	TEV
But even if you do suffer for righteousness' sake, you will be blessed. Have no fear of them, nor be troubled,	But even if you should suffer for doing what is right, how happy you are! Do not be afraid of anyone, and do not worry.

even if you do suffer: this is presented as a possibility, although not a very real one. That is why RSV has even (see also TEV "But even if you should suffer"). "It may be that you will suffer," "It might happen that you will suffer."

for righteousness' sake: "because you do what is right" (see righteousness in 2.24). This means specifically living a Christian life.

you will be blessed: this translates the same expression used in Matthew 5.3-11. It does not so much refer to the blessings which God bestows, as to the feeling of satisfaction a person has, or else to the judgment expressed by someone else: "you are fortunate," "you are to be congratulated," or "consider yourselves fortunate." Instead of the exclamation "how happy you are!" of TEV, it may be better to use an emphatic statement: "you are indeed fortunate" or "you really deserve to be congratulated."

Have no fear of them, nor be troubled: here them may refer specifically to people whom the author knew, people who were persecuting the Christians. They may have been either authorities or hostile citizens. So the translation may be "Don't be afraid of the people who are causing you to suffer." Or else the language may be general and the meaning may be "Don't be afraid of anyone."

nor be troubled: "and don't allow anyone (or, anything) to upset (or, worry) you."

3.15-16 RSV	TEV
but in your hearts reverence Christ as Lord. Always be prepared to make a defense to any one who calls you to account for the hope that is in you, yet do it with gentleness and reverence; 16 and keep your conscience clear, so that, when you are abused, those who revile your good behavior in Christ may be put to shame.	**But have reverence for Christ in your hearts, and honor him as Lord. Be ready at all times to answer anyone who asks you to explain the hope you have in you, 16 but do it with gentleness and respect. Keep your conscience clear, so that when you are insulted, those who speak evil of your good conduct as followers of Christ will become ashamed of what they say.**

but in your hearts reverence Christ as Lord: in some languages it may be better to end verse 14 with a full stop and begin a new sentence in verse 15, as TEV does. The phrase in your hearts goes with the verb reverence and means that the readers are to have a deep respect for Christ as the Lord of their lives. The verb "to reverence" means "to regard as holy"; here the equivalent could be "to regard as divine." It may be difficult, if not impossible, to use one verb in translation that will go naturally with both Christ and as Lord, so it may be necessary to do something like TEV has done: "But have reverence in your hearts for Christ, and honor him as (divine) Lord." Or "Give your complete allegiance to Christ as the Lord of your lives."

make a defense: the word translated defense can be understood in the more general sense of "explanation" or "exposition."

to account for the hope that is in you: "to give a reason for the hope that you have." It may not be natural to speak of hope as an abstract noun, and so it may be better to say "to explain why you have confidence in God" or "to give the reason why you firmly believe that God will keep his promises" (see 1.3,13,21; 3.5). Or else hope here may be equivalent to the Christian faith as such: "to give the reason why you believe in Christ."

yet do it with gentleness and reverence: in RSV this is at the end of verse 15; in TEV it appears at the beginning of verse 16. TEV follows the verse division of the UBS Greek New Testament. Instead of yet do it, it may be better to say "But give that person an answer (or, an explanation)." Or else, "When you answer that person, be gentle and polite" or "...don't be proud or harsh," "...don't be dogmatic and impolite."

keep your conscience clear: this means that the readers are to act in such a way that later on they will not feel guilty, that is, their conscience will not accuse them of having done wrong. When the inward sense of right and wrong, expressed by the word conscience, is not easily represented in a language, it may be better to translate "Be pure in your conduct" or "Behave as a Christian should." "Behave in such a way that later on you will not feel guilty."

abused: this translates the same verb that in 2.12 RSV translates speak against. The abuse is verbal, not physical. "When your enemies speak evil of you" or "...say bad things about you."

those who revile your good behavior: these are the same ones who abuse the believers. "When they say bad things about your moral (or, pure) way of life." In some cases direct speech may be more effective, "those who say 'You are evil,' although you have not done anything evil."

in Christ: "as disciples (or, followers) of Christ," "as believers."

may be put to shame: "will become ashamed of themselves" or "...of what they say" (TEV). This shame that the enemies of Christians will feel will be the result of the clear proof that their accusations are completely wrong.

Verses 15-16 may be translated as follows:

> But have a sincere devotion to Christ as the Lord of your lives. And be ready at all times to explain to anyone who asks you why you are a believer in Christ. 16 Be gentle and polite as you give your explanation, and act in such a way that later you will not feel guilty. In this way those people who insult you and say evil things about your pure (or, holy) way of life as followers of Christ will become ashamed of themselves.

3.17 RSV	TEV
For it is better to suffer for doing right, if that should be God's will, than for doing wrong.	**For it is better to suffer for doing good, if this should be God's will, than for doing evil.**

it is better to suffer for doing right: "it is better for you if you suffer (or, are persecuted) because you do what is right" (see 2.20).

if that should be God's will: "if that happens because God wants it to happen."

than for doing wrong: in some languages it will be necessary to join together the two possible reasons for suffering, as follows: "For it is better if you suffer because you do what is right, than to suffer because you do what is wrong, if, in fact, it is God's will that you should suffer."

3.18

RSV	TEV
For Christ also died[h] for sins once for all, the righteous for the unrighteous, that he might bring us to God, being put to death in the flesh but made alive in the spirit;	**For Christ died[c] for sins once and for all, a good man on behalf of sinners, in order to lead you to God. He was put to death physically, but made alive spiritually,**
[h]**Other ancient authorities read** *suffered*	[c]**died;** *many manuscripts have* **suffered**

In Greek, verses 18-22 are one long sentence and contain many difficult words and phrases. The possibilities for different translations are almost unlimited, and it is obviously impossible to review all the different possibilities here. A translator is urged to consult various translations and, if possible, several commentaries. If this is not possible, the UBS *Translator's Handbook on the First Letter from Peter* offers an excellent exposition of the subject, and the translator should carefully read it before beginning to translate these verses.

For Christ also died: here the writer gives the reason why believers should be willing to suffer, if necessary, for doing good. Christ himself, who was innocent of any wrongdoing, died on behalf of sinners (see the same thought expressed in 2.21-24).

As both the RSV and TEV footnotes indicate, many Greek manuscripts and ancient versions have "suffered" instead of died. There are good reasons for choosing either one of the two readings. The meaning is not greatly affected by one's choice, since it is most likely that here "to suffer" means actually "to die," especially with the following for sins. It may be necessary to expand the statement somewhat, in order to avoid misunderstanding: "For Christ died for our sins," "Christ died so that our sins might be forgiven" or "...so that God could forgive our sins."

once for all: this modifies the verb died and emphasizes the fact that no other sacrifice is necessary in order to obtain the forgiveness of sins. Christ's death was a sufficient and adequate sacrifice and does not have to be repeated.

the righteous for the unrighteous: "a sinless (or, good) man on behalf of sinners." For the meaning of righteous here see the same word in Luke 23.47, which RSV translates innocent and TEV "good."

that he might bring us to God: the purpose of Christ's death was to achieve the forgiveness of sins and thus make it possible for human beings to have fellowship with God. See a similar expression in

Ephesians 2.18. It is likely that "to bring (or, lead) to God" might be understood in a literal sense, and so it may be necessary to use the verb "to reconcile," or else "to make us friends with God" or "to put us into the right relationship with God."

Instead of us TEV has "you," which is the reading preferred by the UBS Greek New Testament. If us is preferred, it should appear in an inclusive form.

being put to death in the flesh but made alive in the spirit: the concise expression in Greek seems to mean, as TEV translates, "He was put to death physically, but made alive spiritually," that is, he was a mortal human being when he was put to death, but he was resurrected as an immortal spiritual being. There are other possible translations. Some see spirit here to mean God's Spirit, and translate "by the Spirit"—but this does not balance with the preceding "in the flesh." Others see spirit to mean Jesus' spirit, or soul, with the meaning "his body was killed (by people), but his spirit was brought (back) to life (by God)." This is not very probable and is not recommended.

The following may serve as a model for translating this verse:

> You must be willing to suffer because you do good, since Christ himself, who was a good man, died for sinners. His death was the full and final means by which our sins are forgiven, and so he has made it possible for us to have fellowship with God. When Christ was put to death, he was a mortal human being; when God raised him to life, he was an immortal spiritual being.

3.19 RSV	TEV
in which he went and preached to the spirits in prison,	**and in his spiritual existence he went and preached to the imprisoned spirits.**

in which: the which may refer back to all of verse 18, or, most likely, to in the spirit. As interpreted by TEV, the phrase means "As a spiritual being" or "In his spiritual existence." The meaning seems to be that at some interval between death and resurrection, Christ went and preached to the spirits in prison, since the next event in Christ's experience is the resurrection in verse 21 and then the ascension to heaven in verse 22. Although this seems to be the most reasonable interpretation, it is not necessarily the correct one. The resurrection and ascension in verses 21-22 are not linked syntactically with Christ's preaching to the imprisoned spirits, but to our salvation and his exaltation.

he went and preached to the spirits in prison: on the various interpretations of this passage see the *Translator's Handbook*. The most natural way to understand this is to take it as a reference to Sheol, or Hades, which in Jewish and early Christian thought was regarded as the destiny of all the dead. But prison is nowhere else used in the Bible as a name of Sheol, the place of dead people. (It should be stated that in nonbiblical Jewish literature Sheol is often referred to as a prison.) In 2 Peter 2.4 reference is made to the rebel angels who are kept chained in darkness, in hell, waiting for the Judgment

Day (see also Jude 6; Rev 20.1-3); and in 2 Peter 2.9 the writer speaks of wicked people being kept for punishment. In accord with Jude 6 and 2 Peter 2.4, many take the spirits here to be the rebel angels; others take them to be human spirits, while still others take them to include both human and angelic spirits. If possible a translation should say only "the spirits who were in prison." But care should be taken not to make it appear that the writer is talking about evil spirits, or demons, and so it may be necessary to say "spirits of dead people" or "human spirits."

preached: either "proclaimed condemnation" or "proclaimed salvation." In light of 4.6, below, it is probable that "proclaimed salvation" is meant.

3.20 RSV	TEV
who formerly did not obey, when God's patience waited in the days of Noah, during the building of the ark, in which a few, that is, eight persons, were saved through water.	These were the spirits of those who had not obeyed God when he waited patiently during the days that Noah was building his boat. The few people in the boat—eight in all—were saved by the water,

who formerly did not obey: the adverb formerly means "in times past," that is, at the time of Noah and the Flood. TEV begins a new sentence here, and this may be better than to continue the sentence from verse 19, since a literal translation such as RSV will be taken to mean that the spirits themselves had been disobedient. The writer is here speaking of the people of Noah's time who did not heed God's warning. So TEV has "These were the spirits of those who had not obeyed God"; or else, "These spirits were of (or, belonged to) the people who long ago disobeyed God." In Jewish teaching, Noah's contemporaries were regarded as the worst of all sinners.

when God's patience waited in the days of Noah: the when goes with formerly, that is, in the past, when Noah lived. It will be better in most languages to say "when God waited patiently" or "when God was patient and waited (for them to obey)." And in the days of Noah may be represented by "the time when Noah lived" or, more simply, "during the time that Noah was building the boat." In some languages the choice of a suitable word for Noah's boat will be determined by the size of the boat (Gen 6.15: 133 meters long, 22 meters wide, 13 meters high).

a few, that is, eight persons: it may not be possible to represent naturally the style of this rather elegant phrase, and so it may be better to say "Only a few persons, eight in all" or "Just eight persons." "Not many people were saved in the boat; there were only eight." Care must be taken to avoid saying that only a few people out of the many in the boat were saved; it should be quite clear that there were only eight people in the boat (Noah and his wife, and their three sons and their wives).

were saved through water: the meaning of the Greek preposition translated through is debatable, but the following verse seems to indicate that through expresses instrumentality: "were saved by means of the water." Others, however, interpret "were saved through the water," that is, were kept safe as the boat went through the water of the Flood.

3.21 RSV	TEV
Baptism, which corresponds to this, now saves you, not as a removal of dirt from the body but as an appeal to God for a clear conscience, through the resurrection of Jesus Christ,	**which was a symbol pointing to baptism, which now saves you. It is not the washing off of bodily dirt, but the promise made to God from a good conscience. It saves you through the resurrection of Jesus Christ,**

Baptism, which corresponds to this: this translates what is literally "which baptism, as an antitype." An "antitype" is a thing or event which is considered to be referred to by a previous thing or event, which is known as a "type." The water of the Flood was a "type" of baptism, so various ways can be used to translate this. TEV "which was a symbol pointing to baptism"; others have "That water represented the water of baptism"; "it was the figure of baptism"; "this water symbolizes baptism."

to this: this is quite ambiguous, and so it will be better to say "to the water of the Flood."

now saves you: this now answers to the formerly of verse 20. A translation should represent the meaning faithfully and say quite clearly "Baptism now saves you." Of course salvation is always God's action, but here baptism, as defined below, is what brings salvation. Some translations prefer saying "saves us" as a more inclusive term; certainly the writer was not saying you in an exclusive sense, and in some languages the inclusive "us" may be more appropriate.

At once the writer defines what he means by baptism saving someone: it is not the physical act of washing dirt off the body, but the spiritual experience of the inner self.

not as a removal of dirt from the body: "Baptism saves, not by washing the dirt off one's body" or "...not by making us clean physically."

but as an appeal to God for a clear conscience: it will be noticed that TEV is quite different: "the promise made to God from a clear conscience." It is not certain what the Greek word translated appeal by RSV means in this context; it may mean "request" or else "response," either as a promise or as a pledge of loyalty. And the Greek genitive phrase "of a good conscience" may mean either "for a good conscience" (RSV) or "from a good conscience" (TEV), or else "a promise (to God) to maintain a good conscience."

The TEV interpretation takes the word translated "promise" to refer to the newly baptized believer's pledge to live a life in obedience to Jesus Christ as Lord. This promise, or pledge, is made without any reservation. The RSV translation understands the word to mean that the newly baptized believer prays that God might help him or her to live a life free of sin and guilt.

through the resurrection of Jesus Christ: as TEV shows, this goes with the main verb "saves," and this should be made quite clear.

The following may serve as a model for the translation of this verse:

> And baptism, which now saves you, is what the water of the Flood symbolized. (Or, And the water of the Flood was a

> figure of baptism, which now saves you.) You are saved because of the resurrection of Jesus Christ (or, because Jesus Christ was raised from death). Baptism does not consist of washing off the dirt from our body, but of our making a sincere promise to God to be a faithful follower of Jesus Christ.

The last sentence of this model follows TEV. If RSV is preferred, the last sentence can be:

> Baptism is not the action of removing dirt from our bodies by means of water; it is the prayer to God asking him to help us live a life free of sin.

3.22 RSV	TEV
who has gone into heaven and is at the right hand of God, with angels, authorities, and powers subject to him.	**who has gone to heaven and is at the right side of God, ruling over all angels and heavenly authorities and powers.**

who has gone into heaven: both RSV and TEV continue the sentence without a break from verse 21. It may be better to begin a new sentence here: "Jesus Christ has gone to heaven, and is at the right side of God." The figure "at the right side" means the place of honor and power (see Psa 110.1; also Acts 7.55; Eph 1.20-21; Phil 2.9-11; Heb 12.2).

with angels, authorities, and powers subject to him: in Greek the verb translated subject is a passive participle meaning "subjected." The implied actor is God: he made the exalted Christ ruler over all spiritual powers (see 1 Cor 15.25-27). It may be that there is no convenient way to represent the three nouns by three separate nouns or titles, so it will be preferable to say "angels and all other spiritual (or, heavenly) authorities" or "angels and other supernatural beings who have authority and power."

Chapter 4

SECTION HEADING

Changed Lives: "Living a Christian Life."

In this section, verses 1-6, the writer calls his readers' attention to the need for pure Christian living. They can do this if they have the same attitude that Christ had. The power of his suffering will enable them to live lives completely different from those of their pagan fellow citizens.

4.1

RSV	TEV
Since therefore Christ suffered in the flesh,[i] arm yourselves with the same thought, for whoever has suffered in the flesh has ceased from sin,	Since Christ suffered physically, you too must strengthen yourselves with the same way of thinking that he had; because whoever suffers physically is no longer involved with sin.

[i]Other ancient authorities add *for us;* some *for you*

Since therefore Christ suffered in the flesh: this refers back to 3.18, which speaks of Christ's sacrificial death. The phrase in the flesh means here the same as it does in 3.18. As the RSV footnote shows, some Greek manuscripts and ancient versions have "suffered for us," and others have "suffered for you." It seems evident that the original copy had only "suffered." But in some translations it may be necessary to add "for us" (inclusive) in order to make clear the nature and purpose of Christ's passion. As in 3.18 the verb "to suffer" here probably has the specific meaning "to die": "Since Christ died physically" or "Christ himself died, and so...." Since Christ's death was not a natural one, it may be necessary to say "Since Christ was put to death."

arm yourselves with the same thought: the writer tells his readers that in order to be able to live good Christian lives they must have the same way of thinking that Christ had. It may be difficult, if not impossible, to refer to an attitude as a weapon, and some adjustments will be necessary: "you must arm yourselves spiritually with the same conviction (or, resolution) that Christ had" or "you must imitate Christ's way of thinking, in order to maintain your own spiritual safety (or, health)." Or else it may be preferable to say "you, too, must be ready to suffer as he was ready to suffer."

for whoever has suffered in the flesh has ceased from sin: this saying has been interpreted in several different ways. One of the difficulties is the uncertainty whether this refers specifically to

Christ or to believers in general. If the reference is to Christ, then the meaning (as in the similar passage, Rom 6.7) is "for Christ, who was put to death, is not involved in sin." But it is more likely that the saying applies to believers, and means that by enduring physical suffering as Christ did, they are enabled to become free of the power of sin. Although the surface meaning of has ceased from sin is "has stopped sinning," it does not seem probable that the writer is saying that such a believer will be sinless. So it seems better to say "is no longer controlled by sin" or "has quit his sinful ways."

4.2 RSV	TEV
so as to live for the rest of the time in the flesh no longer by human passions but by the will of God.	From now on, then, you must live the rest of your earthly lives controlled by God's will and not by human desires.

so as to live: this may go with the imperative verb in verse 1, arm yourselves, or with has ceased from sin. The sense is not greatly affected by the choice of alternatives, but the construction of the sentence should clearly indicate the connection. If the choice is to connect it with arm yourselves, the verse may begin "If you do this" or "If you arm yourselves in this way." If the choice is to relate it to has ceased from sin, the best thing to do is to begin a new sentence in the middle of verse 1 and continue, without a full stop, into verse 2, as follows: "You must do this because whoever suffers physically is freed from the power of sin and is able to live the rest of his life...."

live the rest of the time in the flesh: "live out his physical life," "live the rest of his life." It may be more natural to make this personal, as TEV has done: "you must live the rest of your (earthly) lives" or, more simply, "from now on you must live" or "as long as you live you must...."

no longer by human passions but by the will of God: "no longer ruled (or, dominated) by human desires but by God's will." For passions see 1.14; 2.11. It may be easier to reverse the clauses, as follows: "under the rule of (or, in submission to) God's will and not under the rule of human desires."

4.3 RSV	TEV
Let the time that is past suffice for doing what the Gentiles like to do, living in licentiousness, passions, drunkenness, revels, carousing, and lawless idolatry.	You have spent enough time in the past doing what the heathen like to do. Your lives were spent in indecency, lust, drunkenness, orgies, drinking parties, and the disgusting worship of idols.

Let the time that is past suffice: in this indirect way the writer is telling his readers that they should no longer live as they did in the past; their past lives, as unbelievers, should not carry over into the present but should be completely cut off. The idea may be expressed more naturally and understandably as follows: "You have had time enough in the past" or, in a negative way, "You must no longer do what you did in the past."

the Gentiles: "the heathen" (TEV), "the non-Christians." Here the word is not used in an ethnic sense but in a religious sense. The list that follows includes sexual immorality, debauchery, and idolatry. The writer is saying that in the past his readers committed all those sins.

licentiousness: vice in general or indecent sexual behavior in particular (see 2 Peter 2.2).

passions: the same word used in verse 2, but here with the specific meaning of sexual lust.

drunkenness: "excessive drinking," "intoxication."

revels and carousing form a neat pair in Greek, and both describe orgies, that is, wild parties in which people engage in sexual immorality and excessive drinking.

lawless idolatry: a translation should not imply, as RSV may be taken to imply, that there is "lawful idolatry" as contrasted with lawless idolatry. The adjective translated lawless characterizes the worship of idols as a disgusting, shameful, abominable act. Any such strong expression may be used: TEV "the disgusting worship of idols"; "shameful idolatry," "forbidden worship of idols," or "idolatry, which is a shameful (or, disgusting) thing."

4.4 RSV	TEV
They are surprised that you do not now join them in the same wild profligacy, and they abuse you;	**And now the heathen are surprised when you do not join them in the same wild and reckless living, and so they insult you.**

They are surprised: "the heathen are surprised" (TEV), "They consider it strange," "They don't understand why."

the same wild profligacy: "the same kind of wild and sinful living" or "...of very immoral actions," "...of excessive sinful behavior."

abuse: "speak evil of," "insult" (TEV).

It may be better to reconstruct the verse, as follows: "And now that you no longer join the heathen in their reckless and immoral behavior, they are very surprised and speak evil of you."

4.5 RSV	TEV
but they will give account to him who is ready to judge the living and the dead.	**But they will have to give an account of themselves to God, who is ready to judge the living and the dead.**

The writer says that the heathen, no less than the Christians, will be judged by God.

they will give account: "they will have to defend their case," "they will have to explain what they have done." This refers not only to the way they insult Christians but also to their sinful lives.

to him who is ready to judge the living and the dead: this obviously refers to God, who will judge all people. The phrase the living and the dead is a way of saying "all people who have ever existed" (see Acts 10.42; 2 Tim 4.1). At the Day of Judgment those who are then alive will be judged, and those who have died will be resurrected and also judged. The word ready means "capable," "prepared," "qualified." It may include the idea that Judgment Day is not far away.

4.6 RSV	TEV
For this is why the gospel was preached even to the dead, that though judged in the flesh like men, they might live in the spirit like God.	**That is why the Good News was preached also to the dead, to those who had been judged in their physical existence as everyone is judged; it was preached to them so that in their spiritual existence they may live as God lives.**

The form of this verse in Greek is simple and short (seventeen words, which read as follows: "The gospel was preached to the dead so they might be judged according to men in the flesh, but live according to God in the spirit"). A literal translation makes it appear that the judgment of the dead followed the preaching of the gospel to them.

So far as the preaching of the gospel to the dead is concerned, the idea here is taken to be the same as in 3.19: Christ proclaimed the Good News of salvation to the dead, in Sheol. In 3.19 only the contemporaries of Noah are referred to, while here all the dead are included. The chronological order of events seems to be: (1) they died; (2) they were judged (by God); (3) the gospel was proclaimed to them; (4) so that they might live spiritually.

The this is why points forward to that, and not backward.

though judged in the flesh like men: "though they had been judged (by God), as all human beings are judged." This judgment seems to be the final judgment: "so that they will be judged, as all people are judged." But the phrase in the flesh makes this interpretation unlikely, unless the writer believed that the dead will be raised in a physical body to be judged on Judgment Day. And so it may be, as some scholars believe, that here "judged...in the flesh" is a way of speaking about death itself, which is regarded as judgment for sin. (This certainly makes sense of the passage, but one must admit that the Greek text is quite obscure; it would have been simple for the author to write "died physically, as all people die, so that they might live....") See below for a possible way to represent the judgment as referring to death.

they might live in the spirit like God: "they may in their spiritual existence, live as God lives," "they may live spiritually, as God wants them to live."

The following may serve as a model for translating this verse:

> The gospel was proclaimed (or, Jesus Christ proclaimed the gospel) also to those who had died. Their death, like that of all human beings, was the result of God's judgment. But the gospel was proclaimed to them so that they might be able to live spiritually, as God wants them to live.

SECTION HEADING

Good Managers of God's Gifts: "We Must All Be Willing to Serve One Another."

Now the writer gives some advice on the duty of all believers to use the various gifts they have received from God in such a way as to help one another. Believers have a primary responsibility for their fellow believers and must love one another, pray for one another, and serve one another.

4.7

RSV	TEV
The end of all things is at hand; therefore keep sane and sober for your prayers.	**The end of all things is near. You must be self-controlled and alert, to be able to pray.**

The end of all things is at hand: "The end of the world is near," "Before long this world will come to an end." See similar statements in Romans 13.11-12; 1 John 2.18.

keep sane and sober for your prayers: sane refers to self-control, good judgment; sober means to be alert, watchful (see 1.13). "Be sensible and pay attention"; or, in a negative fashion, "don't get excited or discouraged."

for your prayers: "so that you will be able to pray," or "as you pray," or "and keep on praying."

4.8

RSV	TEV
Above all hold unfailing your love for one another, since love covers a multitude of sins.	**Above everything, love one another earnestly, because love covers over many sins.**

Above all: "The most important thing is," "This is more important than anything else."

hold unfailing your love for one another: "love one another sincerely (or, deeply)," "love your fellow believers with all your heart."

love covers a multitude of sins: this statement is a conscious or unconscious allusion to Proverbs 10.12. The verb "to cover" here means "to forgive" (see James 5.20). Of the various possible meanings, the most likely is "if you love your fellow believers, you are ready to forgive their sins (against you)" (see Matt 18.21-22).

4.9

RSV	TEV
Practice hospitality ungrudgingly to one another.	**Open your homes to each other without complaining.**

Practice hospitality ungrudgingly: "Be always ready to receive your fellow believers into your homes," "Welcome one another as guests in your homes." The adverb ungrudgingly means "without complaining" (TEV) or, in positive terms, "willingly," "gladly," "generously."

4.10

RSV	TEV
As each has received a gift, employ it for one another, as good stewards of God's varied grace:	Each one, as a good manager of God's different gifts, must use for the good of others the special gift he has received from God.

As each has received a gift: "God has given every believer a gift (or, ability)." The main point the writer makes is that all believers have capacities, God-given talents, which they are to use for the common good.

employ it for one another: "use that gift for the good of one another" or "...for the good of your fellow believers."

good stewards: "faithful managers," "responsible administrators." A "steward" is one who is in charge of someone else's property, specifically, a person employed to run a household or business for the owner. So what a steward administers, or manages, is actually not his own. In the same way Christians' talents, or gifts, belong to God, and believers are given the responsibility of managing those gifts.

God's varied grace: here grace means what is given, the gift; "the various gifts of God," that is, what God gives.

The verse may be translated as follows:

> God has given you various gifts, and each one of you must be a good administrator of the particular gift he has received, and use it for the good of all.

4.11

RSV	TEV
whoever speaks, as one who utters oracles of God; whoever renders service, as one who renders it by the strength which God supplies; in order that in everything God may be glorified through Jesus Christ. To him belong glory and dominion for ever and ever. Amen.	Whoever preaches must preach God's messages; whoever serves must serve with the strength that God gives him, so that in all things praise may be given to God through Jesus Christ, to whom belong glory and power forever and ever. Amen.

Here the writer mentions two particular gifts: that of proclaiming the gospel and that of service in the church.

speaks: "preaches" (TEV), "proclaims the gospel." This is the public proclamation of the gospel.

as one who utters the oracles of God: "his words should be as though they were God's own words," "as one who has received his message from God." Or "Whoever preaches should proclaim the very message of God," "Whenever anyone speaks, his words should be as the words of God."

renders service: this is Christian service in the fellowship of the church, such as caring for the needy, the hungry, and the sick. "Those who perform church (or, Christian) service must do so with the strength that God gives."

in order that in everything: this goes with all of the preceding instructions. All Christian life and action should be used for the glory of God.

God may be glorified through Jesus Christ: "to be glorified" means to receive glory, or honor, or praise. So here the translation may be "so that because of everything you do, God will be praised." The praise or the honor is given by people, and instead of the passive form, the active form may be used: "so that everyone will praise (or, honor) God because of everything that you do."

through Jesus Christ: praise, or honor, is offered to God in the name of Jesus Christ, that is, as disciples or followers of Jesus Christ (see 2.5).

To him: this immediately follows the name Jesus Christ and most likely refers to him and not to God (see Rev 1.6).

Instead of To him belong the statement may be made, "Glory and power belong to Jesus Christ forever and ever" or "Jesus Christ has glory and power forever and ever." Here glory means "majesty," "greatness," "magnificence"; dominion means "strength," "power as a ruler."

Amen: "It is so," "So be it"—a way in which prayer is ended.

SECTION HEADING

Suffering as a Christian: "Rejoice in Suffering," "Suffering as Christ Suffered."

Again the writer returns to the subject of suffering (see 2.18-25; 3.8-18). Christians will suffer as Christ did, and they should not be surprised but instead should be glad, for in this way they are living up to their name as followers of Christ. They should not despair, but trust God.

4.12 RSV

Beloved, do not be surprised at the fiery ordeal which comes upon you to prove you, as though something strange were happening to you.

TEV

My dear friends, do not be surprised at the painful test you are suffering, as though something unusual were happening to you.

Beloved: "My dear friends" (TEV), "My dear fellow believers" (see 2.11).

do not be surprised: the same verb used in 4.4.

the fiery ordeal: "the harsh persecution," "the cruel suffering." It is possible that fiery or "burning" might be understood literally. But it seems clear that this is figurative language for persecution, and it is quite appropriate with the relative clause "which is intended to test you." See tested by fire in 1.7.

which comes upon you: "which you are enduring (or, suffering)." This is happening now; it is not a future event.

to prove you means "to put you to the test," "to test you." Persecution and suffering are intended to test Christians' faith and so purify and improve it.

something strange: "something unusual" (TEV), "something that should not happen."

The verse may be translated as follows: "My dear friends, right now you are suffering cruel hardships which put your faith to the test. Don't be surprised, and don't think that this is unusual (or, that this should not happen to you)."

4.13 RSV	TEV
But rejoice in so far as you share Christ's sufferings, that you may also rejoice and be glad when his glory is revealed.	**Rather be glad that you are sharing Christ's sufferings, so that you may be full of joy when his glory is revealed.**

Instead of being surprised, they should rejoice over their sufferings.

in so far as you share Christ's sufferings: "that you are sharing the sufferings of Christ" or "that you have part in Christ's sufferings." There are various ways to understand this statement, but the most probable one is that it means to suffer as Christ suffered (see Rom 8.17; Phil 3.10; Col 1.24).

when his glory is revealed: "when his majesty (or, greatness) is seen." This refers to the final coming of Christ in power. Here glory is "divine majesty" or "divine power."

The verse may be translated as follows: "Be happy that you are suffering as Christ suffered. Then you will be very happy when he comes (again), and you see his divine majesty (or, power)."

4.14 RSV	TEV
If you are reproached for the name of Christ, you are blessed, because the spirit of glory[j] and of God rests upon you.	**Happy are you if you are insulted because you are Christ's followers; this means that the glorious Spirit, the Spirit of God, is resting on you.**

[j]**Other ancient authorities insert** *and of power*

reproached for the name of Christ: "abused (or, reviled) because you are followers of Christ" or "people speak evil of you because you are Christians" (see verse 16, below).

you are blessed: this translates the same Greek word that in 3.14 RSV translates you will be blessed. For the whole statement see Matthew 5.11.

because: this introduces the reason why they are to be congratulated. Their being reviled is proof that they are being guided by God's Spirit.

the spirit of glory and of God rests upon you: this is a literal translation which fails to convey meaning. The meaning is "the glorious Spirit, who is God's Spirit, rests on you" (see TEV). This can be expressed clearly in fewer words as "the glorious Spirit of God." Here "glorious" means "majestic," "powerful," or "wonderful." "God's Spirit" is the Spirit that comes from God or is sent by God.

rests upon you: "remains on you." If the idea of upon is difficult or strange, the translation may say "is (always) with you," "is present with you."

As the RSV footnote shows, many Greek manuscripts and ancient versions add "and of power" after glory. Few modern translations accept this as part of the original text.

4.15 RSV	TEV
But let none of you suffer as a murderer, or a thief, or a wrong-doer, or a mischief-maker;	**If any of you suffers, it must not be because he is a murderer or a thief or a criminal or a meddler in other people's affairs.**

let: see 3.11.

let none of you suffer: the writer is saying that suffering as the result of wrongdoing is not praiseworthy. The only suffering that is worthy of praise is that which comes as a result of positive Christian attitudes and actions. Care must be taken not to translate in such a way as to imply that the writer is only saying that they should avoid being punished for doing the things he condemns. As a matter of fact, they should be punished for those crimes; but no Christian should ever be guilty of such crimes. So it is better, like TEV and others, to translate: "If any of you suffers, it must not be because..." or "If you suffer, it should not be because you...."

murderer...thief: in some languages verbal phrases will be necessary: "kill someone...steal from someone."

wrongdoer: this is a general term and can be translated "criminal" or "one who breaks the law." But in the context it should not imply that a murderer or a thief is not a wrongdoer, and so it may be necessary to say "a murderer, or a thief, or any other kind of criminal."

mischief-maker: there is no certainty about the meaning of the Greek word, which is found nowhere else in the Greek Bible. TEV and others translate "a meddler in other people's affairs." Most languages have expressive terms to describe such a person. The *Translator's Handbook* cites two: "putting one's spoon in someone else's soup" and "looking on while another man counts his money."

4.16 RSV	TEV
yet if one suffers as a Christian, let him not be ashamed, but under that name let him glorify God.	**However, if you suffer because you are a Christian, don't be ashamed of it, but thank God that you bear Christ's name.**

yet if one suffers as a Christian: "but if you suffer (or, are persecuted) because you are a Christian." This is the only valid reason for suffering; only this kind of suffering is worthy of praise.

let him not be ashamed: "don't consider this a disgrace," "this is nothing to be ashamed of."

under that name let him glorify God: the Greek phrase "in this name" could mean "about this matter." But it most probably means "(thank

God that) you are called a Christian" or "...that people call you a Christian."

4.17

RSV	TEV
For the time has come for judgment to begin with the household of God; and if it begins with us, what will be the end of those who do not obey the gospel of God?	The time has come for judgment to begin, and God's own people are the first to be judged. If it starts with us, how will it end with those who do not believe the Good News from God?

The writer once more returns to the subject of judgment. Since there is a change of subject, it may be well to start a new paragraph here, as TEV does.

the time has come for judgment to begin with the household of God: this combines two statements: (1) Judgment Day is near, and (2) God's people will be judged first. So it may be better to have two separate statements in translation, as follows: "The Day of Judgment is near, and God's people will be the first to be judged (or, and God will judge his own people first)." The phrase the household of God means the community of God's people. In 2.5 the same Greek word "house" is used, which here RSV translates household.

if it begins with us: "if we are the first to be judged" or "if God is going to judge us first."

what will be the end...?: this rhetorical question expresses an attitude of dismay and horror: "how terrible it will be...!" The writer only suggests, by means of the rhetorical question, the terrible event awaiting unbelievers. Here the end means "result," "outcome."

those who do not obey the gospel of God: "those who do not believe (or, accept) the Good News that comes from God."

The verse may be translated as follows:

> The Day of Judgment will come soon, and God will judge his own people first. We will be the first to be judged; how terrible will be the punishment (or, ordeal) that awaits the people who do not believe the Good News sent by God!

4.18

RSV	TEV
And "If the righteous man is scarcely saved, where will the impious and sinner appear?"	As the scripture says, "It is difficult for good people to be saved; what, then, will become of godless sinners?"

Here the writer quotes Proverbs 11.31 according to the text of the ancient Greek translation, the Septuagint. As in 2.8 and 3.10, instead of And, a translation should begin with "As the scripture says."

If the righteous man is scarcely saved: scarcely means that there is a difficulty involved. "If it is difficult for a good person to be saved." Although this is phrased as a conditional statement, it is really a statement of fact. It may be better, then, to translate as an affirmation. The difficulty is not that God has a hard time saving good people, but that Christians experience difficulties and hardships before being rewarded with final salvation. So a translation may say "Good people will suffer before God finishes saving them." For righteous see 2.24; 3.12.

where will the impious and sinner appear?: here appear is used in the sense of "turn out"; "how will it turn out for the ungodly and sinners?" Or, more naturally, "what will happen to godless sinners?" Instead of a rhetorical question, an exclamation may be more fitting: "how terrible it will be for godless sinners!"

the impious and sinner: the two can be combined into one phrase: "godless sinners."

4.19 RSV	TEV
Therefore let those who suffer according to God's will do right and entrust their souls to a faithful Creator.	**So then, those who suffer because it is God's will for them, should by their good actions trust themselves completely to their Creator, who always keeps his promise.**

those who suffer according to God's will: "those who are persecuted because that is what God wants for them" (see 2.15; 3.17).

do right and entrust their souls: in Greek the phrase "by doing good" is a prepositional phrase that modifies the verb entrust: that is, doing good is the way they should entrust themselves to God. So TEV has "should by their good actions trust themselves completely...." But the RSV rendering is defensible, and a translation may prefer to follow it. If so, it will be better to translate "continue to do what is right." For entrust see 2.23.

Here, as elsewhere, souls means the persons themselves: "trust themselves" (TEV; see 1.9).

to a faithful Creator: this is a clear reference to God, and the translation should say "to God, who is the faithful Creator." Here faithful means trustworthy, that is, one who can be trusted to keep his promise. And Creator is, specifically, "their Creator" (TEV) or "God, who created them."

Chapter 5

SECTION HEADING

The Flock of God: "Taking Care of the People of God," "Duties and Responsibilities of Christians."

Now the writer gives advice to the readers, addressing the church leaders first (verses 1-4), and then speaking to the younger believers (verse 5a). Beginning at verse 5b he speaks to all church members; the section concludes with a prayer (verses 10-11).

5.1

RSV	TEV
So I exhort the elders among you, as a fellow elder and a witness of the sufferings of Christ as well as a partaker in the glory that is to be revealed.	I, who am an elder myself, appeal to the church elders among you. I am a witness of Christ's sufferings, and I will share in the glory that will be revealed. I appeal to you

exhort: "urge," "advise," "appeal" (TEV). The word carries no idea of an order; it is rather an urgent request.

the elders: these are church leaders, who have general responsibility for the work of the church (see Acts 11.30; 1 Tim 5.17-19; Titus 1.5; James 5.14). There were several of them in each church, and their title and duties were patterned after those of the Jewish elders, the officers of the synagogues.

The word "an older man" is in many languages quite appropriate, since the older men are leaders in the community. Where this is not the case, "church leaders" or "church officers" seems to be the best way to represent the meaning. Or else a phrase can be used: "those who are in charge of the church."

a fellow elder: "I also am a Christian leader."

a witness of the sufferings of Christ: "I saw how Christ suffered," "I saw how Christ was punished (or, persecuted)."

a partaker in the glory that is to be revealed: for glory that is to be revealed see 4.13. The form of the Greek seems to indicate that this event, the coming of Christ, will be soon (see 4.7), and so it may be well to translate "Christ's great power, that will soon become visible to all (or, that soon everyone will see)."

The word partaker may mean (1) he will share in Christ's majestic power, or (2) he and his readers will share in that experience. Although one cannot be dogmatic about it, the first interpretation seems more likely. "When Christ comes (again), I will share in his divine (or, majestic) power."

It is to be noticed that TEV, at the end of verse 1, has repeated "I appeal to you" in order to lead naturally into the exhortations in verse 2. In some languages this will be a convenient way to handle the matter; others will wish to imitate RSV.

5.2 RSV	TEV
Tend the flock of God that is your charge,[k] not by constraint but willingly,[l] not for shameful gain but eagerly,	**to be shepherds of the flock that God gave you and to take care of it willingly, as God wants you to, and not unwillingly. Do your work, not for mere pay, but from a real desire to serve.**
[k]Other ancient authorities add *exercising the oversight*	
[l]Other ancient authorities add *as God would have you*	

Tend the flock of God that is your charge: the language of a shepherd and his flock of sheep is a common one in the Old and the New Testaments. It is used both in a literal sense and in a figurative sense for God and his people, for Israel and the Church, and for the leaders who have the responsibility for the spiritual care of God's people. Wherever possible, this language should be preserved, since it appears so often. In some cases a simile will be better: "Take care of your churches in the same way that a shepherd takes care of his (flock of) sheep." Where it is altogether impossible to use such a figure, then it will be necessary to say "Take good care of your congregations (or, churches)."

that is your charge translates the Greek phrase "among you." Another way of translating this will be "which God has entrusted to you" or "which God has given for you to take care of." The "flock" belongs to God; the elders are the shepherds to whom God has given the responsibility of taking care of his sheep.

As the RSV footnote indicates, many Greek manuscripts and ancient versions have a participle which RSV translates "exercising the oversight." TEV, following the UBS Greek New Testament, includes this, translating "and to take care of it."

not by constraint but willingly: "not because you have to (or, are forced to do it), but because you want to do it."

not for shameful gain but eagerly: "not for the purpose of making money but enthusiastically." For shameful gain see 1 Timothy 3.8; Titus 1.7; the idea of getting rich through Christian service is seen as a shameful thing. The idea can be expressed by "not because you are greedy for money." The contrasting eagerly may be translated "voluntarily" or "enthusiastically"; others translate "out of sheer devotion."

5.3 RSV	TEV
not as domineering over those in your charge but being examples to the flock.	**Do not try to rule over those who have been put in your care, but be examples to the flock.**

not as domineering over those in your charge: "don't act as though you were the boss of your people" or "...of the people you are responsible for."

but being examples to the flock: "instead, be examples to your people," "behave in the way that you want them to behave" (see Titus 2.7).

5.4

RSV	TEV
And when the chief Shepherd is manifested you will obtain the unfading crown of glory.	And when the Chief Shepherd appears, you will receive the glorious crown which will never lose its brightness.

the chief Shepherd: this is an obvious reference to Christ, who is the supreme leader of the people of God. "Christ, who is the Shepherd of us all," "Christ, who is the Shepherd over all (flocks and) shepherds."

is manifested: the same as revealed in 4.13; 5.1. Here the translation can be "comes" or "returns."

you will obtain the unfading crown of glory: this is the reward that Christ will give the elders when he returns. The reward is spoken of as a crown, which is the laurel wreath awarded the winners in athletic contests (see 1 Cor 9.25; 2 Tim 2.5; 4.8). It is called unfading, that is, it will not dry up and wither like a laurel wreath but will always be bright and beautiful. It seems best to understand of glory to mean "glorious" (TEV) or "wonderful."

you will obtain: "you will receive" (TEV); or else, "he will give you," "he will award you."

In cases where crown is only a symbol of power, and the custom of awarding a wreath to a winner in an athletic contest is unknown, it may be necessary to use a general term like "prize" or "reward." "And when Christ, who is the Supreme Shepherd, comes, he will give you the glorious prize (or, reward) that will last forever."

5.5

RSV	TEV
Likewise you that are younger be subject to the elders. Clothe yourselves, all of you, with humility toward one another, for "God opposes the proud, but gives grace to the humble."	In the same way you younger men must submit yourselves to the older men. And all of you must put on the apron of humility, to serve one another; for the scripture says, "God resists the proud, but shows favor to the humble."

Likewise, you that are younger: for Likewise see 3.1,7. Here the writer addresses the rest of the church members who, by definition, are younger than the elders. The term younger could be restricted solely to the younger men of the congregations, but this seems unlikely.

be subject to: the same verb used in 2.13,18; 3.1,5.

the elders: here either the church leaders (RSV) or "the older men" (TEV). It would seem that the form of the Greek favors taking the word in the general sense of "older people."

Clothe yourselves...with humility toward one another: here the writer addresses all the people of the churches (all of you), both the older and the younger. They are all to treat their fellow believers with humility. The figure of clothing comes from the fact that the Greek verb for Clothe is formed from the noun "(servant's) apron." In some languages the figure will be significant (see TEV), but in others it may be strange or misleading. In such cases the translation can be "all of you must serve your fellow believers with humility," "you must all act like humble servants to one another."

To reinforce his advice, the writer quotes Proverbs 3.34 according to the text of the Septuagint. As in similar instances (see 4.18), instead of for, it is better to have "for the scripture says" (TEV). The same passage is quoted in James 4.6.

God opposes the proud: "God is against proud people."

gives grace to the humble: "is good (or, kind) to people who are humble."

5.6 RSV	TEV
Humble yourselves therefore under the mighty hand of God, that in due time he may exalt you.	**Humble yourselves, then, under God's mighty hand, so that he will lift you up in his own good time.**

Humble yourselves...under the mighty hand of God: the writer continues addressing all of his readers. Here he says "Submit yourselves humbly to God's great power," "Accept humbly (or, obediently) God's complete authority over you." God's mighty hand is his power to protect and save his people (and also to punish them).

in due time: "when he wants to," "at the time he chooses." It is God who decides the time and occasion when he will exalt his people. The idea of exalt is "to give victory to" or "to give honor to" or "to make important (or, powerful)."

5.7 RSV	TEV
Cast all your anxieties on him, for he cares about you.	**Leave all your worries with him, because he cares for you.**

Cast all your anxieties on him: troubles and difficulties are referred to as burdens to be carried. The writer is telling his readers that they need not carry these burdens but may transfer them to God—he will carry them.

he cares about you: "he is concerned about you," "he takes care of you." It may be better to reverse the clauses: "God cares for you, and so you should take all your troubles to him (or, leave all your worries with him)."

5.8 RSV	TEV
Be sober, be watchful. Your adversary the devil prowls around like	**Be alert, be on watch! Your enemy, the Devil, roams around**

a roaring lion, seeking some one to devour.	**like a roaring lion, looking for someone to devour.**

Be sober: see 1.13; 4.7.

be watchful: "stay awake (spiritually)," "take care." The writer urges his readers not to relax spiritually but to always be on the alert, constantly watching out for any temptations or dangers that might appear. The two verbs express essentially one thought, and so it is possible to translate "Be continuously on guard," "Always keep alert (or, watchful)."

your adversary the devil: "the Devil, who is your enemy." The Devil is regarded as the ruler of the powers of evil, the enemy of God's people, always trying to make them sin.

prowls around like a roaring lion: if the figure of a roaring lion can be retained, the appropriate verb describing a lion's movement must be used: "prowls" or "roams" (TEV). The main component of roaring is not so much noise but the idea of being fierce, or wild, or hungry.

seeking some one to devour: if the picture of the Devil devouring a person is strange or funny, one may say "destroy" or "kill." This should not be understood, however, as physical destruction or death; it is spiritual ruin, spiritual defeat, that the Devil is trying to inflict on believers.

5.9 RSV	TEV
Resist him, firm in your faith, knowing that the same experience of suffering is required of your brotherhood throughout the world.	**Be firm in your faith and resist him, because you know that your fellow believers in all the world are going through the same kind of sufferings.**

Resist him, firm in your faith: "Keep your faith strong and oppose the Devil," "Keep believing firmly in God, and resist the Devil."

In their fight against the power of evil, the readers should take comfort in the knowledge that their fellow believers all over the world were going through the same kinds of troubles.

the same experience of suffering is required: the verb in the Greek text appears only here in the New Testament. As translated by RSV, the implication is that the suffering is something imposed by God. In a more general sense, as TEV translates, the verb may be taken to mean "are going through," or "are experiencing," "are facing," "have to endure." Instead of experience, it may be better to say "the same kind of sufferings" (TEV) or "are suffering the same things you are."

your brotherhood throughout the world: "your fellow believers in all the world" (TEV).

The verse may be translated as follows: "Resist the Devil, and keep believing firmly in God. Remember that your fellow believers in all the world have to endure the same sufferings that you are enduring."

5.10 RSV	TEV
And after you have suffered a little while, the God of all grace, who has called you to his eternal glory in Christ, will himself restore, establish, and strengthen[m] you.	But after you have suffered for a little while, the God of all grace, who calls you to share his eternal glory in union with Christ, will himself perfect you and give you firmness, strength, and a sure foundation.

[m]Other ancient authorities read *restore, establish, strengthen and settle*

after you have suffered a little while: or "you must suffer for a little while, and after that...." In comparison with the eternal glory that awaits the believers, the sufferings of this life are regarded as short and soon ended.

the God of all grace: here grace stands for God's love, his readiness to bless his people. So the translation may be "God, who always loves us completely" or "God, who is always ready to bless us."

For called see 1.15; 2.9,21; 3.9.

his eternal glory: here glory stands for the life in God's presence, after death. "God has called you to live in his presence forever" or "...to share his majestic power forever."

in Christ: this may mean (1) God calls us by means of Christ, or (2) believers will experience God's glory because they are in union with Christ, that is, they are Christ's followers. The second meaning seems more probable.

restore, establish, and strengthen: as the RSV footnote shows, many Greek manuscripts and ancient versions have another verb, "settle." This is the text translated by TEV. All four verbs have to do with moral and spiritual firmness and strength. The first verb means "to make whole," "to complete," "to make perfect." The other three verbs may be translated by nouns or verbal phrases that express the idea of making something firm, strong, and secure. It is not necessary, however, to try to find three different verbs; one emphatic compound expression may be quite satisfactory: "will give you spiritual health, and make you completely firm and strong."

The following may serve as a model for translating this verse:

> But God, who always loves you completely, has called you to live in his divine (or, majestic) presence forever, after you have suffered a little while. So he will make you spiritually whole, making your faith strong, firm, and steadfast.

5.11 RSV	TEV
To him be the dominion for ever and ever. Amen.	To him be the power forever! Amen.

To him be: as in 4.11, this prayer may be translated, "May God's (or, his) dominion endure forever! Amen." or "May God rule forever! Amen." Or, as a statement, "His power will last forever. Amen."

1 Peter 5.12

SECTION HEADING

Final Greetings: "Closing Words," "Final Instructions."

After a final instruction and a last greeting, the writer closes the Letter with a brief prayer.

5.12 RSV

By Silvánus, a faithful brother as I regard him, I have written briefly to you, exhorting and declaring that this is the true grace of God; stand fast in it.

TEV

I write you this brief letter with the help of Silas, whom I regard as a faithful Christian brother. I want to encourage you and give my testimony that this is the true grace of God. Stand firm in it.

By Silvánus...I have written briefly to you: this means that Silvanus wrote the letter according to Peter's instructions, or as Peter dictated. So a translation may say "Silvanus has written this brief letter for me" or "Silvanus has helped me write this brief letter." In some cases it may be possible to say "Silvanus has written this brief letter as I dictated to him." It will be noticed that TEV uses the more familiar form "Silas" ("Silvanus" is the Latinized form). There is no way of knowing whether or not this is Silas, Paul's companion, or some other man. In Acts he is always called Silas; in 2 Corinthians 1.19; 1 Thessalonians 1.1, and 2 Thessalonians 1.1 he is called "Silvanus."

a faithful brother as I regard him: "who, in my opinion, is a faithful Christian brother," "whom I have always found to be a faithful Christian brother." Probably faithful here means "trustworthy," "one I can always rely on."

exhorting: as in 5.1; here the translation can be "urging," "encouraging."

declaring: "testifying," "giving my witness," "affirming."

this is the true grace of God: "what I have written in this letter has to do with God's true love for you." Such an interpretation takes this to refer to the Letter as a whole, and grace to mean God's love. Or else the translation can be "affirming that the blessings you have received are real proof of God's love for you."

stand fast in it: the idea of standing in God's grace may not be easy to represent, and so it may be necessary to say "never turn away from God's love," "always rely on God's great love."

5.13 RSV

She who is at Babylon, who is likewise chosen, sends you greetings; and so does my son Mark.

TEV

Your sister church in Babylon,[d] also chosen by God, sends you greetings, and so does my son Mark.

[d]**BABYLON:** *As in the book of Revelation, this probably refers to Rome.*

She who is at Babylon: the most widespread interpretation of this is that it refers to the Christian Church in Rome, and the further assumption is made that Peter was in Rome where he wrote. See Revelation 14.8; 17.5; 18.2 for "Babylon" as a name for Rome. Some translations may wish to add a footnote, as do TEV and others. It is not recommended that "Rome" appear in the text.

who is likewise chosen: that is, the believers of the church in Rome have been chosen by God just as the believers to whom Peter is writing. "Who also belongs to God" or "who also has been chosen by God."

sends you greetings: it will be better to say "your fellow believers here in Babylon send you greetings."

my son Mark: here son is probably used in the sense of follower, helper, younger companion. It is generally assumed that this is the same one who appears in Acts and in Paul's letters as Paul's companion, but there is no proof that this is so.

5.14 RSV	TEV
Greet one another with the kiss of love.	**Greet one another with the kiss of Christian love.**
Peace to all of you that are in Christ.	**May peace be with all of you who belong to Christ.**

the kiss of love: "the kiss of Christian love" (TEV) or "a kiss of Christian friendship." If the notion of kissing people in general is strange or offensive, the translation may read "greet one another warmly (or, affectionately)" or "...as dear fellow believers."

Peace is God's gift of spiritual wholeness and well-being.

all of you that are in Christ: "all of you who are in union with Christ" or "...who belong to Christ" (TEV).

The last sentence of this verse may be translated as follows:

> I pray that all of you who are united with Christ may have peace.

An Outline of 2 Peter

1. Introduction 1.1-2
2. The Christian Way of Life 1.3-21
3. False Teachers in the Church 2.1-22
4. The Final Coming of Christ 3.1-16
5. Closing Remarks and Prayer 3.17-18

Title

THE SECOND LETTER FROM PETER

For the title see the comments on the title of 1 Peter.

Chapter 1

1.1 RSV	TEV
Simeon[x] Peter, a servant and apostle of Jesus Christ, To those who have obtained a faith of equal standing with ours in the righteousness of our God and Savior Jesus Christ:[a]	From Simon Peter, a servant and apostle of Jesus Christ— To those who through the righteousness of our God and Savior Jesus Christ have been given a faith as precious as ours:

[x]Other authorities read *Simon*

[a]Or *of our God and the Savior Jesus Christ*

TEV has no section heading for the first two verses. If one is desired, something like "Introduction" or "Opening Greeting" can be used. The Letter begins in the usual way: the writer's name, the readers, and a greeting.

Simeon reflects the Hebrew spelling of the name; "Simon" is the form most commonly used in the New Testament. A translator should feel free to use the usual form here, and not the uncommon one.

a servant: "one who serves." This is Christian service, and the title identifies the writer as a Christian leader.

apostle: here in the sense of one of the twelve original followers of Jesus. The word means "one who is sent" to speak and to act in the name and with the authority of the one who sent him.

The third person form of the Greek may be unnatural in some languages, and so the following may be said: "I, Simon Peter...write this letter to...."

To those who have obtained a faith of equal standing with ours: the letter is written to believers everywhere, and at once the writer declares that he and they all share the same faith, which here means the truths and beliefs which all Christians profess. The verb obtained indicates that the faith they have is a gift from God; so TEV "have been given." If necessary, one may say "to whom God has given."

of equal standing: "as valuable," "as authentic," "as honorable"; or "it is as good as."

with ours: here ours is exclusive and refers to the Apostles or, in a vaguer sense, to the writer and his colleagues. Though the readers had not, like the Apostles, received their faith directly from Jesus Christ, they were not spiritually inferior to the Apostles.

in the righteousness: "because of (or, through) the righteousness." The phrase here means "righteous conduct," that is, fairness, goodness, impartiality: "because our God and Savior Jesus Christ is righteous (or, fair)."

of our God and Savior Jesus Christ: as the RSV footnote indicates, the Greek may be translated, "of our God and the Savior Jesus Christ." But it is most likely that RSV and TEV correctly interpret the Greek (see Titus 2.13), and that Jesus Christ here is called our God and Savior.

Here our is inclusive: it includes all believers. In some languages the phrase our God is not appropriate, since God cannot be possessed. So it will be necessary to say "the God whom we worship, who is Jesus Christ, our Savior."

1.2 RSV	TEV
May grace and peace be multiplied to you in the knowledge of God and of Jesus our Lord.	May grace and peace be yours in full measure through your knowledge of God and of Jesus our Lord.

grace and peace: both are blessings which God gives to people. Grace stands for his love, manifested to all through Jesus Christ, and peace is spiritual well-being, also regarded as God's gift; it may be represented by "spiritual strength" (see 1 Peter 1.2).

be multiplied: "have more and more," "in greater abundance." The following may be said: "I pray that you will know more of God's grace (or, goodness), and that your spiritual strength will always increase."

in the knowledge of God: "through your knowledge of God" (TEV), "because you know God." Care must be taken to use a noun or verb which means "to know God" as a person knows another person through an intimate relationship. A noun or verb which means only "to know about" someone else, in which no personal relationship is implied, should not be used.

Verses 1-2 may be translated as follows:

> I, Simon Peter, a servant and an apostle of Jesus Christ, write this letter. I write to all believers to whom God has given a faith as precious (or, good) as the faith we apostles have. We have all received this same faith because Jesus Christ, who is our God and (our) Savior, is righteous (or, just).
>
> 2 I pray that God will bless you more and more, and that your spiritual strength will keep on growing. It is because of your personal knowledge of God and of Jesus our Lord that God will give you these blessings.

SECTION HEADING

God's Call and Choice: "What Christians Should Be Like," "What God Wants Us to Be."

In this section, verses 3-15, the writer first speaks of how God has saved us (verses 3-4), and then of the need we believers have to keep growing spiritually (verses 5-9). The result of such growth will be admission into the eternal Kingdom of Christ (verses 10-11). The section ends with the writer's explanation of his own desire to keep the readers informed of the truths of the gospel (verses 12-15).

1.3

RSV

His divine power has granted to us all things that pertain to life and godliness, through the knowledge of him who called us to[b] his own glory and excellence,

[b]Or *by*

TEV

God's divine power has given us everything we need to live a truly religious life through our knowledge of the one who called us to share in his own[a] glory and goodness.

[a]**to share in his own;** *some manuscripts have* **through his.**

RSV has verses 3-4 in one sentence; since it is long and complex, it is better to have at least two sentences.

His divine power: this may refer to God (so TEV and others) or to Jesus Christ. It probably refers to Jesus Christ, and a translation should indicate it explicitly. The following may be said: "Jesus Christ has God's power, and he has given us...."

to us: this is probably inclusive, "to (all) us believers"; some, however, take it to refer to the Apostles.

all things that pertain to life and godliness: "everything required for a godly life." The phrase life and godliness is taken to mean "a godly life." The second noun (godliness) serves as an adjective modifying the first noun (life). Here "godly" may be translated "truly religious" (TEV) or "truly Christian."

through the knowledge of: as in verse 2, this means the believers' knowledge of Christ, who is here spoken of as him who called us to his own glory and excellence. According to the Greek text translated in RSV and TEV, Christ calls believers "to share in his own glory and goodness." Glory here may be taken as meaning Christ's divine nature, which Christians are called to participate in. And excellence translates a Greek word that means "virtue," "moral excellence," "upright character."

As the RSV and TEV footnotes show, there are good Greek manuscripts and early versions that have "who called us by means of his glory and goodness." Some commentators and translators prefer this, and it makes sense; but the text translated by RSV and TEV seems preferable.

called: see 1 Peter 1.15.

The verse may be translated as follows:

By means of his divine power, Christ has given us everything we need in order to live a holy (or, Christian) life. All those things are ours because we fully know Christ. He calls us to share his own divine nature and his goodness (or, virtue).

1.4 RSV	TEV
by which he has granted to us his precious and very great promises, that through these you may escape from the corruption that is in the world because of passion, and become partakers of the divine nature.	In this way he has given us the very great and precious gifts he promised, so that by means of these gifts you may escape from the destructive lust that is in the world, and may come to share the divine nature.

by which he has granted to us: the by which may refer back to all things of verse 3, or to glory and excellence. TEV takes it in a general sense of everything that is said in verse 3: "In this way he has given us...."

granted to us his precious and very great promises: "gave us the precious and outstanding (or, excellent) gifts he promised." It is not promises that Christ has given us believers, but the great and precious blessings he promised. And it is by means of these blessings given to Christians, the writer tells his readers, that "you may escape from the destructive lust that is in the world" (TEV).

corruption is moral or spiritual destruction, decay.

passion is "evil desire" or "lust" (TEV). The phrase corruption in the world because of passion may be represented by "the corruption that evil desires have brought into the world" or "moral (or, spiritual) destruction caused by the evil desires in people." Here the world is humanity as such, dominated by sin.

become partakers of the divine nature: "have the divine nature," "share in the very being of God." The goal "becoming like God" may be difficult to express. The writer does not have in mind a transformation that will take place after death, but one that happens in this life. If necessary, one can say "become (true) children of God and be like him."

The followng may serve as a model for translating this verse:

And as a result of all this, he has given us believers the precious and wonderful blessings he promised. In this way we will not be harmed by the spiritual corruption that people's evil desires have brought into the world, and we will be able to share in the nature of God (or, to become like God).

1.5-7 RSV	TEV
For this very reason make every effort to supplement your faith with virtue, and virtue with knowledge, 6 and knowledge with	For this very reason do your best to add goodness to your faith; to your goodness add knowledge; 6 to your knowledge

self-control, and self-control with steadfastness, and steadfastness with godliness, 7 and godliness with brotherly affection, and brotherly affection with love.

add self-control; to your self-control add endurance; to your endurance add godliness; 7 to your godliness add brotherly affection; and to your brotherly affection add love.

These three verses form one sentence which is long but not complicated. It will be noticed that TEV uses the verb "add" with every new quality, and has semicolons to divide the sentence. RSV uses the verb supplement only once, and so uses commas to divide the sentence. If it is more natural, periods can be used, thus dividing the sentence into several complete sentences.

For this reason: "Because you are meant to share the divine nature."

supplement...with: "add to," "supply in addition." The verb indicates the personal effort of Christians to add these Christian virtues to their basic faith in Christ.

supplement your faith with virtue: the basic quality is Christian faith, given by God (verse 1), to which Christians must try to add seven qualities. The first one is virtue, that is, goodness, moral excellence (see verse 3). Instead of abstract qualities it may be more natural to use verbal phrases. So the list can begin "God gave you faith, and you must do your best also to be good (or, to live a pure life)."

knowledge: of God and his will for his people.

self-control: "a disciplined life," "mastery (or, control) of one's desires." It may be that the control of sexual desire is in focus here.

steadfastness: "endurance" (TEV), "perseverance."

godliness: as in verse 3.

brotherly affection: "affection for your fellow believers."

love in the deepest and most inclusive sense, as deep and broad as God's love for all people.

Verses 5-7 may be translated as follows:

> Because Christ has done all this, you must do your best to keep believing in him and also to live a pure (or, moral) life; you must also know God's will; 6 you must be able also to control your desires (or, appetites); you must persevere despite difficulties; you must live a Christian life; 7 you must treat all fellow believers with affection; and you must love all people.

1.8 RSV

For if these things are yours and abound, they keep you from being ineffective or unfruitful in the knowledge of our Lord Jesus Christ.

TEV

These are the qualities you need, and if you have them in abundance, they will make you active and effective in your knowledge of our Lord Jesus Christ.

if these things are yours and abound: "if you possess these qualities (or, virtues) in abundance" or "if you keep on having more and more of these qualities."

they keep you from being ineffective and unfruitful: instead of the double negative it is probably better to use a positive expression: "they will make you effective and fruitful."

ineffective translates a Greek word meaning "not working," "not active"—lazy, incompetent, useless.

unfruitful means "producing no results," "doing nothing good."

in the knowledge of our Lord Jesus Christ: as in verses 1,3. The preposition in here means that their lives are determined by their personal knowledge of Christ, and they will be active and effective believers if they have a growing supply of the Christian virtues listed in verses 5-7.

The verse may be translated as follows:

> If you have these qualities, and if they keep growing (or, developing), they will keep you active and effective, as your personal knowledge of our Lord Jesus Christ rules your lives (or, ...as you know our Lord Jesus Christ better and better).

1.9 RSV	TEV
For whoever lacks these things is blind and shortsighted and has forgotten that he was cleansed from his old sins.	**But whoever does not have them is so short-sighted that he cannot see and has forgotten that he has been purified from his past sins.**

these things: the virtues listed in verses 5-7.

is blind and shortsighted: logically these two words are incompatible. A blind person cannot see and so cannot be shortsighted. A short-sighted person can see clearly only things that are near, but not things that are far off. It may be well to translate "is like a person who is blind or short-sighted" or "is like a person who cannot see well, or cannot even see at all." The translation should not lead the reader to think that the writer is talking about physical blindness; he is talking about being blind about spiritual matters, the inability or unwillingness to be aware of God and his will for people.

cleansed: "purified" (TEV), "washed clean." The writer is probably thinking of baptism, when all past sins were washed away.

By has forgotten the writer does not mean that such a person has forgotten that he or she was baptized, but has forgotten what baptism meant in terms of the forgiveness of sins. That person lives as though his or her sins had never been forgiven.

The verse may be translated as follows:

> The believer who doesn't have these qualities is like a person who can't see very well, or who cannot see at all. Such a believer has forgotten that his past sins were washed away (or, that God had forgiven his sins and made him pure).

1.10 RSV

Therefore, brethren, be the more zealous to confirm your call and election, for if you do this you will never fall;

TEV

So then, my brothers, try even harder to make God's call and his choice of you a permanent experience; if you do so, you will never abandon your faith.[b]

[b]abandon your faith; *or* fall into sin.

brethren: "my dear fellow believers," "my Christian brothers and sisters."

be the more zealous: "try even harder" (TEV), "do the best you can." This is like the exhortation in verse 5.

confirm: "make certain of," "make sure," in the sense of showing that it is real and effective. The Christian's call and election come from God; the Christian must do everything possible to prove that God's action is real in his or her life. There is no significant difference of meaning here between call and election; both refer to God's initiative in salvation (see verse 3 who called us). The decision and choice are God's but the believer must do his or her best to make God's decision evident.

you will never fall: this may be taken to mean "you will never fall into sin" (see the TEV footnote); but in connection with verse 11, it seems more probable that the meaning is "you will never fall away," in the sense of abandoning the Christian faith.

1.11 RSV

so there will be richly provided for you an entrance into the eternal kingdom of our Lord and Savior Jesus Christ.

TEV

In this way you will be given the full right to enter the eternal Kingdom of our Lord and Savior Jesus Christ.

so: "In this way" (TEV), "as a result," "because of this," that is, because you do your best to make God's call and choice a real fact in your lives.

will be richly provided: this translates the verb which in verse 5 is translated supplement. The actor in this passive expression is God, or Christ; "God will give you the full right (or, privilege)."

the eternal kingdom: life in the presence of God and Christ in heaven, after death.

of our Lord: the kingdom belongs to him, that is, he is the king. Here our includes all Christians.

1.12 RSV

Therefore I intend always to remind you of these things, though you know them and are established in the truth that you have.

TEV

And so I will always remind you of these matters, even though you already know them and are firmly grounded in the truth you have received.

In verses 12-15 the writer tells his readers that he will provide them with an account of the basic gospel truths, so they will never forget what they have been taught. Notice in verse 12 remind; in verse 13 reminder, and in verse 15 recall.

If desired, these three verses can be a separate section entitled "Always Remember What You Learned."

remind you of these things: "make you remember these things." By these things the writer means the instructions and exhortations he has given them in verses 3-11.

though you know them: the writer admits that they know the truths of the gospel, but he still wants to remind them of it.

are established: "are sure of," "cannot be shaken from." The truth that you have is the gospel, or the Christian faith, and their lives are securely founded on it. They received this truth from the apostles. Instead of the truth that you have, it is better to translate the Greek "the truth that has come to you" or "the truth that you were taught" (see similar idea in Col 1.5-6; Jude 3).

1.13-14 RSV	TEV
I think it right, as long as I am in this body,[c] to arouse you by way of reminder, 14 since I know that the putting off of my body[c] will be soon, as our Lord Jesus Christ showed me.	**I think it only right for me to stir up your memory of these matters as long as I am still alive. 14 I know that I shall soon put off this mortal body, as our Lord Jesus Christ plainly told me.**

[c]Greek *tent*

I think it right: "I think I should," "I think it is my duty."

as long as I am in this body: "as long as I am alive." As the RSV footnote shows, the Greek word translated body is "tent," a temporary residence (see similar language in 2 Cor 5.1-4).

to arouse you by way of a reminder: either "to stimulate you to action by reminding you" or "to stir up your memory by reminding you." The latter seems preferable, and so the translation may be "to stir up (or, refresh) your memory by reminding you of these matters."

the putting off of my body: again the writer uses the figure of a tent in speaking of his death. The language of RSV and TEV ("I shall soon put off this mortal body") may not be natural or understandable, and so it may be necessary to say "I shall soon die" or "I won't live much longer," "I will soon depart this life."

showed me: "revealed to me," "told me" (TEV), "made plain to me."

The two verses may be restructured and translated as follows: "I know that I do not have long to live, for our Lord Jesus Christ told me. And so, before I die, I think I should stir up your memory by reminding you of these matters."

1.15 RSV	TEV
And I will see to it that after my departure you may be able at any	**I will do my best, then, to provide a way for you to remember**

time to recall these things.	these matters at all times after my death.

I will see to it: this translates the verb that in verse 10 is translated be...zealous to (and see also verse 5 make every effort). So TEV "I will do my best."

after my departure: "after I die."

The writer promises his readers that he will provide a way for them to recall his teachings after his death. This could be done either by training a younger colleague to transmit his teachings, or else by leaving a written record. This Letter itself is not what he is talking about; what he promises is something he will do later on.

SECTION HEADING

Eyewitnesses of Christ's Glory: "Those Who Saw Christ's Greatness," "The Apostolic Message Is True."

In this section, verses 16-21, the writer shows that the apostolic message about Jesus is based on the firsthand testimony of eyewitnesses and not on invented tales. The apostles saw the transfiguration of Jesus, and this confirmed the Old Testament prophecies about him. These can be understood only if their interpreters are guided by the same Spirit who moved the prophets to speak.

1.16

RSV	TEV
For we did not follow cleverly devised myths when we made known to you the power and coming of our Lord Jesus Christ, but we were eyewitnesses of his majesty.	We have not depended on made-up stories in making known to you the mighty coming of our Lord Jesus Christ. With our own eyes we saw his greatness.

we did not follow: "we did not depend on," "we were not using." Here we means the Apostles.

cleverly devised myths: "fabricated tales," "invented stories," "legends," "fictional accounts." Here myths means something invented, with no basis in fact (see 1 Tim 1.4).

the power and coming: this is a way of saying "the powerful coming" (see a similar instance of this kind of expression in verse 3). The word translated coming is regularly used in the New Testament for the return of Christ at the end of the age, which is commonly spoken of as the Second Coming. The apostolic message about the Lord's return in power was not based on cleverly fashioned legends, but on the firsthand witness of Christ's divine majesty on the Mount of Transfiguration. This experience was a guarantee that the Lord Jesus would return in power.

we were eyewitnesses: this refers to the Apostles; only three of them saw Jesus' transfiguration (Mark 9.2-7).

majesty: "power," "greatness" (TEV).

The verse may be translated as follows:

When we taught you that our Lord Jesus Christ will come in power, we did not depend on invented stories; we knew what we were talking about because with our own eyes we had seen his divine majesty.

1.17 RSV	TEV
For when he received honor and glory from God the Father and the voice was borne to him by the Majestic Glory, "This is my beloved Son,[d] with whom I am well pleased,"	We were there when he was given honor and glory by God the Father, when the voice came to him from the Supreme Glory, saying, "This is my own dear Son, with whom I am pleased!"

[d]Or *my Son, my (or the) Beloved*

he received honor and glory from God the Father: "God the Father gave him honor and glory." Here honor and glory are synonymous. In the setting of the transfiguration of Jesus, the statement means "God the Father honored him and glorified him." This may be stated, "God the Father showed how great and wonderful Jesus is." It may be, as some commentators say, that the honor consisted in what God said about Jesus, and the glory was the light that shone there (see Luke 9.30-32).

God the Father: "God, his Father" or "God, who is his Father."

the voice was borne to him: "when the voice spoke to him" or "when the voice said to him."

by the Majestic Glory: this clearly refers to God, and it may be better to make it explicit: "from the majestic presence of God" or "the majestic and glorious God spoke." Or the title may be only a way of speaking about God, without any specific reference to his divine qualities. So the translation may be "God."

This is my beloved Son, with whom I am well pleased: as in Matthew 17.5. As the RSV footnote indicates, the translation can be "This is my Son, my (or, the) Beloved"; it can also be translated, "This is my only Son." The words are not addressed to Jesus but to the others there on the mount.

RSV continues the sentence until the end of verse 18. TEV begins verse 17 with the words "We were there when..." so as to end verse 17 with a full stop and begin verse 18 as a new sentence.

1.18 RSV	TEV
we heard this voice borne from heaven, for we were with him on the holy mountain.	We ourselves heard this voice coming from heaven, when we were with him on the holy mountain.

we heard this voice borne from heaven: "we heard this voice that came from heaven." It may not be possible to speak of a voice coming from heaven, so the verb "to speak" may be better: "we heard this voice when it spoke from heaven." Or if it is not natural to say "a voice spoke," the translation can be "we heard what God said when he spoke from heaven."

we were with him: "we were there with Jesus."

the holy mountain: because of what happened there, it is called holy or sacred. There the divine power and glory were made visible. The translation can be "God's own mountain."

1.19 RSV	TEV
And we have the prophetic word made more sure. You will do well to pay attention to this as to a lamp shining in a dark place, until the day dawns and the morning star rises in your hearts.	**So we are even more confident of the message proclaimed by the prophets. You will do well to pay attention to it, because it is like a lamp shining in a dark place until the Day dawns and the light of the morning star shines in your hearts.**

we have the prophetic word made more sure: the Greek allows two interpretations, one of which would say that the prophets' message supports the truth revealed at the Mount of Transfiguration. But it is more likely that the meaning expressed by TEV and other translations is correct: "So we are even more confident of the message proclaimed by the prophets"; or "So we believe all the more firmly in what the prophets said." The transfiguration of Jesus, that is, the revelation of his divine nature, confirmed what the prophets had said about the coming Messiah. Here we refers to all believers.

You will do well to pay attention to this: here this refers to the message of the prophets. You will do well may be translated "You will be helped if..." or "It will be good for you to...." Pay attention to means "to hold on to," "to heed (or, follow)," "to regard as true and so to believe."

as to a lamp: it is better, with TEV, to represent this as a comparison: "It is like a lamp." The lamp at that time was a wick lamp, whose fuel was olive oil. Any general word for lamp may be used, but nothing that would mean a light powered by electricity or batteries (such as a flashlight, or electric torch).

until the day dawns: the thought here is that the prophetic message is like a lamp shining in a dark place, and so it is exceedingly useful and important. But eventually the sun will rise, the day will dawn, and the lamp itself will not be needed. This obviously refers to the day of the coming of the Lord Jesus.

the morning star rises in your hearts: this figure may be difficult to represent. TEV "the light of the morning star shines in your hearts" is somewhat easier but still difficult. The morning star (Venus) is seen at dawn, before the sun rises. This passage combines the figures of the morning star and of the dawn to represent the day of the Lord's return. The morning star represents Christ (see Rev 22.16; see also Luke 1.78-79; Eph 5.14). If the figure of the light of the star shining in your hearts is so strange as to cause difficulties for the readers, it may be necessary to say "and the light of the morning star shines on you" or "and you see the morning star shining." Or the comparison may be made explicit: "that the light of Christ, like the light of the morning star, will shine in your hearts."

1.20 RSV	TEV
First of all you must understand this, that no prophecy of scripture is a matter of one's own interpretation,	Above all else, however, remember that no one can explain by himself a prophecy in the Scriptures.

First of all: "This is important," "Pay attention to this," "Above everything else."

understand: the writer is explaining something to his readers, either as a new fact or, less probably, as something they already know.

prophecy of scripture: "prophetic passage in the Scriptures," "prophecy written in the Scriptures," or "what the prophets wrote in the Scriptures." It should be remembered that scripture here is the Old Testament, not the whole Bible.

is a matter of one's own interpretation: "can be (rightly) interpreted by a person alone." The writer is saying (as the next verse makes clear) that the help of the Holy Spirit is needed for a correct interpretation of biblical prophecy; one's own interpretation means "interpretation without (the Holy Spirit's) help." The translation can be "No one can interpret (or, explain) a passage of prophecy in the Scriptures without the help of the Holy Spirit."

1.21 RSV	TEV
because no prophecy ever came by the impulse of man, but men moved by the Holy Spirit spoke from God.[e] [e]Others authorities read *moved by the Holy Spirit holy men of God spoke*	For no prophetic message ever came just from the will of man, but men were under the control of the Holy Spirit as they spoke the message that came from God.

no prophecy ever came by the impulse of man: "no prophetic message was ever produced by a person speaking alone," or "the prophets did not speak on their own," or "the prophets' message was not the result of their own will."

men moved by the Holy Spirit: "men guided (or, controlled) by the Holy Spirit," "men who were under the direction of God's Spirit."

spoke from God: "spoke a message that came from God."

The two clauses can be combined into one, as follows: "For the prophets always spoke their messages as they were guided by the Holy Spirit, and not under their own direction."

As the RSV footnote indicates, there is a variant Greek text; the text represented by RSV and TEV, however, has greater manuscript support.

Chapter 2

SECTION HEADING

False Teachers: "Warnings against False Teachers," "The Danger of Wrong Teachings."

In this section, verses 1-22, the writer warns his readers against the false teachers whose heretical doctrines and immoral way of life are very dangerous to the Christian faith. But it is not only their teachings that are dangerous but also their immoral way of life. There is no way of determining exactly what heretical doctrines those false teachers were spreading among the Christians of that time.

Some translators may wish to indicate that this section is parallel to Jude 4-13. This can be done by placing this reference within parentheses immediatly below the section heading.

2.1

RSV

But false prophets also arose among the people, just as there will be false teachers among you, who will secretly bring in destructive heresies, even denying the Master who bought them, bringing upon themselves swift destruction.

TEV

False prophets appeared in the past among the people, and in the same way false teachers will appear among you. They will bring in destructive, untrue doctrines, and will deny the Master who redeemed them, and so they will bring upon themselves sudden destruction.

false prophets: this means either men who claimed to be prophets and were not, or else prophets whose message was false. Probably the former is meant: "men who claim to have a message from God but do not" (see "false apostles" in 2 Cor 11.13; "false prophets" in Matt 24.11).

arose: "appeared" (TEV). Or "There were false prophets...."

the people: "the people of Israel."

false teachers: "who claim to teach (Christian) truths but do not."

will secretly bring in: this translates the verb that in 1.5 is translated supplement (TEV "add"). The idea of secrecy is not necessarily part of the meaning of the Greek verb, but in this context it is probably intended: "they will introduce without anyone noticing it."

destructive heresies: "teachings that are untrue and dangerous." The nature of the heretical teachings is not defined, but they are so strong and so dangerous that they can destroy genuine Christian faith. It may be necessary to say explicitly in translation in what way the heretical doctrines are destructive.

denying: "rejecting," "disowning." These people have abandoned the Christian faith.

the Master who bought them: the title Master (see Jude 4) for Jesus Christ goes well with the function attributed to him by the verb bought; he is like a master who buys a slave. Here the verb is used in a spiritual sense, "redeemed" (TEV), "freed," or "saved" (see the same verb in 1 Cor 6.20; see a similar idea in 1 Peter 1.18-19).

bringing upon themselves: "as a result they will bring upon themselves." Their destruction by God will be their own fault. He will condemn them to be punished for their sins (see 3.7).

The verse may be translated as follows:

> Among the people of Israel there were men who falsely claimed to be God's messengers. In the same way there will come into your group leaders who will teach false doctrines. They will spread false and dangerous teachings among you, and they will even reject Jesus Christ as their Master, the one who saved them from their sins.

2.2 RSV	TEV
And many will follow their licentiousness, and because of them the way of truth will be reviled.	**Even so, many will follow their immoral ways; and because of what they do, others will speak evil of the Way of truth.**

TEV "Even so" is meant to emphasize the sin of those believers who will imitate the evil ways of the false teachers.

many will follow their licentiousness: "many believers will imitate their immoral behavior" or "...will do the same immoral things they do."

licentiousness is immoral behavior, a complete disregard for morality, especially in sexual conduct.

because of them: that is, because of the way the many believers will behave, as they imitate the false teachers. So TEV has "and because of what they do."

the way of truth: the gospel, the Christian faith.

will be reviled: "will be insulted" by nonbelievers (see similar idea in Rom 2.24). "People will speak evil of the Way of truth." It may be clearer to say "people will say bad things about the gospel, which teaches the true way people should live."

The verse may be translated as follows:

> Many believers will do the same immoral things the false teachers do. And nonbelievers will see the believers acting this way, and they will say evil things about the Christian faith.

2.3 RSV	TEV
And in their greed they will exploit you with false words; from of old their condemnation has not been idle, and their destruction has not been asleep.	**In their greed these false teachers will make a profit out of telling you made-up stories. For a long time now their Judge has been ready, and their Destroyer has been wide awake!**

in their greed: "because they are greedy." The writer is talking about the false teachers, and the translation should make this clear.

will exploit you: "they will make a profit off of you." It seems fairly clear here that the verb is used in the sense of making money. The false teachers will enrich themselves through teaching their heresies to the readers of this Letter.

false words: "false teachings," "heretical doctrines." These are doctrines that they themselves make up; they are not the true teachings of the Christian faith.

from of old: the condemnation of these false teachers was predicted long ago.

has not been idle: "has been ready" (TEV), "was not made lightly," "is not an empty threat." The writer means that the condemnation that God long ago decided for them was not a meaningless threat, but was real and will be put into effect.

their destruction has not been asleep: "the destruction that awaits them is still in effect." The text speaks of the abstract concepts of condemnation and destruction, which are actually events; it may be easier to speak of God, who condemns and destroys. So TEV has used personal terms, "their Judge" and "their Destroyer."

The verse may be translated as follows:

Those false teachers are greedy, and they will make money out of teaching you false doctrines. Long ago God condemned them and decided to destroy them. God does not sleep, and he will punish them as he said he would.

2.4

RSV	TEV
For if God did not spare the angels when they sinned, but cast them into hell[f] and committed them to pits of nether gloom to be kept until the judgment;	God did not spare the angels who sinned, but threw them into hell, where they are kept chained in darkness,[c] waiting for the Day of Judgment.
[f]Greek *Tartarus*	[c]chained in darkness; *some manuscripts have* in dark pits.

RSV follows the structure of the Greek text and has verses 4-10 as one sentence, which is made up of several conditional statements, if...if...if...if (verses 4,5,6,7), followed by the conclusion, then the Lord knows how (verses 9-10a). Verse 8 is a parenthetical statement, designed to explain more fully Lot's predicament.

This is a very complicated sentence, and no translation should try to imitate it. TEV divides the material into six sentences, but even these may need further restructuring into simpler sentences.

God did not spare: "God punished," "God did not let go unpunished."

the angels when they sinned: it is better to translate "the angels who sinned" (TEV). The writer does not say what sin the angels committed, but the reference is probably to the story about the sons of God or "heavenly beings," in Genesis 6.1-4. Jude 6 speaks of "the angels who did not stay within the limits of their proper authority" (TEV). According to certain Jewish writings not found in the Old Testament some angels rebelled against God and were punished by him.

hell: as the RSV footnote shows, the Greek text says "Tartarus," which in Greek mythology was the lowest place in Hades, reserved for the gods who were defeated by Zeus.

pits of nether gloom: "dark holes in hell." Here a further description of hell, or Tartarus, is given. TEV follows a different Greek text, "in chains of darkness," which it translates "chained in darkness." This is the text of the UBS Greek New Testament, and it has better manuscript support.

to be kept until the judgment: "to be imprisoned (or, chained) until the Day of Judgment," at which time they will be punished.

The verse may be translated as follows:

> We know (or, You remember) that God punished the angels who sinned. He threw them into hell, where they are kept chained in the darkness until the Day of Judgment.

2.5 RSV	TEV
if he did not spare the ancient world, but preserved Noah, a herald of righteousness, with seven other persons, when he brought a flood upon the world of the ungodly;	God did not spare the ancient world, but brought the flood on the world of godless people; the only ones he saved were Noah, who preached righteousness, and seven other people.

if he did not spare the ancient world: following the proposal for verse 4, this could begin: "We know that God punished (the people of) the ancient world" or "...the people who lived a very long time ago." This is the world of the time of Noah.

preserved Noah...with seven other persons: these are Noah and his wife, and their three sons and their wives, a total of eight (Gen 7.7; 8.18).

a herald of righteousness: "a man who proclaimed righteousness," which here means right conduct, moral behavior, as commanded by God. So the translation can be "a man who told people how God wanted them to live."

brought a flood upon the world of the ungodly: "caused a great flood to cover the world, which was inhabited by ungodly people."

The following may serve as a model for translating this verse:

> We know (or, You remember) that God also punished the godless people who lived a very long time ago. He sent a great flood on all of them, which killed them, but he rescued Noah and seven other people. Noah was a man who proclaimed a righteous way of life.

2.6 RSV	TEV
if by turning the cities of Sodom and Gomorrah to ashes he condemned them to extinction and made them an example to those who were to be ungodly;	God condemned the cities of Sodom and Gomorrah, destroying them with fire, and made them an example of what will happen to the godless.

by turning the cities of Sodom and Gomorrah to ashes: "he caused fire to burn up the cities of Sodom and Gomorrah." The Greek verb "reduce to ashes" means "to burn up completely," "to completely destroy by fire." The account is found in Genesis 19.24-25.

condemned them to extinction: "condemned them to be destroyed."

those who were to be ungodly: "godless people who would live at a later time." The word translated example can be "warning" (see Jude 7) or "object lesson." All godless people are to be destroyed as were the godless people of Sodom and Gomorrah.

The verse may be translated as follows:

We know (or, You remember) that God condemned (the people of) the cities of Sodom and Gomorrah, and he destroyed them with fire. In this way he made them an example (or, a warning) of what will happen to godless people.

2.7 RSV	TEV
and if he rescued righteous Lot, greatly distressed by the licentiousness of the wicked	**He rescued Lot, a good man, who was distressed by the immoral conduct of lawless people.**

he rescued righteous Lot: "he rescued Lot, a good (or, moral) man." The story is told in Genesis 19.1-16,29.

greatly distressed: this refers to Lot, who was upset by the immoral behavior of the people of Sodom.

licentiousness: see 2.2.

the wicked: "lawless people" (TEV), "morally corrupt."

The verse may be translated as follows:

We know (or, You remember) that God rescued Lot, who was a good man. Lot was greatly upset by the immoral behavior of the wicked (or, lawless) people (of Sodom).

2.8 RSV	TEV
(for by what that righteous man saw and heard as he lived among them, he was vexed in his righteous soul day after day with their lawless deeds),	**That good man lived among them, and day after day he suffered agony as he saw and heard their evil actions.**

RSV places this verse within parentheses, which makes it very difficult to connect verse 7 to verse 9. It seems better to follow the example of TEV and make of verse 8 a separate sentence.

that righteous man: as in verse 7.

he was vexed in his righteous soul: this repeats essentially the statement in verse 7, greatly distressed. The verb here in verse 8 is a strong one, "he suffered" (TEV), "he was tormented."

their lawless deeds: "their wicked (or, evil) actions."

The various elements in this verse should be carefully connected to one another, and this verse should follow naturally after verse 7. Needless repetitions should be avoided. Something like the following may be said: "That good man lived among those evil people. Day after day he suffered great agony because of the evil things he saw and heard them doing."

2.9 RSV	TEV
then the Lord knows how to rescue the godly from trial, and to keep the unrighteous under punishment until the day of judgment,	And so the Lord knows how to rescue godly people from their trials and how to keep the wicked under punishment for the Day of Judgment,

then the Lord knows how: it is better to begin a new sentence here. This is the conclusion of the series of "if" clauses beginning at verse 4: "All of this shows (or, proves) that the Lord knows how." Here the Lord is God.

rescue: as in verse 7.

trial: "difficulties," "hardships."

to keep the unrighteous under punishment: "to punish evil people as he guards them (or, keeps them imprisoned) until the Day of Judgment." It may be that the Greek text means "to keep evil people imprisoned until the Day of Judgment, when they will be punished."

2.10a RSV	TEV
and especially those who indulge in the lust of defiling passion and despise authority.	especially those who follow their filthy bodily lusts and despise God's authority.

those who indulge in the lust of defiling passion: here the writer picks out those who are particularly deserving of punishment. It may be well to begin a new sentence: "Above all, God will punish the people who indulge in filthy (or, immoral) sexual habits." The phrase defiling passion may be translated "lusts (or, desires) that corrupt a person spiritually." This may be a reference to homosexual acts (see Jude 7).

despise authority: TEV takes this to mean "despise God's authority." It could be human authority, either of the state or of the church.

2.10b RSV	TEV
Bold and wilful, they are not afraid to revile the glorious ones,	These false teachers are bold and arrogant, and show no respect for the glorious beings above; instead, they insult them.

Bold and wilfil, they: the writer is talking about the false teachers, and it is necessary to make this explicit: "Those false teachers are bold and arrogant."

they are not afraid to revile the glorious ones: by the glorious ones the writer means angels, perhaps of a certain order. TEV translates "the glorious beings above" (see Jude 8). This could be "the powerful angels in heaven." Since these are distinguished from the angels of verse 11, it is possible that they belong to a distinct class. TEV takes the verbal phrase "they are not afraid of" (literally "they do not tremble at") to have "glorious beings" as the object: "show no respect for the glorious beings above." The following participle, "insulting," is taken by TEV to represent an additional idea, "they insult (them)." But the exegesis represented by RSV is also possible and most translations follow it.

2.11 RSV	TEV
whereas angels, though greater in might and power, do not pronounce a reviling judgment upon them before the Lord.	**Even the angels, who are so much stronger and mightier than these false teachers, do not accuse them with insults in the presence of the Lord.**

angels...greater in might and power: that is, they are greater and more powerful than the false teachers (see TEV). The respect shown by the angels is in contrast with the arrogant attitude of the false teachers.

do not pronounce a reviling judgment on them: "do not accuse (or, condemn) them with insulting words."

before the Lord: "in God's presence." This seems to imply a scene in heaven, where the glorious ones are being tried. There is no indication of what the writer had in mind: the passage probably refers to what is found in Jude 9.

2.12 RSV	TEV
But these, like irrational animals, creatures of instinct, born to be caught and killed, reviling in matters of which they are ignorant, will be destroyed in the same destruction with them,	But these men act by instinct, like wild animals born to be captured and killed; they attack with insults anything they do not understand. They will be destroyed like wild animals,

these: the false teachers.

irrational animals: "wild animals" (TEV), "animals without reasoning powers."

creatures of instinct: "they act by instinct."

born to be caught and killed: this applies to the wild animals, to whom the writer is comparing the false teachers. "They are like wild animals that are born to be captured and killed" or "...that exist only to be captured and killed."

reviling in matters of which they are ignorant: "they insult things they do not understand," "they speak evil of matters they know nothing about" (see Jude 10).

will be destroyed in the same destruction with them: the writer is not saying that the false teachers will be killed when the wild animals are killed, as RSV says. The meaning, as TEV and others express it, is "the false teachers will be killed (or, destroyed) like wild animals (or, as wild animals are)."

A translator should notice that there is no way of knowing whom these and them in the RSV text refer to. See TEV for a clear way to express them.

2.13 RSV	TEV
suffering wrong for their wrong-doing. They count it pleasure to revel in the daytime. They are blots and blemishes, reveling in their dissipation,[g] carousing with you.	and they will be paid with suffering for the suffering they have caused. Pleasure for them is to do anything in broad daylight that will satisfy their bodily appetites; they are a shame and a disgrace as they join you in your meals, all the while enjoying their deceitful ways!

[g]Other ancient authorities read *love feasts*

suffering wrong for their wrongdoing: "they will be made to suffer because of the suffering they caused others" or "because they caused others to suffer, they will also suffer." This phrase, in connection with the preceding they will be destroyed, refers to the final punishment which God will condemn them to on the Judgment Day.

revel translates a noun which in this context means feasting and luxury (see Luke 7.25 "live in luxury"), or any kind of excess including sexual activity. Here it is a matter of carousing, of eating and drinking too much. So TEV has "satisfy their bodily appetites." They do these things in the daytime, whereas they are normally done at night; this is seen as another indication of how immoral these false teachers are.

blots and blemishes: the writer compares them to dirty spots and stains (see in 3.14 the opposite of these two words, without spot or blemish). TEV has abandoned the literal figure and says "a shame and a disgrace" in order to bring out the moral connotation of the two terms.

their dissipation: the Greek word RSV translates dissipation is taken by TEV to mean deception ("their deceitful ways"), and this is more in keeping with the use of the word elsewhere in the New Testament. TEV "enjoying" translates the Greek participle that RSV translates reveling.

carousing with you: "as they feast with you." The Greek verb means "to feast together with." It seems that here the language describes the same situation found in Jude 12, that is, these false teachers joined in the fellowship meals with other believers but were carousing together (see the similar situation in 1 Cor 11.18-22). It does not mean, as RSV seems to indicate, that the false teachers and the readers of this Letter were all carousing together at the fellowship meal.

As the RSV footnote shows, instead of "deceptions," some Greek manuscripts and early versions have "love feasts" (as in Jude 12). RSV and TEV follow the Greek text which has the better manuscript support.

The last sentence (in RSV) in this verse may be translated as follows: "They even join in your fellowship meals, but their conduct is shameful and disgraceful. They enjoy the ways in which they deceive you."

2.14 RSV	TEV
They have eyes full of adultery, insatiable for sin. They entice	They want to look at nothing but immoral women; their appetite

unsteady souls. They have hearts trained in greed. Accursed children!

for sin is never satisfied. They lead weak people into a trap. Their hearts are trained to be greedy. They are under God's curse!

They have eyes full of adultery: this literal translation is intelligible, but in most languages it is not a natural expression. "They can't look at a woman without wanting her," "They want to have sex with every woman they see."

insatiable for sin: this reinforces the preceding statement: "their lust is never satisfied."

They entice unsteady souls: "They trap people whose faith is weak." The "trap" into which the false teachers lead these people is sin and, eventually, destruction. Their victims are weak, that is, their convictions and faith are not firm, and so they are easily misled.

hearts trained in greed: this may not be very intelligible, and so it may be necessary to say "they are ruled (or, dominated) by greed," "they are accustomed to being greedy," "they are experts in getting what they want."

Accursed children!: the Greek phrase "(they are) children of a curse" reflects a Hebrew way of saying "they are cursed by God." In the Bible God's curse is his pronouncement of judgment and punishment on people; so "They will be punished by God," "God will punish them," "They are doomed to destruction."

2.15 RSV

Forsaking the right way they have gone astray; they have followed the way of Balaam, the son of Beor, who loved gain from wrongdoing,

TEV

They have left the straight path and have lost their way; they have followed the path taken by Balaam son of Beor, who loved the money he would get for doing wrong

the right way is the way of the gospel, of the truth.

gone astray: "are lost," "don't know which way to go."

they have followed the way of Balaam, the son of Beor: "they have done what Balaam, the son of Beor, did." Since at the close of verse 16 Balaam is called a prophet, the translation here can be "the prophet Balaam, son of Beor."

loved gain from wrongdoing: "coveted the money he would get by doing the wrong thing." It was for the sake of money that Balaam led the people of Israel to worship false gods (see Num 22—24; 31.16; Jude 11; Rev 2.14).

2.16 RSV

but was rebuked for his own transgression; a dumb ass spoke with human voice and restrained the prophet's madness.

TEV

and was rebuked for his sin. His donkey spoke with a human voice and stopped the prophet's insane action.

was rebuked for his own transgression: this refers to Balaam's donkey, who reprimanded Balaam (see Num 22.28).

a dumb ass spoke: here dumb means "mute," "unable to speak." A donkey does not speak human language; in this case, however, one did.

restrained the prophet's madness: "stopped Balaam from his insane (or, stupid) action," "he kept Balaam from acting foolishly."

Verses 15-16 may be translated as follows:

These false teachers have left the right way, the way of the gospel, to follow the way taken by the prophet Balaam, son of Beor. Balaam was willing to commit sin in order to make money (or, Balaam wanted to make money by doing what was wrong). 16 But his donkey stopped him from acting foolishly. The animal spoke with a human voice, and scolded him for his sin.

2.17

RSV	TEV
These are waterless springs and mists driven by a storm; for them the nether gloom of darkness has been reserved.	**These men are like dried-up springs, like clouds blown along by a storm; God has reserved a place for them in the deepest darkness.**

are waterless springs: it may be better to use a simile, "they are like dried-up springs," "they are like pools without water," "they are like waterless fountains."

mists driven by a storm: "like clouds blown along by a strong wind." Both figures, the dried-up springs and the clouds, indicate that the false teachers are worthless and that they will disappear.

the nether gloom of darkness: "the darkest places in hell" (see Jude 13). Sheol was thought of as a dark pit in the depths of the earth.

has been reserved: by God (see TEV). That is where God will send them on the Judgment Day (see verse 9).

2.18

RSV	TEV
For, uttering loud boasts of folly, they entice with licentious passions of the flesh men who have barely escaped from those who live in error.	**They make proud and stupid statements, and use immoral bodily lusts to trap those who are just beginning to escape from among people who live in error.**

uttering loud boasts of folly: "with loud shouts they make foolish boasts," "they make proud and stupid claims."

entice: as in verse 14.

licentious passions of the flesh: "immoral bodily desires," "evil desires and sexual lusts (or, cravings)."

barely escaped from those who live in error: this is a way of referring to recent converts to the Christian faith, people who by accepting the faith have freed themselves from the doom that awaits the pagan society in which they live. The adverb barely here is more an indication of time than of chance of success: "they have just begun to escape," "they recently escaped."

those who live in error: this is a description of the pagans, who did not follow the truth of the gospel. The recent converts to the Christian faith had been pagans, but now are no longer like them.

2.19 RSV	TEV
They promise them freedom, but they themselves are slaves of corruption; for whatever overcomes a man, to that he is enslaved.	**They promise them freedom while they themselves are slaves of destructive habits—for a person is a slave of anything that has conquered him.**

They promise them freedom: "The false teachers promise people spiritual freedom." This is not physical freedom, but freedom from rules and regulations.

are slaves of corruption: "are controlled by sin." Here corruption may be thought of as meaning sins that corrupt and defile spiritually (see 1.4); it is possible that it means "destruction" (as in verse 12), but this seems unlikely.

whatever overcomes a man: "any force (or, power) that conquers a person." It is more natural to reverse the elements in this statement and say "a person becomes a slave to anything that conquers him."

2.20 RSV	TEV
For if, after they have escaped the defilements of the world through the knowledge of our Lord and Savior Jesus Christ, they are again entangled in them and overpowered, the last state has become worse for them than the first.	**If people have escaped from the corrupting forces of the world through their knowledge of our Lord and Savior Jesus Christ, and then are again caught and conquered by them, such people are in worse condition at the end than they were at the beginning.**

Verses 20-21 say that converts to the Christian faith who abandon the faith are worse off than people who never became Christians.

the defilements of the world: this is a way of speaking about sin, which defiles and corrupts a person spiritually (see defiling in 2.10).

through the knowledge of: "because they know." This is the way Christians escape being corrupted by the sinful world. A noun or verb for knowledge should be used that means to know intimately and personally (see 1.2). This is the kind of knowledge that saves, a knowledge that leads to a personal relationship of trust and obedience.

our Lord and Savior Jesus Christ: the our includes all Christians.

entangled: the defilements are thought of as a noose, or as chains that tie a person up. Or the translation may say "gets involved with those things," "gets caught up in them." It means to go back to former sinful habits.

<u>the last state has become worse</u>: "they are in worse condition at the end" or "their condition becomes worse than it was at the beginning."

The verse may be translated as follows:

> People are saved from the corrupting sins of the world because of their knowledge of (or, relation to) our Lord and Savior Jesus Christ. But if they go back to their old ways and become slaves to sinful habits again, then their situation is much worse than it was before they knew Jesus Christ.

2.21

RSV	TEV
For it would have been better for them never to have known the way of righteousness than after knowing it to turn back from the holy commandment delivered to them.	It would have been much better for them never to have known the way of righteousness than to know it and then turn away from the sacred command that was given them.

<u>the way of righteousness</u>: this is the way of the gospel, "the right way," "the way that God wants people to live."

<u>after knowing it to turn back</u>: "to turn back to their old (sinful) way after they had started following the right way."

<u>the holy commandment delivered to them</u> is the one contained in the gospel message, with its spiritual and moral requirements, handed down from Jesus Christ by the apostles to believers. See Jude 3.

The verse may be translated as follows:

> Those people would be in a better condition if they had never known the gospel, which shows the way God wants people to live. But when they turn away from the gospel message, which they received (from the apostles), then they are in a worse condition than at first.

2.22

RSV	TEV
It has happened to them according to the true proverb, The dog turns back to his own vomit, and the sow is washed only to wallow in the mire.	What happened to them shows that the proverbs are true: "A dog goes back to what it has vomited" and "A pig that has been washed goes back to roll in the mud."

<u>according to the true proverb</u>: since two proverbs are quoted, it may be better to use the plural "proverbs," as TEV does. "What happens to them shows that the following proverbs are true." "In their case the truth of these two proverbs is shown."

The first proverb is "A dog goes back to what it has vomited" (see Prov 26.11).

The second proverb is "A pig that has been washed goes back to roll in the mud" (TEV). In each case, the implied conclusion is: "A dog that goes back...is in a worse condition" and "A pig that goes back... is in a worse condition"—and this may need to be said explicitly. Or, after citing the proverbs, the verse can end as follows: "Both animals are then in a worse condition then they were at first."

Chapter 3

SECTION HEADING

The Promise of the Lord's Coming: "Be Ready for the Lord's Return," "Jesus Christ Will Come Soon."

In this section, verses 1-18, the writer stresses the fact that the Lord's coming will be sudden and unexpected. There are people who will make fun of this hope and say that Christ's return had been promised a long time ago, yet he had not returned. The Lord is being patient with his people, and believers should always be ready for his coming.

3.1

RSV	TEV
This is now the second letter that I have written to you, beloved, and in both of them I have aroused your sincere mind by way of reminder;	My dear friends, this is now the second letter I have written you. In both letters I have tried to arouse pure thoughts in your minds by reminding you of these things.

the second letter that I have written to you: this refers to 1 Peter as the first letter.

beloved: "dear friends" (TEV), "dear fellow believers."

I have aroused...by way of reminder: "I have stirred up...by reminding you"—as in 1.13. It is better to translate "I have tried (or, attempted) to stir up...."

your sincere mind: the adjective translated sincere may mean "pure" as TEV has it ("arouse pure thoughts in your minds"), but in this context it most probably means "correct," "sound," "orthodox." "I have reminded you of these matters, so that you will (continue to) think right (or, have correct thoughts)." The writer does not want them to be misled by the heresies of the false teachers.

3.2

RSV	TEV
that you should remember the predictions of the holy prophets and the commandment of the Lord and Savior through your apostles.	I want you to remember the words that were spoken long ago by the holy prophets, and the command from the Lord and Savior which was given you by your apostles.

that you should remember: RSV continues the sentence through verse 2. It is not very long or complex, and a translator may find it natural to follow RSV's example. But in some languages it may be better to begin a new sentence in verse 2, as TEV does: "I want you to remember."

the predictions of the holy prophets: a prophet is a person who proclaims God's message; sometimes, as in this case, it is a message about things that will happen in the future. The reference here is probably to the Hebrew prophets of the Old Testament, but it could be to Christian prophets of New Testament times. Although not specifically stated, the subject of the prophets' predictions probably is the matter of the day of the Lord (3.10). Here holy is a title of respect, given to the great Hebrew prophets (see Luke 1.70).

the commandment of the Lord and Savior: "what our (or, your) Lord and Savior commanded you to do." This is essentially the gospel message, regarded not only as the Good News of salvation, but also as a way for Christians to live. The reference here is not to one specific command but to the whole moral and spiritual demands of the Christian faith.

through your apostles: the literal translation, as in TEV and RSV, may be taken to mean that these are apostles that were sent out by the readers, or that belonged to the group of the readers. But the meaning here is that Christ's apostles had delivered the gospel message to the readers (see 1.16). So the translation should be "by means of the apostles who delivered (or, proclaimed) the gospel to you."

The verse may be translated as follows: "I want you to remember (or, I want to remind you of) the messages that the holy prophets proclaimed in the past, and of the teaching of our Lord and Savior which was given (or, passed on) to you by the apostles."

3.3 RSV	TEV
First of all you must understand this, that scoffers will come in the last days with scoffing, following their own passions	**First of all, you must understand that in the last days some people will appear whose lives are controlled by their own lusts. They will make fun of you**

First of all: as in 1.20.

scoffers will come...with scoffing: "people who make fun of you (or, of the gospel) will come to you." The phrase with scoffing is a literal translation of the Greek construction, which is an emphatic way of describing them as people whose only interest is in making fun of the Christian faith, or of Christians.

in the last days: this is the time of the Lord's coming, and the writer takes it for granted that the time has already come; he and his readers will see the Lord's return.

following their own passions: "controlled by their (evil) desires," "who serve only their own selfish interests" (see Jude 18).

Verse 3 may be translated as follows:

> It is very important for you to remember this. In the last days people who want only to satisfy their evil desires will come to you. They will make fun of you (or, of your faith).

3.4 RSV

and saying, "Where is the promise of his coming? For ever since the fathers fell asleep, all things have continued as they were from the beginning of creation."

TEV

and will ask, "He promised to come, didn't he? Where is he? Our fathers have already died, but everything is still the same as it was since the creation of the world!"

Where is the promise of his coming?: obviously the text doesn't mean what the RSV literal translation means. The question is not where the promise is, but where is the person or event that has been promised. In English the idiomatic expression is natural: "What happened to the promise that Christ would come (or, return)?" The text itself does not say who made the promise: either Christ himself (see Matt 24.34) or his apostles. If a translation has to be specific, it would seem preferable to name Christ as the one who made the promise (see verse 9, below).

ever since the fathers fell asleep: in this context, the fathers means the immediately preceding generation. "Our fathers (and mothers) have already died." Or "The previous generation has passed away."

all things have continued as they were: "everything is the same as it was," "nothing is different from what it was," "nothing has changed." The people who are making fun of the belief in Christ's return are saying that the world-wide changes promised for the Day of the Lord have not taken place; nothing has changed. The promise had been that Christ would return soon.

the beginning of creation: "the creation of the world" (TEV), "the beginning of time."

3.5-6 RSV

They deliberately ignore this fact, that by the word of God heavens existed long ago, and an earth formed out of water and by means of water, 6 through which the world that then existed was deluged with water and perished.

TEV

They purposely ignore the fact that long ago God gave a command, and the heavens and earth were created. The earth was formed out of water and by water, 6 and it was also by water, the water of the flood, that the old world was destroyed.

They deliberately ignore this fact: "They are not willing to consider this fact." In some languages a figurative expression may be quite meaningful: "They close their eyes to this fact." The writer says that those scoffers purposely ignore a very important fact.

by the word of God: "by means of his word, God" or "God spoke (or, gave an order)." This refers to the account of creation in Genesis 1, where God created the world by his commands.

heavens existed long ago: "the heavens were created a long time ago." The plural heavens follows Hebrew usage (see Gen 1.1); it may reflect the concept of several heavens (either three or seven), from the lowest, the visible sky, to the highest, the dwelling place of God. Here, however, it seems likely that the meaning is best expressed in English by "heaven." The two, heaven and earth, are the whole universe, the whole creation.

There are several ways in which this part of verse 5 may be interpreted. (1) "Heaven has existed from ancient times, and by means of God's word (or, command) the earth was created out of water and by means of water." (2) As RSV and TEV interpret the text: "By means of his command, a very long time ago God created heaven, and he created the earth out of water and by means of water." The second interpretation is followed by most modern translations. It does not seem probable that the writer would have said that heaven had existed from the beginning, and that God's creative command applied only to the earth.

formed out of water: this seems to reflect the creation account in Genesis 1.9-10, that the earth was submerged under the water that covered everything, and at God's command on the third day the water was brought together in one place and the earth emerged, coming up out of the water.

by means of water: or "with water." This seems to be what the Greek text means, that is, that water was the means by which the earth was formed. Some take it to mean "between the waters," that is, the water above the firmament and the water below (see Gen 1.6-7).

through which: RSV is difficult to understand. In Greek the phrase is plural and seems to refer to the water that came down from above and the water that surged up from the depths below (Gen 7.11). The Greek phrase for through which points to water as the means by which the world ...perished. The phrase with water repeats the idea that water is the means of destruction; it is not a separate statement. This repetition is part of the writer's style.

the world that then existed was deluged...and perished: this refers to the Flood, when all life on earth was destroyed, except for the animals and the eight people that survived in Noah's ark.

Verses 5 and 6 may be translated as follows:

> 5-6 These people willfully (or, deliberately) ignore the fact that by means of his command God created heaven and earth (or, created the universe) a very long time ago. He made the earth appear out of the water, and formed it with (or, by means of) water. And it was water, the water of the Flood, that destroyed that world.

3.7 RSV	TEV
But by the same word the heavens and earth that now exist have been stored up for fire, being kept until the day of judgment and destruction of ungodly men.	But the heavens and the earth that now exist are being preserved by the same command of God, in order to be destroyed by fire. They are being kept for the day when godless people will be judged and destroyed.

by the same word: that is, the command of God.

the heavens and earth that now exist: the writer speaks of the original heaven and earth at the time of creation (verse 5); then of the earth that was destroyed by the Flood (verse 6). Here he talks about the universe now in existence, but which will be destroyed at the end.

have been stored up: here this means "kept," "preserved" (TEV). The agent is God's command: "God, by means of his command, is keeping the heaven and earth that exist now."

for fire: "to be destroyed (or, burned up) by fire." The world was destroyed once by water (Gen 7.21-23); it will be destroyed again by fire.

being kept: this repeats the idea expressed by have been stored up (see 2.4).

the day of judgment: as in 2.9. RSV, closely following the Greek text, translates the day of judgment and destruction. TEV expresses the same idea: "the day when godless people will be judged and destroyed." But another way may be used: "the Day of Judgment, when godless people will be destroyed" or "...will be condemned to destruction." God is the one who will destroy them.

ungodly men: "godless people" (TEV), "people who reject (or, do not obey) God" (as in 2.5).

3.8

RSV	TEV
But do not ignore this one fact, beloved, that with the Lord one day is as a thousand years, and a thousand years as one day.	But do not forget one thing, my dear friends! There is no difference in the Lord's sight between one day and a thousand years; to him the two are the same.

do not ignore this one fact: the writer calls the readers' attention to a very important fact that shows how silly is the argument of the people who make fun of the belief in Christ's return.

beloved: see 3.1.

the Lord: Jesus Christ, as in verse 2.

one day is as a thousand years, and a thousand years as one day: the writer is saying that the Lord does not measure time as human beings do; he is not bound by time. From his point of view there is no difference between one day and a thousand years. The verse reflects the thought of Psalm 90.4. If the exact figure one thousand years is difficult or impossible to express, it may be necessary to say something like this: "The Lord doesn't measure time as we do. For him there is no difference between one day and many years. We think a day is a short time and many years are a long time, but they are the same to him." Such wording leads forward naturally to the next verse.

3.9

RSV	TEV
The Lord is not slow about his promise as some count slowness, but is forbearing toward you,[h] not wishing that any should perish, but that all should reach repentance.	The Lord is not slow to do what he has promised, as some think. Instead, he is patient with you, because he does not want anyone to be destroyed, but wants all to turn away from their sins.

[h]Other ancient authorities read *on your account*

is not slow about his promise: "does not delay to keep his promise," "is not slow to do what he promised" (TEV).

as some count slowness: "as some people say (or, think) he is." He is referring to the people who were mocking.

is forbearing toward you: "is patient with you" (TEV). As the RSV footnote shows, some Greek manuscripts and early versions have "is patient on your account." The writer explains that the delay in the coming of Christ is not because he is not prompt to keep his promise, but because he is merciful. He does not want to condemn and destroy anyone; he wants all people to repent of their sins and be saved.

perish: this refers to spiritual death, eternal death.

repentance: "turning away from sin," "changing one's mind (or, attitude)." The phrase reach repentance means "to repent," "to turn from sin and to God."

3.10

RSV

But the day of the Lord will come like a thief, and then the heavens will pass away with a loud noise, and the elements will be dissolved with fire, and the earth and the works that are upon it will be burned up.

TEV

But the Day of the Lord will come like a thief. On that Day the heavens will disappear with a shrill noise, the heavenly bodies will burn up and be destroyed, and the earth with everything in it will vanish.[d]

[d]**vanish;** *some manuscripts have* **be found;** *others have* **be burned up;** *one has* **be found destroyed.**

the day of the Lord: "the day of the Lord's return (or, coming)," "the day when the Lord will come."

will come like a thief: that is, suddenly and without advance warning (see Matt 24.43-44; Luke 12.39-40). It may be necessary to make the manner of coming explicit: "it will come as unexpectedly as a thief." If the figure like a thief is difficult for the readers, the idea may be expressed by "will come when no one is expecting it," "will come (suddenly and) unexpectedly."

the heavens will pass away with a loud noise: "heaven will disappear with a roar." The word translated a loud noise means "a rushing sound." Since the destruction is by fire, it may be that the word is descriptive of the crackling noise made by flames.

the elements: the Greek word may be used in the sense that the Greek philosophers used it, referring to the four elements out of which all matter (in their opinion) is composed: earth, air, water, fire. Another meaning of the word is the heavenly bodies: the sun, moon, and stars. This is how TEV and others translate it; some say simply "the stars," which may be preferable in some translations.

will be dissolved with fire: "will be destroyed by fire," "will burn up and be destroyed" (TEV).

the earth and the works that are upon it: "the earth and everything on it." This includes all natural features and all man-made constructions.

will be burned up: as the TEV text ("will vanish") and footnote show, there is considerable uncertainty about the original text here. The text with the best evidence in its favor is "will be found." Some translations take this to mean "will be laid bare," "will be exposed." Others take it to mean "will be subject to God's judgment" or "will be disclosed." There are attempts to make sense of the verb (in the passive voice) "to find," but they do not seem convincing. Another way of dealing with this text is to punctuate it as a rhetorical question, "Will the earth and everything on it remain (or, survive)?" The implied answer is "No." This solution seems most unlikely.

The best solution is to follow either the RSV will be burned up or TEV "will vanish." A footnote should be added, indicating that there is uncertainty about the original text.

3.11 RSV	TEV
Since all these things are thus to be dissolved, what sort of persons ought you to be in lives of holiness and godliness,	**Since all these things will be destroyed in this way, what kind of people should you be? Your lives should be holy and dedicated to God,**

Since all these things are thus to be dissolved: "Since everything is going to be destroyed like this." The writer is saying: the universe will be destroyed; that is a fact. What effect should that fact have on believers?

RSV continues an uninterrupted sentence to the end of verse 12. It is better to divide and simplify, as TEV has done. Instead of the TEV question and answer form, however, some other construction may be better. "We know that everything (or, the whole universe) will be destroyed in this way. This means, then, that you should be holy and godly in your behavior." The two words holiness and godliness are here quite synonymous; see godliness in 1.3. The meaning may be expressed by "lives completely dedicated to God." "You should always obey God's will." This kind of life has already been described in 1.5-7.

3.12 RSV	TEV
waiting for and hastening[i] the coming of the day of God, because of which the heavens will be kindled and dissolved, and the elements will melt with fire!	**as you wait for the Day of God and do your best to make it come soon—the Day when the heavens will burn up and be destroyed, and the heavenly bodies will be melted by the heat.**

[i]Or *earnestly desiring*

waiting for: "as you wait for" (TEV).

hastening the coming of the day of God: this seems to be what the Greek text means (the RSV footnote has another possible interpretation of the text, but this seems less likely). So TEV has "do your best to make it come soon." The thought behind this is that by holy living and the active proclamation of the gospel, believers will make the Lord come sooner.

the day of God is the same as the day of the Lord (Jesus) in verse 10. Here it may be necessary to say "the day when God will judge the world."

because of which: this is difficult to understand, and it is better to begin a new sentence here: "That day will be the time when," or "That is the day when," or, more simply, "On that day."

the heavens will be kindled and dissolved: "heaven will be destroyed by fire," "a blazing fire will destroy heaven."

the elements will melt with fire: see the similar statement in verse 10. Here the verb "to melt" is used; there the verb "to destroy" is used.

3.13 RSV	TEV
But according to his promise we wait for new heavens and a new earth in which righteousness dwells.	But we wait for what God has promised: new heavens and a new earth, where righteousness will be at home.

According to his promise: "because he promised it."

we wait: this includes all believers. "We look forward to," "we expect."

new heavens and a new earth: this means that believers look forward to living in a new universe, after the present one has been destroyed by fire.

righteousness: as in 2.5, this is God's rule, God's will. In essence this is the same as the Kingdom of God. It may be impossible to speak of the abstract quality righteousness living, or dwelling, somewhere. So it may be necessary to say "In that new world (or, universe) everything will be done according to God's will." Or "Everyone will obey God completely in that new universe (or, world)."

3.14 RSV	TEV
Therefore, beloved, since you wait for these, be zealous to be found by him without spot or blemish, and at peace.	And so, my friends, as you wait for that Day, do your best to be pure and faultless in God's sight and to be at peace with him.

beloved: as in 3.1,8.

since you wait for these: "as you wait for that Day" (TEV), "as you wait for those things to happen."

be zealous to be found by him: "do your best that God will find you" or "...that in God's sight you will be...." This idiomatic use of the verb "to find" means to be in a certain situation or condition, as judged by the one who "finds." The reference is to the final Day and to the kind of people they will be when they face God on that Day. The verb translated be zealous is the same one that in verse 12 is translated by TEV "do your best."

without spot or blemish: "pure and faultless" (TEV), "completely without sin" (see 2.13).

at peace: "at peace with God." Or it could mean the believer's inner security and confidence.

The verse may be translated as follows:

> My dear fellow believers, we are all (confidently) waiting for the day of God to come. While you wait, do your best to appear before God on that Day at peace with him, and without any sins or faults.

3.15 RSV	TEV
And count the forbearance of our Lord as salvation. So also our beloved brother Paul wrote to you according to the wisdom given him,	Look on our Lord's patience as the opportunity he is giving you to be saved, just as our dear brother Paul wrote to you, using the wisdom that God gave him.

count...as salvation: "consider (or, regard)...an opportunity for you to be saved." Here salvation refers to the final act of the process, where believers will be in the very presence of God.

the forbearance of our Lord: see 3.9.

To strengthen his appeal, the writer reminds his readers of what our beloved brother Paul had written to them. Here our is inclusive.

according to the wisdom given him: "in keeping with the wisdom that God gave him." Or, as a complete sentence: "God made Paul wise, and so he wrote you about this same matter" or "...he gave you good advice when he wrote you about this."

The following may serve as a model for translating this verse:

> The Lord is patient, and you must regard his patience as an opportunity he gives for you to be saved. Our dear brother Paul wrote the same thing to you, guided by the wisdom that God had given him.

3.16 RSV	TEV
speaking of this as he does in all his letters. There are some things in them hard to understand, which the ignorant and unstable twist to their own destruction, as they do the other scriptures.	This is what he says in all his letters when he writes on the subject. There are some difficult things in his letters which ignorant and unstable people explain falsely, as they do with other passages of the Scriptures. So they bring on their own destruction.

speaking of this as he does in all his letters: it is better to follow TEV and end verse 15 with a full stop, beginning verse 16 as a new sentence. "This is what he says in all his letters as he writes about these matters (or, subjects)." The subject is the Lord's coming.

things...hard to understand: "matters which are hard to understand." The writer does not say what subjects Paul wrote about that are difficult to understand.

ignorant and unstable: "ignorant and immature." The same Greek word for unstable is used in 2.14, unsteady. Here also it means Christians who are not mature and have no firm convictions or beliefs.

twist: "misinterpret," "misapply," "change the meaning of," "explain wrongly." The word seems to mean a willful misinterpretation of the text.

to their own destruction: by misinterpreting what Paul wrote, these people are bringing about their own destruction on Judgment Day.

as they do the other scriptures: that is, they also misinterpret the other scriptures. Scriptures could refer to some New Testament writings, but it probably refers to the Old Testament. The word other implies that Paul's letters are classified as Scriptures. The Greek could mean "as they also misinterpret his other writings," but the most natural reading is, as RSV and TEV have it, the other scriptures.

The verse may be translated as follows:

> Some passages in Paul's letters are hard to understand. Untrained and immature people change the meaning of those passages, as they do other passages of the Scriptures. Because they do this they are bringing about their own destruction on the Day of Judgment.

3.17 RSV	TEV
You therefore, beloved, knowing this beforehand, beware lest you be carried away with the error of lawless men and lose your own stability.	But you, my friends, already know this. Be on your guard, then, so that you will not be led away by the errors of lawless people and fall from your safe position.

beloved: as in 3.1.

knowing this beforehand: "since you have been warned about this ahead of time," "because you already know these matters."

beware: "take care," "be careful," "look out for yourselves."

be carried away with the error of lawless men: "be led into error by lawless (or, evil) people." Here, as in 2.7 (RSV the wicked, TEV "lawless people"), the lawless are the morally corrupt false teachers, spoken about in chapter 2.

lose your own stability: this is moral and spiritual firmness and integrity, which the readers have as opposed to unsteady (2.14) and unstable (3.16) people. See 1.12, established in the truth.

3.18 RSV	TEV
But grow in the grace and knowledge of our Lord and Savior Jesus Christ. To him be the glory both now and to the day of eternity. Amen.	But continue to grow in the grace and knowledge of our Lord and Savior Jesus Christ. To him be the glory, now and forever! Amen.

grow: "develop," "continue to go forward," "progress."

in the grace and knowledge of our Lord and Savior Jesus Christ. It may not be possible to use one verb for both of these ideas. To grow in the grace of Jesus Christ means to develop spiritually, to keep on experiencing more of Christ's great love (see 1.2). In a broader sense, grace here can be understood to be equivalent to the Christian experience as a whole. The command then means "keep on becoming better Christians" or "keep on living more closely to Christ, who loves you."

The second command, to grow in the knowledge of Jesus Christ, means to continue to develop a closer, or better, relationship with Christ, to know him better through a personal relationship to him.

It is possible to take the Greek to mean "Grow in grace, and grow also in your knowledge of our Lord and Savior Jesus Christ." But this does not seem as probable as the interpretation followed by RSV and TEV. In some languages the two titles Lord and Savior may have to be expressed by a verbal phrase, "Jesus Christ, who saved us and rules over us."

To him be the glory: this is a prayer, and it may be taken as a prayer of thanksgiving, "Let us praise Christ for his glory." Here glory means "majesty," or "greatness," or "divine power." Or the meaning can be expressed, "Let us praise and honor Christ."

both now and to the day of eternity: "now and until the end of time," "now and forever" (TEV).

Amen: "So be it," "It is so."

The following may serve as a model for the translation of this verse:

> You must live in such a way that you will experience more and more of the love of our Lord and Savior Jesus Christ and know him better. Let us praise and honor Christ, now and for all time to come. Amen.

An Outline of Jude

1. Introduction 1-2
2. False Teachers Condemned 3-16
3. Exhortation to Christian Living 17-23
4. Closing Doxology 24-25

Title

THE LETTER FROM JUDE

For the title see comments on the title of 1 Peter.

1-2

RSV

Jude, a servant of Jesus Christ and brother of James,

To those who are called, beloved in God the Father and kept for Jesus Christ:

2 May mercy, peace, and love be multiplied to you.

TEV

From Jude, servant of Jesus Christ, and brother of James—

To those who have been called by God, who live in the love of God the Father and the protection of Jesus Christ:

2 May mercy, peace, and love be yours in full measure.

TEV has no section heading here; if one is desired, something like "Greetings" or "Opening Salutation" may be used. The Letter begins in the usual way, with the writer's name, the recipients, and a greeting.

Jude translates the name in Greek which is also translated Judas (Mark 3.19) and Judah (Matt 1.2-3). In addition to the Jude mentioned in this verse, there are eight men referred to in the New Testament by this name. In English translations, the form Jude has been used only here. Jude and his brother James in this verse have traditionally been identified as brothers of Jesus (Matt 13.55; Mark 6.3; see comments on James 1.1). Languages that have distinct terms for younger and older brother should here assume that James is older than Jude (see Mark 6.3, which suggests, if it does not prove, that James was the oldest of the four brothers listed).

a servant: "one who serves" or "I serve." This refers to Christian ministry and identifies the writer as a Christian leader.

The third person form of the greeting may not be satisfactory, and so it may be better to begin: "I, Jude, a servant of Jesus Christ and a brother of James, write this letter to...." In some languages it will be more natural to have "a servant of Jesus Christ" after "a brother of James."

to those who are called: that is, to Christians. It is God who "calls" a person to salvation, or life, through faith in Christ.

beloved in God the Father: "who are loved by God the Father," "whom God our Father loves." It may be better to say "God our Father" or "God, who is our Father." TEV "who live in the love of God the Father" may be better rendered as "who are certain that God our Father loves them."

It is to be noticed that instead of beloved some Greek manuscripts have "sanctified." There is no doubt that beloved is the original text.

and kept for Jesus Christ: it seems better to translate "and protected by Jesus Christ" or "and whom Jesus Christ protects (or, keeps safe)." This "protection" is of a spiritual nature and may be represented by "cared for by Jesus Christ."

mercy, peace, and love: it may be impossible to speak of these abstract qualities as such, and so it may be necessary to represent them as personal qualities, and to translate each term as a complete clause. Mercy is God's compassion, or kindness; peace is the condition of spiritual well-being which God's people are meant to enjoy; and love is primarily God's love, but may be by extension also the love which Christians have for one another.

be multiplied: see 2 Peter 1.2.

The two verses may be translated as follows:

> I, Jude, a servant of Jesus Christ and a (younger) brother of James, write this letter to all Christians, who are loved by God our Father and are protected by Jesus Christ. I pray that God will always be good to you, that your spiritual well-being will increase, and that your love for one another will grow stronger.

SECTION HEADING

False Teachers: "Warning against False Teachers," "The Danger of Wrong Teachings."

In this section, verses 3-16, Jude explains to his readers why he felt compelled to write to them at this time (verses 3-4). He then goes on to describe and condemn the false teachers who had somehow made their way into the Christian fellowship (verses 5-16).

3

RSV	TEV
Beloved, being very eager to write to you of our common salvation, I found it necessary to write appealing to you to contend for the faith which was once for all delivered to the saints.	**My dear friends, I was doing my best to write to you about the salvation we share in common, when I felt the need of writing at once to encourage you to fight on for the faith which once and for all God has given to his people.**

Beloved: "My dear friends" (TEV), "My dear brothers and sisters," "My dear fellow Christians."

being very eager to write to you: "I was anxious to write to you" or "I was getting ready to write a letter to you."

of our common salvation: "of the salvation we share with one another." Here salvation is synonymous with "the Christian faith (or, religion)"; see common faith in Titus 1.4.

I found it necessary: something happened which caused Jude to write a letter somewhat different from the one he had originally planned. It seems that he received news of the activities of the false teachers, and so he decided to write immediately a letter of warning and condemnation.

appealing: "urging," "exhorting," "encouraging."

contend: "fight for," "defend," "uphold." The Christian faith is being attacked by false teachers, and all true believers should do their best to preserve it.

the faith which once for all was delivered to the saints: the gospel is called the faith, which is regarded as a body of doctrines which all Christians accept and proclaim. The passive verbal phrase once for all delivered means that God is the one who determined the contents of the Christian faith, and he gave it to believers in Jesus Christ to accept and transmit without change.

the saints: "God's people," "believers in Jesus Christ," "Christians." The word reflects the Old Testament designation of the Israelites as a people dedicated to God, a people who belong only to him.

The verse may be translated as follows:

> My dear fellow believers: I was feeling a strong urge to write a letter to you about the (Christian) faith which all believers have. But right now I feel I must write in order to encourage you to do your best to defend the faith which God has given to his people, a faith which cannot be changed.

4 RSV

For admission has been secretly gained by some who long ago were designated for this condemnation, ungodly persons who pervert the grace of our God into licentiousness and deny our only Master and Lord, Jesus Christ.[a]

[a]Or *the only Master and our Lord Jesus Christ*

TEV

For some godless people have slipped in unnoticed among us, persons who distort the message about the grace of our God in order to excuse their immoral ways, and who reject Jesus Christ, our only Master and Lord. Long ago the Scriptures predicted the condemnation they have received.

admission has been secretly gained: this impersonal English phrase translates a Greek verb which means "to enter without being noticed," "to join under false pretenses," "to sneak in," "to creep in undetected." TEV "among us" is inclusive, that is, "among us believers." However, it may be possible that this should be "among you" or "into your group."

long ago were designated for this condemnation: this refers to the punishment that awaits these people, a punishment which had been predicted a long time before. It seems probable that, as TEV indicates, the prediction was made in the Scriptures, and the condemnation, or sentence, passed on them is probably the one prophesied by Enoch (see verses 14-15). The expression this condemnation is a bit strange, since Jude has not mentioned any condemnation explicitly. It may be better to translate "the condemnation they will receive."

pervert the grace of our God into licentiousness: here the grace of our God seems to be a way of speaking about the gospel message concerning God's great love, his goodness to all. The false teachers were distorting the gospel message to justify their immorality. Christian freedom was being made an excuse for immoral behavior.

deny: "disown," "reject," "no longer obey (or, follow)." These people have deserted the faith.

our only Master and Lord, Jesus Christ: although possible, it is not probable that the alternative translation in the RSV footnote is correct: "the only Master and our Lord Jesus Christ."

Both RSV and TEV have all verse 4 in one sentence, and it may be better to restructure the material into two or more sentences, as follows:

> Certain people have joined our group (or, fellowship) without being noticed. A long time ago the punishment of these godless people was predicted in the Scriptures. These people use the message about the goodness (or, love) of God as an excuse for their immoral behavior, and they deny that Jesus Christ is our only Master and Lord.

5

RSV

Now I desire to remind you, though you were once for all fully informed, that he[b] who saved a people out of the land of Egypt, afterward destroyed those who did not believe.

[b]Ancient authorities read *Jesus* or *the Lord* or *God*

TEV

For even though you know all this, I want to remind you of how the Lord[a] once rescued the people of Israel from Egypt, but afterward destroyed those who did not believe.

[a]the Lord; *some manuscripts have* Jesus, *which in Greek is the same as* Joshua.

remind you: "bring again to your attention," "cause you to remember."

you were once for all fully informed: this translates a Greek text that differs from the text translated by TEV. The Greek adverb once for all modifies the verb saved in the text translated by TEV ("once rescued"); in the text translated by RSV it modifies the verb "you know." Most modern translations follow the text translated by TEV.

that he who saved: this translates a conjectural Greek text, that is, one that is not found in any known Greek manuscript but is thought by some scholars to have been the original text. The text with the strongest support in Greek manuscripts is the one cited in the TEV footnote: "that Jesus, who saved." But it is very difficult to think that the writer meant to say that Jesus led the Israelites out of Egypt. As the TEV footnote observes, the proper name in Greek may mean "Joshua" as well as "Jesus"; but Joshua cannot be the one referred to in the statement kept by him in verse 6. (In the Greek text the subject of the verb saved in verse 5 is also the subject of the verb "he has kept" in verse 6.) The Greek text translated by TEV has "the Lord" as the subject of the verb "saved." This is the text adopted by the UBS Greek New Testament and is followed by most modern translations. Here "the Lord" is God.

saved a people out of the land of Egypt: this refers to the Israelites, and so it is better to translate "who rescued the people of

Israel from Egypt" or "who brought the Israelites out of Egypt" or "...out of slavery in Egypt" (see Exo 12.51).

The destruction of those who did not believe is what happened to all the adult Israelites who left Egypt, with the exception of Joshua and Caleb (Num 14.26-35; see 1 Cor 10.5-11; Heb 3.16—4.2). They did not believe that God would give them the victory over the inhabitants of the country they were about to invade.

This verse shows how God dealt with his rebellious people; even though he saved them, he destroyed those who were unfaithful to him.

6 RSV	TEV
And the angels that did not keep their own position but left their proper dwelling have been kept by him in eternal chains in the nether gloom until the judgment of the great day;	Remember the angels who did not stay within the limits of their proper authority, but abandoned their own dwelling place: they are bound with eternal chains in the darkness below, where God is keeping them for that great Day on which they will be condemned.

Jude shows how God dealt with rebellious angels. This story is not told in the Old Testament. Genesis 6.1-4 speaks of heavenly beings who married human females. Based on this account, later Jewish writings not in the Old Testament developed further stories of how angels rebelled and were punished by God (see also the comments on verse 14).

did not keep their own position: "were not content with the place of power that God had given them," "did not observe the proper limits of their authority" (see TEV). The Greek word translated position means "authority," "office," "place of power." The passage does not say why the angels rebelled.

their proper dwelling: "their own dwelling place" (TEV), that is, heaven, in the presence of God. The verb left is somewhat neutral; something like "deserted" or "abandoned" carries greater emotional force.

By implication (see verse 7) the angels indulged in sexual immorality and perversion, which seems to refer to Genesis 6.1-4.

The fate of these rebellious angels is described vividly. God has bound them with eternal chains and placed them in a dark region below, where they will stay until they are condemned on the great Day of Judgment. The dark region below (RSV nether gloom) is Sheol, the world of the dead, or else Tartarus (see 2 Peter 2.4), the special place for rebellious angels.

7 RSV	TEV
just as Sodom and Gomorrah and the surrounding cities, which likewise acted immorally and indulged in unnatural lust, serve as an example by undergoing a	Remember Sodom and Gomorrah, and the nearby towns, whose people acted as those angels did and indulged in sexual immorality and perversion: they suffer the

punishment of eternal fire.	punishment of eternal fire as a plain warning to all.

RSV continues verse 7 as part of the sentence beginning with verse 6, but it is better to start a new sentence here: "They will be punished, like Sodom and Gomorrah" or, like TEV, "Remember Sodom and Gomorrah."

The account of the immoral behavior of the citizens of Sodom and Gomorrah is told in Genesis 19.1-25. The surrounding cities were Admah and Zeboiim (Deut 29.23; see Hos 11.8).

likewise: that is, like the rebellious angels; so TEV "whose people acted as those angels did."

acted immorally and indulged in unnatural lust: "indulged in sexual immorality and perversion" (TEV) or "...and crimes against nature." This is generally interpreted as a reference to homosexual acts (see Rom 1.26-27; 1 Cor 6.9); perhaps bestiality is also intended (Exo 22.19; Lev 20.15-16).

serve as an example: the destruction of these cities and their inhabitants is an example of how God punishes rebellious and immoral people. This example is a warning to others.

eternal fire: Sodom and Gomorrah and the nearby towns were destroyed by fire; it was thought that the fires had kept burning ever since their destruction.

The verse may be translated as follows:

> The people of Sodom and Gomorrah and of the nearby cities acted like those angels; they also indulged in sexual immorality and perversion. Those cities and their inhabitants were destroyed by a fire that burns forever. This punishment serves as a plain warning to all sinners.

8 RSV	TEV
Yet in like manner these men in their dreamings defile the flesh, reject authority, and revile the glorious ones.[c]	In the same way also, these people have visions which make them sin against their own bodies; they despise God's authority and insult the glorious beings above.

[c]Greek *glories*

these men: that is, the false teachers, the godless people referred to in verse 5.

in their dreamings defile the flesh. It is probable that these dreamings are visions (see TEV) or revelations, which they claim to have and through which they gain spiritual knowledge. They claim that their visions justify their immoral conduct, which seems to be what defile the flesh means. TEV represents this by "sin against their own bodies," that is, the immoral use of their sexual powers.

reject authority: that is, God's authority, whether represented by angels or by human beings.

revile the glorious ones: "speak evil of the angels," "say bad things about the heavenly beings." As the RSV footnote shows, the Greek word is "glories"; so TEV "the glorious beings above." This can be translated "the glorious angels in heaven." It is not certain exactly how the false teachers insulted the angels; Jude says that such a thing is blasphemy.

9 RSV	TEV
But when the archangel Michael, contending with the devil, disputed about the body of Moses, he did not presume to pronounce a reviling judgment upon him, but said, "The Lord rebuke you."	Not even the chief angel Michael did this. In his quarrel with the Devil, when they argued about who would have the body of Moses, Michael did not dare condemn the Devil with insulting words, but said, "The Lord rebuke you!"

Some early Christian writers state that the story of Michael's argument with the Devil over the body of Moses is found in a first-century A.D. writing called "The Assumption of Moses." Only parts of this writing remain today, and this story is missing. Michael, who was one of the chief angels, and the Devil both claimed the right to Moses' body. According to the story, the Devil said the body was his because Moses had committed murder.

The point Jude is making is that Michael, even though provoked to anger, did not himself denounce and insult the Devil, who was also regarded as a supernatural being. Instead he called down God's judgment on him.

pronounce a reviling judgment on him: "condemn him with insulting words."

The Lord rebuke you: "May God punish you." The verb usually translated "to rebuke" may here have the stronger meaning of "to punish." There is a clear parallel between this and Zechariah 3.2.

10 RSV	TEV
But these men revile whatever they do not understand, and by those things that they know by instinct as irrational animals do, they are destroyed.	But these people attack with insults anything they do not understand; and those things that they know by instinct, like wild animals, are the very things that destroy them.

these men: the false teachers.

revile whatever they do not understand: "speak evil about matters they do not understand," "attack with insults anything they do not understand" (TEV). It is not clear what the matters are that the false teachers did not understand. The implication seems to be that they were the revealed truths about the Christian faith, the gospel.

The false teachers' knowledge is limited to matters they know by instinct. They are like wild animals, without reasoning powers. Ironically enough, the very things they do know will destroy them, will bring about their ruin.

The verse may be translated as follows: "These people speak insulting words about matters they know nothing about. They do know some things, but they are like wild (or, irrational) animals, and know those things only by instinct. Those very matters will finally destroy them."

In this context, their instinctive knowledge seems to be primarily of sexual activities. Their immoral behavior will finally bring their ruin.

11

RSV	TEV
Woe to them! For they walk in the way of Cain, and abandon themselves for the sake of gain to Balaam's error, and perish in Korah's rebellion.	How terrible for them! They have followed the way that Cain took. For the sake of money they have given themselves over to the error that Balaam committed. They have rebelled as Korah rebelled, and like him they are destroyed.

Woe to them!: "How terrible for them!" (TEV). "They will be punished severely!"

they walk in the way of Cain: "they act as Cain did," "they do the same thing that Cain did," "they follow Cain's example." In late Judaism and early Christianity, Cain was a symbol of treachery and greed. It is difficult to see how Cain's murder of Abel could have been the comparison intended by Jude. Perhaps in a general way Jude is talking about anger and violence (see 1 John 3.12).

Balaam's error was covetousness; for the sake of gain, that is, out of love for money, he led the people of Israel to worship false gods (Num 22—24; 31.16; see 2 Peter 2.15; Rev 2.14). Instead of error or "mistake," one can say "deceit" or "lie."

Korah led a rebellion against Moses and Aaron (Num 16.1-35).

perish in Korah's rebellion is misleading; Jude means "they rebel as Korah did, and they will be destroyed as he was."

12

RSV	TEV
These are blemishes[d] on your love feasts, as they boldly carouse together, looking after themselves; waterless clouds, carried along by winds; fruitless trees in late autumn, twice dead, uprooted;	With their shameless carousing they are like dirty spots in your fellowship meals. They take care only of themselves. They are like clouds carried along by the wind, but bringing no rain. They are like trees that bear no fruit, even in autumn, trees that have been pulled up by the roots and are completely dead.

[d]Or *reefs*

These are: RSV uses metaphors in verses 12-13; TEV uses similes, "they are like."

blemishes on your love feasts. As the RSV footnote points out, the Greek word translated blemishes (TEV "dirty spots") may be understood to mean "reefs," that is, hidden dangers (a reef is a rock in the sea just below the surface of the water, on which a ship can be wrecked). There is no way to decide which meaning is preferable, and translations vary. Either figure makes sense in this context. It is better, like TEV, to use a simile: "These men are like dirty spots (or, stains)" or "These men are like dangerous reefs." Or else the figure may be dropped: "These men are a shameful sight" or "These men are a dangerous threat."

love feasts were meals which believers ate together, ending with a celebration of the Lord's Supper.

boldly carouse together: like the people Paul spoke of in 1 Corinthians 11.18-21, these people at the church fellowship meals kept to themselves, eating and drinking to excess, without any regard for the spiritual purpose of the meal.

looking after themselves: "taking care only of themselves," "looking after their own needs"—without considering the needs of their fellow believers.

waterless clouds: "clouds that bring no rain," "clouds that don't produce rain." This is a figure of worthlessness.

RSV carries the sentence on to the end of verse 13. Although long, it is not complex, and the semicolons clearly mark the five figures being used. Some translations, like TEV, may prefer to have a separate sentence for each figure.

carried along by winds: the point of the comparison here is that these people are moved by external forces and have no will power of their own.

fruitless trees in late autumn: autumn is the time for trees to bear fruit. If there is no fruit late in the season, the tree is clearly worthless. So those teachers never produce anything worthwhile.

twice dead, uprooted: here Jude seems to be thinking specifically of the false teachers. It may be that by twice dead he means their spiritual death before conversion and their spiritual death as a result of their abandoning the Christian faith. By the figure of uprooted Jude means they are completely separated from the source of spiritual life and vitality. If the figure of a tree is still uppermost, the trees may be said to be twice dead in the sense that their fruitlessness is a first form of death, and once pulled up by the roots, they are indeed dead.

It may be better to follow TEV: "trees that have been pulled up by the roots and are completely dead."

13 RSV	TEV
wild waves of the sea, casting up the foam of their own shame; wandering stars for whom the nether gloom of darkness has been reserved for ever.	**They are like wild waves of the sea, with their shameful deeds showing up like foam. They are like wandering stars, for whom God has reserved a place forever in the deepest darkness.**

wild waves of the sea: the figure here is of waves that dash themselves against the shore and leave dirt and debris (see Isa 57.20).

the foam of their own shame: "their sinful actions are like (dirty) foam." This figure may be translated as follows: "Their shameful deeds are like the dirty foam produced (or, left on the shore) by wild waves of the sea."

wandering stars: "stars that have wandered off their course," "stars that follow no fixed orbit." Or the writer may have been thinking of meteors.

the nether gloom of darkness: as in verse 6, the depths of Sheol.

has been reserved: by God (see TEV). This is the same verb used in verse 6.

14-15

RSV

It was of these also that Enoch in the seventh generation from Adam prophesied, saying, "Behold, the Lord came with his holy myriads, 15 to execute judgment on all, and to convict all the ungodly of all their deeds of ungodliness which they have committed in such an ungodly way, and of all the harsh things which ungodly sinners have spoken against him."

TEV

It was Enoch, the sixth direct descendant from Adam, who long ago prophesied this about them: "The Lord will come with many thousands of his holy angels 15 to bring judgment on all, to condemn them all for the godless deeds they have performed and for all the terrible words that godless sinners have spoken against him!"

The quotation is from a nonbiblical work called *The Book of Enoch* (also known as *I Enoch*), which was read and esteemed by Jews and Christians at that time. It seems clear that in verse 4 reference is made to this writing.

Enoch in the seventh generation from Adam: see the genealogy in Genesis 5.1-24; 1 Chronicles 1.1-3. Enoch belonged to the seventh generation, so TEV has "the sixth direct descendant from Adam." Where it may not be possible to indicate the precise generation, it may be sufficient to say "a descendant of Adam, who lived not very long after him"; possibly, "the great-grandson of Adam's great-grandson."

The quotation is mainly from Enoch 1.9; there are similar statements in 5.4; 27.2.

Behold: this translates a word that serves as an attention getter. Some translate "I saw," meaning that it was a vision that Enoch had.

The Lord came with his holy myriads: "I saw the Lord come with thousands of his angels." Or, like TEV, "The Lord will come...," since in the context of the book of Enoch this describes the future coming of God to judge.

In verse 15 some form of the word "ungodly" appears three times (as in verses 8-10 there are three occurrences of forms of the word "blaspheme"); in the Greek text translated by RSV, there are four occurrences of the term. The whole sentence does not flow very smoothly, but it is not difficult to translate.

to execute judgment on all: "to judge all people," "to pass sentence on everyone."

to convict: "to condemn" (TEV), "to punish."

all the ungodly...deeds of ungodliness...ungodly way: the repetition of the word may not be effective in some languages, and synonymous expressions may be preferable: "to condemn all godless people for the sins they committed in their wickedness, and for all the harsh (or, insolent) words those sinners have spoken against him."

16 RSV

These are grumblers, malcontents, following their own passions, loud-mouthed boasters, flattering people to gain advantage.

TEV

These people are always grumbling and blaming others; they follow their own evil desires; they brag about themselves and flatter others in order to get their own way.

grumblers, malcontents: "always complaining, never happy," "always criticizing, always blaming others." The text does not say what or who is the object of their complaints and criticism. Probably the two words are used in a general way, meaning that the false teachers criticize people who don't agree with them, and complain about everything.

passions: "desires," "evil desires" (TEV). They are completely selfish, seeking only to satisfy their own desires.

loud-mouthed boasters: "they brag a lot about themselves," "they are always claiming they are important." These people are vain and arrogant.

flattering people to gain advantage: "they say nice things about others to gain their own ends." This probably refers to the way these false teachers would, for selfish purposes, flatter rich and influential people.

SECTION HEADING

Warnings and Instructions: "Instructions to the Readers."

In this section, verses 17-23, Jude speaks directly to his readers and tells them how they should meet the danger posed by the false teachers. Not only are the readers to look after themselves, but they must also be ready to help any of their fellow believers who may be in danger of being led astray by the false teachers.

17 RSV

But you must remember, beloved, the predictions of the apostles of our Lord Jesus Christ;

TEV

But remember, my friends, what you were told in the past by the apostles of our Lord Jesus Christ.

Jude recalls what the apostles had said about the last days, namely, the time at which he writes this Letter.

beloved: "my dear friends," "my dear fellow believers."

the predictions: "what they said in the past." The Greek phrase, "the words spoken before," could mean, as RSV has it, the predictions, but it seems probable that it means only "words spoken in the past." As the beginning of verse 18 shows, the readers of Jude had themselves heard the apostles (they said to you). Here it may be preferable to imitate TEV "what you were told in the past by the apostles" or "what the apostles of our Lord Jesus Christ told you in the past."

apostles: these are the twelve close disciples of Jesus. In many passages of the New Testament, the word also includes others (such as Paul) who were not immediate followers of Jesus Christ. Here the word refers to the Twelve. The way the writer speaks of them makes it clear that he himself was not one of them, and that he is writing after their time.

our includes all Christians.

18

RSV	TEV
they said to you, "In the last time there will be scoffers, following their own ungodly passions."	They said to you, "When the last days come, people will appear who will make fun of you, people who follow their own godless desires."

the last time: "the last days" (TEV), "the end of the age," "as the world is about to end." This is like 1 Timothy 4.1; 2 Timothy 3.1-5.

scoffers: "people who (will) make fun of you" or "...make fun of the gospel."

following their own ungodly passions: "living according to their own godless desires." The language here is very much like that in verses 15,16.

19

RSV	TEV
It is these who set up divisions, worldly people, devoid of the Spirit.	These are the people who cause divisions, who are controlled by their natural desires, who do not have the Spirit.

set up divisions: "create divisions in the fellowship (or, the church)." By their way of life, and by their attitude toward other Christians, these false teachers separated themselves from others, on the assumption that they were superior Christians.

worldly people, devoid of the Spirit: these are two ways of describing a single characteristic of the false teachers. Instead of worldly, the Greek adjective is better represented by "people who follow their own instincts" (see the corresponding adverb in verse 10, translated by instinct). The Greek participial phrase "not having the Spirit" means "they are not guided by God's Spirit," "they do not have the Spirit of God."

20 RSV	TEV
But you, beloved, build yourselves up on your most holy faith; pray in the Holy Spirit;	But you, my friends, keep on building yourselves up on your most sacred faith. Pray in the power of the Holy Spirit,

But you, beloved: as at verse 17.

build yourselves up on your most holy faith: this refers to growth in Christian life or spirituality, and the figure is that of Christians helping one another to grow, or develop, in their faith. The Christian community is here compared to a building which is in the process of being constructed (see similar language in 1 Cor 3.9b-17; Eph 2.20-22; Col 2.7; 1 Peter 2.5). The foundation on which the building stands is your most holy faith, a way of speaking about the Christian religion (see verse 3). This may be translated "your Christian faith, which is very sacred (or, holy)."

If it is not possible to use the metaphor of build...up, it will be necessary to use the figure of growth: "grow (or, develop) in your Christian faith." But since the figure of building is used several times in the New Testament, the translator should try to preserve it.

pray in the Holy Spirit: here in may mean "guided by the Holy Spirit" or "by means of the power of the Holy Spirit." They are to follow the guidance of the Holy Spirit as they pray.

21 RSV	TEV
keep yourselves in the love of God; wait for the mercy of our Lord Jesus Christ unto eternal life.	and keep yourselves in the love of God, as you wait for our Lord Jesus Christ in his mercy to give you eternal life.

keep yourselves in the love of God: God loves them, and their lives and actions must show that his love controls them, and that they wish to be pleasing to him. In verse 1 Jude stresses God's part in this relationship; here he stresses the believer's part. If his readers do this, they will live under the influence of God's love and will continue to receive his blessings.

wait for the mercy of our Lord Jesus Christ unto eternal life: this unclear English sentence is a literal translation of the Greek text. What Jude means is "Wait for the day (or, time) when our Lord Jesus Christ, in his mercy, will give you eternal life." The gift of eternal life is seen as something still in the future. It will be given them by our Lord Jesus Christ, who has mercy on them. Here mercy may be represented as "compassion," "goodness," or "kindness," or even "grace" or "love." For wait for see Titus 2.13, in *A Translator's Guide to Paul's Letters to Timothy and Titus*.

The verse may be translated as follows:

> You must live in such a way that God's love will always be with you (or, that you will never depart from God's love). And wait confidently for the gift of eternal life, which our Lord Jesus Christ will give you. He will do so because he is good (or, because he is merciful).

22-23 RSV	TEV
And convince some, who doubt; 23 save some, by snatching them out of the fire; on some have mercy with fear, hating even the garment spotted by the flesh.[e]	Show mercy toward those who have doubts; 23 save others by snatching them out of the fire; and to others show mercy mixed with fear, but hate their very clothes, stained by their sinful lusts.

[e]The Greek text in this sentence is uncertain at several points

As the RSV footnote indicates, the form and meaning of the Greek text of these two verses is unclear in places. In verse 22 RSV and TEV translate different Greek texts. RSV translates a Greek text whose main verb is convince; TEV's Greek text has "be merciful to," "show mercy toward." Most modern translations follow the Greek text translated by TEV.

If RSV is preferred, convince some, who doubt may be "try to reassure (or, convince) those Christians who have doubts (about the Christian faith)."

If the TEV text is preferred: "Be kind (or, compassionate) to your fellow believers who have doubts (about the Christian faith)."

snatching them out of the fire: here the fire is a figure of eternal destruction, and represents the fires of Gehenna, that is, hell. The vivid language should be preserved, if possible. "Keep others from going to hell; bring them back to the right way." Or "If some of your fellow believers are headed for hell, pull them back and save them."

have mercy with fear: as they try to help their sinning fellow believers, they themselves must be careful to keep from being influenced or harmed by their sins. They must have compassion for them, but they must use caution and not bring back into their fellowship people who might lead the believers to commit sin.

hating even the garment spotted by the flesh: this is similar to the language of verse 8. The flesh refers to their sins, especially those of immorality. The Greek word translated garment means the short piece of clothing worn next to the skin. It may not make much sense to translate literally stained by the flesh, as RSV does, and so it may be better to translate "soiled by their filthy lusts."

Verses 22-23 may be translated as follows:

> Some in your fellowship have doubts about the Christian faith: treat them gently (or, kindly). 23 Others are in danger of going to hell: pull them back to the right way, and save them. And there are others who are ruled by their filthy lusts: show mercy to them, but be careful, and avoid being contaminated (or, polluted) by their sinful lives.

SECTION HEADING

Prayer of Praise: "Benediction," "Closing Prayer."

Jude ends the Letter with a prayer of adoration and thanksgiving.

24-25 RSV	TEV
Now to him who is able to keep you from falling and to present you without blemish before the presence of his glory with rejoicing, 25 to the only God, our Savior through Jesus Christ our Lord, be glory, majesty, dominion, and authority, before all time and now and for ever. Amen.	To him who is able to keep you from falling and to bring you faultless and joyful before his glorious presence—25 to the only God our Savior, through Jesus Christ our Lord, be glory, majesty, might, and authority, from all ages past, and now, and forever and ever! Amen.

Both RSV and TEV follow the order of the Greek text: Now to him... be glory, etc. It may be better to reverse the order, as proposed in an alternative translation below.

to him who is able (verse 24) refers to the only God, our Savior (verse 25).

keep you from falling: "keep you from abandoning the (Christian) faith," "keep you from committing sins"; or "keep you loyal to Christ."

present you without blemish before the presence of his glory: this means to bring them spotless and sinless into the very presence of God on the Day of Judgment (see Col 1.22). The glory of God is his revealed nature, described in terms of bright, shining light: "into the glorious (or, majestic) presence of God."

with rejoicing: as translated by RSV, this could be taken to refer to God, but it refers to the readers: "you will be very happy."

to the only God: he alone is God, there is no other.

Savior is used of God eight times in the New Testament; it is used of Christ fifteen times.

The qualities of glory, majesty, dominion, and authority are ascribed to God, that is, he is praised for these qualities, which are his from all times past and forever and ever in the future. Instead of abstract nouns, adjectives and verbs may be preferable: "he is glorious (or, great) and majestic, he rules over all and has authority over all" or "...he rules with complete authority over all."

RSV connects through Jesus Christ our Lord with our Savior; while possible, this does not seem very probable. Christians offer prayers of praise and thanksgiving to God through Jesus Christ our Lord, that is, in his name, or as his followers.

before all time: "before the world was created," "from the very beginning."

and now: "at this present time."

for ever: "for all future time."

Amen means "So be it," "It is so."

Verses 24-25 may be translated as follows:

> Let us now praise the one God our Savior! He can keep you from abandoning your faith, and can bring you completely sinless (or, pure) and happy into his own majestic presence. 25 Through Jesus Christ our Lord let us all praise God for his glory, greatness, power, and authority, which he has had before the world was created, and which are his now and will be his for all time to come! Amen.

Selected Bibliography

Text

The Greek New Testament. Third edition 1975. K. Aland, M. Black, C.M. Martini, B.M. Metzger, and A. Wikgren, editors. Stuttgart: United Bible Societies.

Lexicon

Arndt, W.F., and F.W. Gingrich. Second edition 1979. A Greek-English Lexicon of the New Testament and Other Early Christian Literature. Chicago: University of Chicago Press.

Commentaries

Arichea, D.C., and E.A. Nida, 1980. A Translator's Handbook on the First Letter of Peter. New York: United Bible Societies.

The best commentary for a translator. Indispensable. Knowledge of Greek is not required.

Barnett, A.E. 1957. The Second Epistle of Peter (Interpreter's Bible, vol. 12). New York: Abingdon.

Good but brief commentary and exposition. No knowledge of Greek required.

Beare, E.G. 1947. The First Epistle of Peter. Oxford: Basil Blackwell.

Knowledge of Greek is required: full exegetical and textual notes. Excellent Introduction; see especially "The Theology of the Epistle."

Bigg, Charles. Second edition 1902. The Epistles of St. Peter and St. Jude (International Critical Commentary). Edinburgh: T. & T. Clark.

Knowledge of Greek is required. A complete exegetical and expository treatment of the Letter.

Bibliography

Carr, A. 1930. The General Epistle of St. James (Cambridge Greek Testament). Cambridge: University Press.

No knowledge of Greek required. Good, although brief, exegetical notes. Very good Introduction; see chapter 5, "St. James and St. Paul: Faith and Works."

Easton, B.S. 1957. The Epistle of James (Interpreter's Bible, vol. 12). New York: Abingdon.

Excellent exposition. No knowledge of Greek needed. Two Special Notes: "Elders" and "Unction."

Hort, F.J.A. 1898. The First Epistle of St. Peter I.1—II.17. London: Macmillan.

Full exegetical notes on part of the Greek text.

Hunter, A.M. 1957. The First Epistle of Peter (Interpreter's Bible, vol. 12). New York: Abingdon.

Good exegesis and exposition of the Letter; no knowledge of Greek required.

James, M.R. 1912. The Second Epistle General of Peter and the General Epistle of Jude (Cambridge Greek Testament). Cambridge: University Press.

Very good Introduction, with a discussion of the relation between 2 Peter and Jude, and between 2 Peter and 1 Peter. Brief notes, but good. A knowledge of Greek is necessary.

Mayor, J.B. 1897. The Epistle of St. James. London: Macmillan.

A massive and elaborate commentary on the Greek text. The section called Comment (pp. 183-232) includes a paraphrase of the text, section by section; for this part no knowledge of Greek is required. Includes a full index of the Greek words of the Letter.

Moffatt, James. n.d. The General Epistles of James, Peter, and Judas (Moffatt New Testament Commentary). New York: Harper & Brothers.

Based on Moffatt's own translation; no knowledge of Greek required. Good commentary, even though brief.

Reicke, Bo. 1964. The Epistles of James, Peter, and Jude (The Anchor Bible, vol. 37). Garden City, NY: Doubleday.

Very good general Introduction covering the historical setting and the form and content of the Letters. Running commentary, section by section. A translation is given, but it hardly qualifies as a dynamic equivalence translation.

Ropes, J.H. 1916. The Epistle of St. James (International Critical Commentary). Edinburgh: T. & T. Clark.

A very complete exegesis of the Greek text; the best of the commentaries used for this Guide.

Selwyn, E.G. 1947. The First Epistle of St. Peter. London: Macmillan.

The best commentary in English of the Greek text. Excellent Additional Notes, and complete Introduction. See especially chapter 4, "Theology and Ethics of the Epistle" (pp. 64-115).

Glossary

This Glossary contains terms which are technical from an exegetical or a linguistic viewpoint. Other terms not defined here may be referred to in a Bible dictionary.

abstract noun is one which refers to a quality or characteristic, such as "beauty" or "darkness."

active. See voice.

actor. See agent.

adjective is a word which limits, describes, or qualifies a noun. In English, "red," "tall," "beautiful," and "important" are adjectives.

adverb is a word which limits, describes, or qualifies a verb, an adjective, or another adverb. In English, "quickly," "soon," "primarily," and "very" are adverbs.

adverbial refers to adverbs. An adverbial phrase is a phrase which functions as an adverb. See phrase.

agent is one who accomplishes an action, whether the grammatical construction is active or passive. In the expressions "John struck Bill" (active) and "Bill was struck by John" (passive), the agent in either case is "John." See also causative agent, instrument.

ambiguous describes a word or phrase which in a specific context may have two or more different meanings. For example, "Bill did not leave because John came" could mean either (1) "the coming of John prevented Bill from leaving" or (2) "the coming of John was not the cause of Bill's leaving." It is often the case that what is ambiguous in written form is not ambiguous when actually spoken, since features of intonation and slight pauses usually make clear which of the two or more meanings is intended. Furthermore, even in written discourse, the entire context normally serves to indicate which meaning is intended by the writer.

ancient versions. See versions.

causative relates to events and indicates that someone or something caused something to happen, rather than that the person or thing did it directly. In "John ran the horse," the verb "ran" is a causative, since it was not John who ran, but rather it was John who caused the horse to run.

causative agent is a person who causes an action by means of someone else. For example, in "The man had John plant the garden," the "man" is the causative agent, and "John" is the immediate or active agent. See also agent, instrument.

clause is a grammatical construction, normally consisting of a subject and a predicate. The main clause is that clause in a sentence which could stand alone as a complete sentence, but which has one or more dependent or subordinate clauses related to it. A subordinate clause is dependent on the main clause, but it does not form a complete sentence.

common language translation is one that uses only that portion of the total resources of a language that is understood and accepted by all native speakers as good usage. Excluded are features peculiar to a dialect, substandard or vulgar language, and technical or highly literary language not understood by all.

conditional refers to a clause or phrase which expresses or implies a condition, in English usually introduced by "if."

conjectural text is a text not found in any known ancient manuscript, but thought by some scholars to have been the original text. See also text, textual.

conjunctions are words which serve as connectors between words, phrases, clauses, and sentences. "And," "but," "if," and "because" are typical conjunctions in English.

context is that which precedes and/or follows any part of a discourse. For example, the context of a word or phrase in Scripture would be the other words and phrases associated with it in the sentence, paragraph, section, and even the entire book in which it occurs. The context of a term often affects its meaning, so that a word does not mean exactly the same thing in one context that it does in another context.

copyists were people who made handwritten copies of books, before the invention of printing. See manuscripts.

cultural equivalent is a kind of translation in which certain details from the culture of the source language are changed because they have no meaning or may even carry a wrong meaning for speakers of the receptor language. A cultural equivalent translation should be used only when absolutely necessary for conveying the intended meaning, and it may be important to add an explanatory note.

direct address, direct discourse, direct speech. See discourse.

discourse is the connected and continuous communication of thought by means of language, whether spoken or written. The way in which the elements of a discourse are arranged is called discourse structure. Direct discourse is the reproduction of the actual words of one person quoted and included in the discourse of another person; for example, "He declared *'I will have nothing to do with this man.'*" Indirect discourse is the reporting of the words of one person within the discourse of another person, but in an altered grammatical form rather than as an exact quotation; for example, "He said *he would have nothing to do with that man.*"

emphasis (emphatic) is the special importance given to an element in a discourse, sometimes indicated by the choice of words or by position in the sentence. For example, in "Never will I eat pork again," "Never" is given emphasis by placing it at the beginning of the sentence.

exegesis is the process of determining the meaning of a text (or is the result of this process), normally in terms of "who said what to whom under what circumstances and with what intent." A correct exegesis is indispensable before a passage can be translated correctly.

exclusive first person plural excludes the person(s) addressed. That is, a speaker may use "we" to refer to himself and his companions, while specifically excluding the person(s) to whom he is speaking. See inclusive.

explicit refers to information which is expressed in the words of a discourse. This is in contrast to implicit information. See implicit.

figure or figurative expression involves the use of words in other than their literal or ordinary sense, in order to bring out some aspect of meaning by means of comparison or association. For example, "raindrops dancing on the street," or "his speech was like thunder." Metaphors and similes are figures of speech.

first person. See person.

full stop, or period, is a marker indicating the end of a sentence.

future tense. See tense.

generic has reference to a general class or kind of objects, events, or abstracts; it is the opposite of specific. For example, the term "animal" is generic in relation to "dog," which is a specific kind of animal. However, "dog" is generic in relation to the more specific term "poodle."

goal is the object which receives or undergoes the action of a verb. Grammatically, the goal may be the subject of a passive construction ("John was hit," in which "John" is the goal of "hit"), or of certain intransitives ("the door shut"), or it may be the direct object of a transitive verb ("[something] hit John").

idiom or idiomatic expression is a combination of terms whose meaning cannot be understood by adding up the meanings of the parts. "To hang one's head" and "to have a green thumb" are English idioms. Idioms almost always lose their meaning or convey a wrong meaning when translated literally from one language to another.

imperative refers to forms of a verb which indicate commands or requests. In "Go and do likewise," the verbs "Go" and "do" are imperatives. In many languages, imperatives are confined to the grammatical second person; but some languages have corresponding forms for the first and third persons.

These are usually expressed in English by the use of "may" or "let"; for example, "May we not have to beg!" or "Let them work harder!"

implicit (implied) refers to information that is not formally represented in a discourse, since it is assumed that it is already known to the receptor, or evident from the meaning of the words in question. For example, the phrase "the other son" carries with it the implicit information that there is a son in addition to the one mentioned. This is in contrast to explicit information, which is expressly stated in a discourse. See explicit.

inclusive first person plural includes both the speaker and the one(s) to whom that person is speaking. See exclusive.

indicative refers to forms of a verb in which an act or condition is stated as an actual fact rather than as a potentiality, a hope, or an unrealized condition. The verb "won" in "The king won the battle" is in the indicative form.

indirect discourse. See discourse.

instrument (instrumentality) is the object used in accomplishing an action. In the sentence "John opened the door with a key," the "key" is the instrument. See also agent, causative agent.

irony (ironic) is a sarcastic or humorous manner of discourse in which what is said is intended to express its opposite; for example, "That was a smart thing to do!" when intended to convey the meaning "That was a stupid thing to do!"

literal means the ordinary or primary meaning of a term or expression, in contrast with a figurative meaning. A literal translation is one which represents the exact words and word order of the source language; such a translation is frequently unnatural or awkward in the receptor language.

manuscripts are books, documents, or letters written by hand. Thousands of manuscript copies of various Old and New Testament books still exist, but none of the original manuscripts. See text, textual.

manuscript evidence (manuscript support) is also called textual evidence. See text, textual.

metaphor is likening one object, event, or state to another by speaking of it as if it were the other; for example, "flowers dancing in the breeze." Metaphors are so commonly used and so well established in all languages that speakers and writers often use them without being conscious of the fact that they are using figurative language. See simile.

modify is to affect the meaning of another part of the sentence, as when an adjective modifies a noun, or an adverb modifies a verb.

noun is a word that names a person, place, thing, or idea, and often serves to specify a subject or topic of discussion.

parallel generally refers to some similarity in the content and/or form of a construction; for example, "Hear this, all peoples! Give ear, all inhabitants of the world." The structures that correspond to each other in the two statements are said to be parallel. Parallels, or parallel passages, refers to two or more portions of biblical text that resemble each other, often by using a series of words that are identical. For example, the Lord's Prayer as recorded in Matthew 6.9-13 has as its parallel Luke 11.2-4.

parenthetical statement is a statement that interrupts a discourse by departing from its main theme. It is frequently set off by marks of parenthesis, round brackets: ( ).

participial indicates that the phrase, clause, construction, or other expression described is governed by a participle.

participle is a verbal adjective, that is, a word which retains some of the characteristics of a verb while functioning as an adjective. In "singing children" and "painted house," "singing" and "painted" are participles.

passive. See voice.

person, as a grammatical term, refers to the speaker, the person spoken to, or the person or thing spoken about. First person is the person(s) speaking (such as "I," "me," "my," "mine," "we," "us," "our," or "ours"). Second person is the person(s) or thing(s) spoken to (such as "thou," "thee," "thy," "thine," "ye," "you," "your," or "yours"). Third person is the person(s) or thing(s) spoken about (such as "he," "she," "it," "his," "her," "them," or "their"). The examples here given are all pronouns, but in many languages the verb forms have affixes which indicate first, second, or third person and also indicate whether they are singular or plural.

personal pronoun is one which indicates first, second, or third person. See person and pronoun.

phrase is a grammatical construction of two or more words, but less than a complete clause or a sentence. A phase is usually given a name according to its function in a sentence, such as "noun phrase," "verb phrase," or "prepositional phrase."

plural refers to the form of a word which indicates more than one. See singular.

predicate is the part of a clause which complements the subject. The subject is the topic of the clause, and the predicate is what is said about the subject. For example, in "The small boy ran swiftly," the subject is "The small boy," and the predicate is "ran swiftly." See subject.

preposition is a word (usually a particle) whose function is to indicate the relation of a noun or pronoun to another noun, pronoun, verb, or adjective. Some English prepositions are "for," "from," "in," "to," and "with."

pronouns are words which are used in place of nouns, such as "he," "him," "his," "she," "her," "we," "them," "who," "which," "this," or "these."

relative clause is a dependent clause which describes the object to which it refers. In "the man whom you saw," the clause "whom you saw" is relative because it relates to and describes "man."

restructure. See structure.

rhetorical question is an expression which is put in the form of a question but which is not intended to ask for information. Rhetorical questions are usually employed for the sake of emphasis.

second person. See person.

sentence is a grammatical construction composed of one or more clauses and capable of standing alone.

Septuagint is a translation of the Hebrew Old Testament into Greek, made some two hundred years before Christ. It is often abbreviated as LXX.

simile (pronounced SIM-i-lee) is a figure of speech which describes one event or object by comparing it to another, using "like," "as," or some other word to mark or signal the comparison. For example, "She runs like a deer," "He is as straight as an arrow." Similes are less subtle than metaphors in that metaphors do not mark the comparison with words such as "like" or "as." See metaphor.

singular refers to the form of a word which indicates one thing or person, in contrast to plural, which indicates more than one. See plural.

specific is the opposite of general, generic. See generic.

structure is the systematic arrangement of the elements of language, including the ways in which words combine into phrases, phrases into clauses, and clauses into sentences. Because this process may be compared to the building of a house or bridge, such words as structure and construction are used in reference to it. To separate and rearrange the various components of a sentence or other unit of discourse in the translation process is to restructure it.

subject is one of the major divisions of a clause, the other being the predicate. In "The small boy walked to school," "The small boy" is the subject. Typically the subject is a noun phrase. It should not be confused with the semantic agent, or actor. See predicate.

synonyms are words which are different in form but similar in meaning, such as "boy" and "lad." Expressions which have essentially the same meaning are said to be synonymous. No two words are completely synonymous.

tense is usually a form of a verb which indicates time relative to a discourse or some event in a discourse. The most common forms of tense are past, present, and future.

text, textual, refers to the various Greek and Hebrew manuscripts of the Scriptures. Textual evidence is the cumulative evidence for a particular form of the text. Textual variants are forms of the same passage that differ in one or more details in some manuscripts. See also manuscripts.

third person. See person.

translation is the reproduction in a receptor language of the closest natural equivalent of a message in the source language, first, in terms of meaning, and second, in terms of style.

variant. See text, textual variants.

verbal has two meanings. (1) It may refer to expressions consisting of words, sometimes in distinction to forms of communication which do not employ words ("sign language," for example). (2) It may refer to word forms which are derived from verbs. For example, "coming" and "engaged" may be called verbals, and participles are called verbal adjectives. See verbs.

verbal phrases. See phrase.

verbs are a grammatical class of words which express existence, action, or occurrence, such as "be," "become," "run," or "think."

versions are translations. The ancient, or early, versions are translations of the Bible, or of portions of the Bible, made in early times; for example, the Greek Septuagint, the ancient Syriac, or the Ethiopic versions.

voice in grammar is the relation of the action expressed by a verb to the participants in the action. In English and many other languages, the active voice indicates that the subject performs the action ("John hit the man"), while the passive voice indicates that the subject is being acted upon ("The man was hit").

wordplay in a discourse is the use of the similarity in the sounds of two words to produce a special effect.

Index

This index includes concepts, key words, and terms for which the Guide contains a discussion useful for translators.

Index

Printed in the United States of America